P9-DNS-643

PRAISE FOR *POPULAR ECONOMICS*

"*Popular Economics* is an essential twenty-first century complement to Henry Hazlitt's *Economics In One Lesson*. In a book that is happily free of charts and incomprehensible equations, John Tamny uses exciting stories from the world around us to show the reader that nothing is easier than economic growth. *Popular Economics* is the answer for those confused by the 'dismal science.'"

—Arthur Laffer

"John Tamny offers a wide-ranging analysis of some of the most pressing issues facing the American economy today, from income inequality and job creation to budget deficits and tax reform. Through engaging examples and stories, he provides a thought-provoking argument in favor of a free-market approach to economic growth. Whether you agree with him or not, there is no question that his perspective needs to be part of the discussion on American economic policy in the new millennium."

—Enrico Moretti, professor of economics, Cal-Berkeley, and author of *The New Geography of Jobs*

"In a revelatory analysis of the so-called 'financial crisis,' John Tamny makes the unexpected case that the actual crisis was the huge banking blunder of betting the investment capital of the U.S. economy on housing, a retrospective consumption good already grossly in oversupply. Confirming the blunder, government under both Bush and Obama bailed out the banks and debauched the dollar, devaluing the entire entrepreneurial economy of the future. Rare is a book so contrary, so pithy, and so true."

—George Gilder, author of *Knowledge and Power*

"Want to understand the vital purpose of stable money in a free-market economy? Read John Tamny's chapters on the importance of reliable standards—whether you are measuring ingredients for a chicken wings recipe, constructing a house, or timing athletes running the forty-yard dash—and you will fully comprehend that money is meant to provide a dependable measure of value. Tamny's writing throughout this brilliant book rings with clarity and consistency; you will be left wondering why these same qualities don't apply to our money."

—Judy Shelton, author of *Money Meltdown*

"Ignore John Tamny's easy to read *Popular Economics* at your own moral peril. It's as close to spiritual as you get in this realm—a better tutorial than any econ text. I'd make it mandatory for the 95 percent of econ majors—right up through PhDs—who never really got the basics. While making you edgy toward the endless societal consensus nonsense that it cuts through like a guillotine, it also frees you to see the true creative beauty of reality all around us."

—**Ken Fisher**, founder and CEO, Fisher Investments

"In this entertaining and provocative new book, John Tamny makes the powerful case for freedom as the font of social and economic growth. *Popular Economics* draws upon a rich collection of both spectacular successes and devastating failures to show how easily attainable prosperity is."

—**David Resler**, retired chief economist,
Nomura Securities International

"John's book is many things. It's a great way to learn economics, it's a very strong case for economic liberty, and it is an epic myth-buster. I will be giving it out to friends, of all viewpoints, for a long, long time."

—**Cliff Asness**, managing principal, AQR Capital

POPULAR ECONOMICS

POPULAR ECONOMICS

What the ROLLING STONES, DOWNTON ABBEY, and LEBRON JAMES can teach you about economics

JOHN TAMNY

A Division of Salem Media Group

Library of Congress Cataloging-in-Publication Data

Tamny, John.
Popular economics : what the Rolling Stones, Downton Abbey, and LeBron James can teach you about economics / John Tamny.
pages cm
Summary: "John Tamny uses entertaining stories from sports, movies, popular culture, and famous businesses to explain the basic principles of economics. His Popular Economics is an everyman's guide to how money really works-a lesson politicians try (and fail) to grasp every day. "-- Provided by publisher.
ISBN 978-1-62157-337-1 (hardback)
1. Economics. I. Title.
HB171.T24 2015
330--dc23

Published in the United States by
Regnery Publishing
A Division of Salem Media Group
300 New Jersey Ave NW
Washington, DC 20001
www.Regnery.com

Manufactured in the United States of America

10 9 8 7 6 5 4 3 2

Books are available in quantity for promotional or premium use. For information on discounts and terms, please visit our website: www.Regnery.com.

Distributed to the trade by
Perseus Distribution
250 West 57th Street
New York, NY 10107

To my wife, Kendall. Thank you for all of your love and support, and most of all for the inspiration without which there would be no book.

CONTENTS

Part III: Trade

Part IV: Money

FOREWORD BY STEVE FORBES

You hold in your hands one of the most subversive economics treatises since Karl Marx's *Communist Manifesto*, published in 1848, or John Maynard Keynes's *General Theory of Employment, Interest and Money*, published in 1936. While Marx desired to undermine the social order of free markets, property rights, and minimal government, John Tamny wants to restore what was in place before the past century's Great Depression and two world wars. Indeed, he would strengthen the freedom-enhancing and prosperity-creating institutions and practices that flourished before these twentieth-century calamities. While Keynes wanted government to steer the economy—as a driver does an automobile (an utterly illusory goal)—through manipulations of money, interest rates, taxes, and government spending, Tamny wishes to do the opposite: slash tax rates, radically simplify the tax code, let markets set interest rates (the Federal Reserve would ultimately be consigned to the Smithsonian), institute a gold standard to stabilize our money, end government bailouts of all kinds, and cut government to the minimalist role originally envisioned by our Founders.

There are many people who share Tamny's goals. However, he sets about his liberty revolution by unleashing a most potent weapon: this book. Tamny makes the supposedly complex, arcane, equation-dense subject of economics—a discipline that allegedly can only be mastered by a handful of brilliant high priests like Janet Yellen and Ben Bernanke—into something *everyone* can fully understand. In spirit, Tamny does for economics what the Gutenberg printing press did for the Bible, making a previously inaccessible subject open to all. Equally important, he does to economists what Toto did to the *Wizard of Oz*: pulling aside the curtain to expose the fraud that has become modern economics.

Tamny understands what all too many don't these days: We improve our standard of living by trading with one another. For instance, say you want to bake and sell cakes. You have to trade to get the ingredients, such as eggs, sugar, flour, and cream; the necessary pieces of equipment, such as an oven and a refrigerator; utensils, such as measuring spoons and cups, and on and on. Billions of such transactions take place every day. We'd still be living in caves if we didn't trade with one another.

Barter, however, is hopelessly cumbersome. Money makes trading products, services, and financial instruments infinitely easier. Money is a claim on these things, just as a coat-check ticket at a restaurant is a claim on the coat you "deposited." With money, investing becomes feasible on a massive scale, and it's only through investing that we make the advances that increase the standard of living for all. Unstable money impedes trade and investment.

On subject after subject Tamny delightfully demolishes the destructive accepted wisdom of today. A few examples:

- Governments don't create wealth. Too often they get in the way of its creation. They can seize it, spend it, and redistribute it, but they can't produce real resources.
- Budget deficits aren't the real problem, the level of government spending is. Whether these outlays are financed by taxes, borrowing, or central banks' creating reserves out of thin air, the result is the same: Resources are taken away from the people who created them. The inevitable result is the waste and inefficient use of those resources, and we are the poorer for it. Milton Friedman famously said that he preferred a trillion-dollar budget that came with a big deficit than a two-trillion-dollar budget that was in balance.
- Trade is good whether transacted in our hometown, within our country, or overseas. Economists' and politicians' obsession with the international balance of payments is a monumentally destructive waste of time. All that counts is that trade balances globally. If you buy a pair of socks from China and the Chinese merchant then buys a share of stock in the United States, economists will fret about a trade deficit and capital account deficit, even though you got your socks and

the Chinese seller got a financial asset in return. Each party gained something from the transaction.

- Saving is good. Capital creation through savings by individuals and profits from business is essential. Keynesians have the notion that savings go into a black hole and do nothing for the economy. Preposterous, Tamny rightly rejoins. Capital creators are the heroes who enable the rest of us to earn more and to get access to products like the iPod, which we could never have conceived of before entrepreneurs like Steve Jobs offered them to us in the marketplace.
- Progress requires destroying the old to make way for the new. Buggies and automobiles are an obvious example. Those of us who grew up in the world of print media have witnessed first-hand with the internet what Joseph Schumpeter famously called "creative destruction." But the internet has also enabled millions of people to interact with one another instantly and become content creators. Journalism, information accessibility, and debate are flourishing as never before. This is the very essence of democracy.

Innovation is messy. People must experiment to discover what works and what doesn't. As Tamny points out, we've had more than two thousand different auto manufacturers in the United States. This shows that the idea that the economy—if guided by the wise in government—will avoid ups and downs and booms and recessions is nonsense. Turbulence is part and parcel of progress. When governments don't let capital go where the opportunities are, we end up less well off.

Tamny takes on many other shibboleths, pointing out, for example, that abolishing the estate tax—the purported purpose of which is to make sure that the wealth of the rich doesn't stay concentrated—would be a highly effective tool for income redistribution. Another of his counterintuitive insights is that outsourcing is good for workers.

Here's one that will raise hackles: Pursuing energy independence is destructive. If people outside the United States can provide energy more cheaply than we can, we should let them do so. That way we can focus our scarce capital on cutting-edge opportunities. Britain gave up trying to be "food independent" in the early 1840s, when it abolished its tariffs on food imports, the so-called Corn Laws. Workers loved the availability of cheaper food, and Britain went on to become the mightiest nation in the world, helping the Allies win the twentieth century's two world wars, despite being dependent on food imports to survive.

Tamny's book also, thankfully, gets matters right on exactly what inflation and deflation are. Hint: Inflation isn't the Consumer Price Index going up. Nor are falling prices necessarily bad if they're the result of productivity.

Commerce isn't another form of warfare, Tamny correctly avers. Rather, commerce creates conditions for peace by breaking down barriers between peoples (you may not love your neighbor, but you sure would like to sell to him), making us all richer.

The book also puts doom-and-gloom predictors in proper perspective. No one can predict the details of a particular disaster, because there's no way to know for sure what the relevant players will do. Take the financial crisis of 2008–2009. The housing bubble created by the Federal Reserve's weak-dollar policy had already burst, and the economy was painfully adjusting to the fallout. What turned this U.S.

disaster into a globe-girdling calamity were the steps taken by Washington policymakers. In early 2008 the U.S. Treasury Department and the Fed bailed out the creditors of Bear Stearns, a large but hardly critical Wall Street investment house. Then came the government takeovers of Fannie Mae and Freddie Mac. Everyone then expected that Lehman Brothers, a far more consequential outfit than Bear Stearns, would receive similar treatment. Instead, it was allowed to file for bankruptcy. Washington, days later, reversed course again, taking over mammoth AIG. Markets were left with no idea what authorities would do next, and panic set in. In the months that followed no one knew which institutions would be saved and which would go under. The notorious Troubled Asset Relief Program, whereby the federal government forced equity investments on banks, whether they were weak or strong, added to the confusion. More mistakes followed, leaving us with a punk economy that still can't get out of second gear and a government that has amassed massive, growth-suffocating powers. No one could have foreseen those particulars. As Tamny points out, had Bear been allowed to fail without government intervention, Lehman would have scrambled to effect its own rescue, probably through a fire sale-like merger with another bank.

What makes this book so special is that it avoids all the mind-numbing jargon of traditional economics books. You won't find such pretentious or just plain wrong-headed economic axioms as "the marginal propensity to consume," "the paradox of thrift" (a particularly pernicious Keynesian nostrum that savings can be bad for economic growth), "the marginal product theory of the single firm," "nonoptimality of competitive laissez-faire pricing," "the law of diminishing marginal utility," "the acceleration principle," "the marginal propensity to save," "the law of increasing (relative) demand," or "the law of marginal-physical-product."

Tamny doesn't suffer from science envy, as most economists do. Economists are obsessed with mathematical formulas and equations because they give their discipline the supposed prestige of a hard science. Equations render the illusion of pin-point precision, which is entirely absent from most of human behavior.

As an example, look at this question posed in the classic college textbook so many of us groaned under, Paul Samuelson's *Economics* (eighth edition): "If $C = a + bY = 200 + 2/3\ Y$ and $I = \bar{I} = 100$, solve $Y = C + I = 200 + 2/3\ Y + 100$ to get $Y^* = 900$. Increase $\bar{I}$ by 10 and verify that Y^* goes up by 30. What is the multiplier? Why? (Note: Y is NNP in billions of \$)."

And to think this guy landed a Nobel prize for stuff like that!

What makes Tamny's book worthy of becoming a classic that will be referred to for a long time to come is its brilliant use of stories to illustrate points. People are always interested in well-told tales about others and the lessons to be learned from their experiences. Here you'll read about Jerry Jones and his seemingly crazy decision decades ago to buy the Dallas Cowboys, a move that today looks blindingly obvious but was originally ridiculed by experts and sophisticated investment bankers. Tamny's subjects are numerous and include Paris Hilton, Larry King, the late Al Neuharth (founder of *USA Today*), Michael Bloomberg, J. K. Rowling, Patrick Soon-Shiong (who became a billionaire through his breakthroughs in fighting cancer), and Bill Rasmussen (founder of ESPN). Tamny's illustrative arsenal is full of enlightening references to sports, movies, and the TV series *Downton Abbey*. He discusses failures as well, because there are lessons to be learned from them, both about people who rebounded from failure and about those who did not.

The discipline of economics is not a hard science like physics, chemistry, biology, or engineering. Tamny rightfully and brilliantly recognizes that economics concerns the ways in which people strive, as Abraham Lincoln put it, to improve their lot in life. What enables this innate desire to flourish and what stands in the way of its being fulfilled is the fruitful, legitimate focus of economics. Visit virtually any poor country in the world and you'll quickly see that it has considerable entrepreneurial energy, as people trade in stalls and on street corners. Why doesn't such activity translate into vigorous economic growth? Because government-made barriers, such as obstacles to setting up a legal business, onerous taxation, the lack of basic property rights, and rampantly unstable currencies stand in the way. The proper role of government is to create a conducive environment in which commerce among consenting adults can take place and to then stand aside. Prosperity is certain to follow.

Sadly, this basic insight is ignored or hobbled by all too many credentialed economists and political leaders. The International Monetary Fund, for instance, is notorious for its anti-growth prescriptions of currency devaluation and higher taxes. Look around the world today and you'll find governments everywhere that have erected extremely harmful structural barriers to the practice of commerce. Japan, for example, is doubling its national sales tax and boosting its payroll levies from the already nose-bleed level of 30 percent to an even more catastrophic 37 percent. Is it any wonder the world's third-largest economy has stagnated for twenty years and is now falling into recession?

By breaking the mold of what modern economics has become and by explaining in an engaging way what economics truly is, Tamny has done humanity an inestimable service.

Read this book. Absorb its basic lessons. And then promote it in every way you can. You don't have to agree with every particular in it to know that *Popular Economics* will rank with George Gilder's

Wealth and Poverty and *Knowledge and Power*, Warren Brookes's *The Economy in Mind*, Jude Wanniski's *The Way the World Works*, and a handful of other books as a signal contribution to the cause of liberty and to a beneficent, opportunity-rich civilization for all.

INTRODUCTION

Macroeconomics is a tautology and a myth, a dangerous one at that, sustaining the illusion that prosperity is necessarily linked with territory, national units, and government spending in general.
—Reuven Brenner, *Labyrinths of Prosperity*

A relatively weak economy has diminished the confidence of the American people. The refrain of some of the best-known economists in the United States is that the future holds only stagnation because we've allegedly forgotten how to grow. In short, economic growth has become difficult to achieve.[1]

Happily, the prevalent view within the economics profession is false. Economic growth is not only simple, it is also easy to understand. There is nothing mysterious about economics. It is all around us—in the movies and sports we watch, the products we enjoy, and in what we do each day.

The problem, strangely enough, is the economics profession itself. Increasingly reliant on charts, graphs, indecipherable equations, and incomprehensible numbers, economists have turned what is perfectly basic and a matter of common sense into something that is mystifying.

In truth, nothing is less complicated than the subject of economics, and therefore nothing is easier than economic growth. This is particularly true in the United States. A country of individuals descended from immigrants, or immigrants themselves, America is populated by people who wanted something better, who abandoned the familiarity of home to migrate to a place that has long prized personal and economic freedom.

Entrepreneurs are by definition risk takers, and immigrants have in many ways taken the ultimate risk. When talented and entrepreneurial people from all over the world populate a country, it's not surprising that they make it wealthy.

Another human trait, one that we all share and that makes economic growth easy, is that our wants are unlimited. We always desire something more, and the exchange of our labor for the food, clothing, and shelter that we do not possess makes economic growth a simple matter of reducing the barriers to production.

At the most basic level, a person must first supply something of value before he can purchase something else. The path to economic growth, then, is stimulating the *supply* side of the economy. Governments can stimulate the supply side by reducing tax, regulatory, trade, and monetary barriers to production.

Taxes are nothing more than a penalty on work. When politicians talk about raising our income taxes, they are really saying that they are going to increase the cost of getting up and going to work each morning.

Regulations are similarly a tax placed on economic activity, a cost of doing business. They rarely achieve their stated objectives, but they succeed insofar as they suffocate the economy. Regulations rob workers and businesses of time and resources that could otherwise go into producing goods desired by the marketplace.

Trade is, in many ways, the simplest of the four basics of economic growth. Each of us is a free trader because trade is the purpose of our work. We go to work each day precisely because there is so much that we want but do not have. Government tariffs on imported goods penalize our work and make it less desirable in the process.

The purpose of money is to facilitate the exchange of consumable goods. Money itself is not wealth. It is how we measure our own work and then trade products. McDonald's does not seek my writing skills in return for the Quarter Pounders it provides me. Money serves as the broadly accepted medium of exchange for all producers. It is a unit of measure, and a unit of measure cannot perform its function well if it changes all the time. Until 1971, the U.S. dollar had a constant value tied to gold. When we dissolved that connection to gold, we sent the dollar—and our economy—on a never-ending roller coaster ride.

In modern times, economics has become too intimidating. It should not be. We are all microeconomists in our daily lives, and we are surrounded by economic lessons. Indeed, the purpose of this book is to shed sunlight on what is so logical, free of charts, and mostly free of statistics. Nothing is easier to understand than economics. It's everywhere you look.

PART I

Taxes

CHAPTER ONE

Taxes Are Nothing More Than a Price Placed on Work

The wages of labour are the encouragement of industry, which, like every other human quality, improves in proportion to the encouragement it receives.
—**Adam Smith**, *The Wealth of Nations*

In the music industry, there's a pecking order that everyone understands. In Los Angeles, my hometown, the easiest way to measure musical success, other than consulting *Billboard*, is to look at the venues where various bands and singers perform in concert. Bands that are up and coming but still not well known might find themselves at the Whiskey A Go Go on Hollywood's Sunset Strip. The next step has often been the Hollywood Palladium, with its five-thousand-person capacity, and the really successful groups play at the Staples Center downtown.

But for the biggest bands, even arenas the size of Staples can't hold their legions of fans. Those bands play in stadiums, from the Rose Bowl in Pasadena to the Coliseum near downtown LA. The Rolling Stones are a stadium band, and the story of their staggering success can teach us something about taxation. Taxes are the price we charge people to work, and that price affects where they work and whether they work at all. As the Stones' lead guitarist, Keith Richards, explained in his endlessly fascinating autobiography, *Life*, "The tax rate [in Britain] in the early '70s on the highest earners was 83 percent, and that went up to 98 percent for investments and so-called unearned income. So that's the same as being told to leave the country."[1]

That statement is full of economic lessons. For one, raising the price of something doesn't mean you'll get that price. General Motors could increase the sticker price of its Chevy Malibu to one hundred thousand dollars, but its customers would laugh and go next door to the Ford dealership.

The same is true for taxes. Politicians may raise the cost of work for their citizens, but if the cost is too high, those citizens won't stick around to be fleeced, especially if they're well to do. Like the car shoppers, they'll go elsewhere. Richards and the Rolling Stones did just that.

> The last thing I think the powers that be expected when they hit us with super-tax is that we'd say fine, we'll leave. We'll be another one not paying tax to you. They just didn't factor that in. It made us bigger than ever, and it produced *Exile on Main St.*, which was maybe the best thing we did. They didn't believe we'd be able to continue as we were if we didn't live in England. And in all honesty,

> we were very doubtful too. We didn't know if we would make it, but if we didn't try, what would we do? Sit in England and they'd give us a penny out of every pound we earned? We had no desire to be closed down. And we upped and went to France.[2]

England's political class perhaps grew a little arrogant in their belief that they could put any price on work they pleased. As it turned out, raising the cost of working to 83 percent meant the Inland Revenue Service collected 83 percent of *nothing* from the Rolling Stones.

Politicians try to justify high taxes by asserting that the top rates will affect only the highest earners, who can most afford them. They often complement this economic falsehood with the absurd argument that hiking taxes on the richest is all about fairness. It's only fair, they say, for the highest earners to pay the lion's share of taxes. The reality, unfortunately, is not so simple. Progressive taxation, in fact, is most unfair to middle- and lower-income taxpayers.

The Rolling Stones were not always the *Rolling Stones*. In the early 1960s, Richards recalls, "the poverty seemed constant, unmovable."[3] He writes, "I even kept accounts of the money we earned at gigs, the pounds, shillings and pence. Often it just said '0' when we played at tiny end-of-term school dances."[4]

Most people do not begin life on top. Politicians who raise income tax rates on top earners in the name of "fairness" are telling the strivers lower down that they will incur a penalty for succeeding. Those who are already rich can hire the best tax accountants to circumvent outlandish rates and can move, as the Stones eventually did.

Taxes are not only a price on work. They are also a price on the productive use of wealth. Great Britain's political leaders in the 1970s apparently forgot what goes into producing a record album. The Rolling Stones needed sound engineers, backup instrumentalists and singers, gofers and personal assistants, not to mention catering companies, drivers, public relations specialists, and many others who achieve employment when the rich deploy their capital. High tax rates gave all those jobs to the French and later, when post-production of *Exile on Main St.* moved to Los Angeles, to the Americans. The rich are highly mobile, and they will put their capital to work in the most favorable environment. When the government hits them with high taxes, it's the non-rich who feel the most pain.

You could be excused if you thought that people in the movie business want to pay more taxes. Hollywood is near monolithic in its left-wing politics, and its leading lights fund and campaign for the politicians who promise to raise their income taxes the most. Yet moviemakers are actually quite adept at finding low-tax havens in which to practice their craft. The Academy Award–winning director, writer, and actor Ben Affleck is an unabashed liberal, but here is what he told the *Los Angeles Times* in late 2013 about why he was going to Georgia to shoot *Live by Night*:

> You just follow the money. What happens is that you're faced with a situation of shooting somewhere you want to shoot, versus shooting somewhere you'd less rather shoot—and you get an extra three weeks of filming. It comes down to the fact that you have *x* amount of money to make your movie in a business where margins are really thin.[5]

Affleck is not alone in seeking tax advantages before rolling the camera. Chris Moore, the producer of the *American Pie* franchise, summarized matters neatly for the *Los Angeles Times*: "If you have a $100 million Brad Pitt movie, you just call 15 different film offices, and you're going to have the governor calling you at home saying, 'Hey, man, here's why you should do it in Iowa.'"[6]

Actor Rob Lowe talked about the large crews required to make films in his 2011 autobiography, *Stories I Only Tell My Friends*. In it Lowe recalled that:

> It takes an army to make a movie. Camera crews, lighting crews, wardrobe crews, makeup crews, hair crews, painters, builders (called grips), a crew to provide the props, a crew to provide the furnishings (the art department), electricians, special-effects people, stunt performers, stand-ins, the accountant, scheduling and finance (called the unit production manager), catering and someone to provide snacks and drinks (called craft service), and the team of walkie-talkie-armed Gestapo that police the second-by-second momentum of shooting: the assistant director staff.[7]

California, the longtime home of the film business, is run by politicians who are eager to reach into the pockets of its most productive industries. Though many of the industry's best and brightest choose to live and work in California, they often make their movies outside the Golden State. The *Los Angeles Times* reports that the "number of top-grossing films shot in California has plummeted 60% in the last 15 years."[8] The alarming part of this story is how non-rich Californians suffer from the state's aggressive taxation of some of its highest earners.

The *Times* goes on, "Hollywood's trade workers—the electricians, carpenters, caterers and others who work behind the scenes—

have long complained that they've lost their livelihoods as states vie for film business with ever-richer incentives."[9]

Wealthy filmmakers, like top-earning bands, have the mobility to avoid the tax rates meant for them. Not the lower earners, who suffer the consequences of the naïve effort to soak the rich.

As a matter of fact, those with less are better off when the rich keep more of their income. Does that seem counterintuitive? Consider Uber, the popular car service that's a substitute for traditional taxis. A tap on your smartphone's Uber app tells you instantly how many cars are nearby and how long you'll have to wait for one. Another tap dispatches an SUV, a black town car, or a cab ready to whisk you to your destination. The fare and tip are automatically charged to your credit card. No frantic hunt for an available taxi, no fumbling for cash or calculating a tip.

City dwellers might shrug their shoulders—they can walk outside and find plenty of cabs. But if you live in the suburbs or a smaller city, Uber is a dream come true. Before Uber, you had to call a cab company and deal with a surly dispatcher, who was often vague about when your taxi would arrive, if it arrived at all. Not with Uber.

It is often said that capitalism is colorblind. Cabdrivers have been known to pass by black customers eager to hail a taxi, but Uber drivers show up without regard to race. Even better, drivers *and* customers can rate one another. If your ride is unsatisfactory—the car's a mess, the driver doesn't run the air conditioning on a hot day, the radio's too loud—you can give the driver a low rating. Too many poor ratings bring about the driver's dismissal by Uber.[10]

By the same token, a passenger who is habitually rude to drivers, makes a mess of the car, throws up, or is unreasonably demanding can receive a negative rating by the driver. Uber can "fire" customers who cause problems for its drivers—a reminder that capitalism is a two-way street.

In December 2011, just eighteen months after Travis Kalanick founded Uber, he announced that Jeff Bezos, the founder of Amazon.com, and others were investing thirty-two million dollars in his nascent firm.[11] With a net worth of nearly thirty billion dollars,[12] Bezos will be fine whether he is paying 10 percent or 50 percent of his income to the federal government. Of course, that is not the point. There's no such thing as idle capital. The growing number of Uber drivers is testimony to the opportunities Bezos can create if we let him keep his money. Punishing taxes on the rich reduce investment in new ideas that enrich and empower others.

Skeptics need look no further than Apple Computer. Back in the 1970s, Steve Jobs was a college dropout bursting with ideas. But he wouldn't have gone anywhere without capital. The venture capitalist Arthur Rock invested $57,600 in Apple Computer, and the rest is history.[13]

Jobs left Apple for a time, but he returned in 1997; and some of his greatest innovations followed. From the iPod to the iPhone to the iPad, Jobs's revolutionary vision transformed how people buy music, talk on their phones, and use computers. Apple's stock predictably soared as Jobs quarterbacked all of these exciting technological advances, and it now vies for the title of the world's most valuable company.

The envious might respond that Jobs invented playthings for the leisure class, that Apple employs the highly trained techno-elite, and the primary beneficiaries of Apple's share-price revival are the infamous 1 percent. That response is wrong in almost every particular, but for now, let's consider how Apple's rise supports the much-maligned notion of "trickle-down economics."

Enrico Moretti, an economist at the University of California at Berkeley, explains in *The New Geography of Jobs* that Apple's more than twelve thousand employees in Cupertino, California, are only the beginning of the story of the company's contribution. Apple's success, Moretti found, accounts for at least sixty thousand other jobs in Cupertino. "In essence," he writes, "in Silicon Valley, high-tech jobs are the *cause* of local prosperity, and the doctors, lawyers, roofers, and yoga teachers are the *effect*."[14]

Thank goodness Arthur Rock got to keep some of his substantial earnings! A major theme of this book is that all companies and the jobs they make are the certain result of investment. Since money never lies idle, it is an economic truism that the less governments tax those with the most disposable income, the more likely they are to invest that income in job-creating ideas. It's the rich, by definition, who have the excess funds that the next Steve Jobs is looking for. The government may impose heavy taxes on the rich in the name of fairness, but that "fairness" comes at the expense of the economy and those not yet rich.

CHAPTER TWO

When We Tax Corporations, We Rob Them of Their Future

The advantages and gains that are realized today are due to capital that was invested previously.
—Mark Spitznagel, *The Dao of Capital*

The brothers Charles and Frank Duryea completed the first gasoline-powered American car in Springfield, Massachusetts, on September 20, 1893.[1] By 1896 they had sold thirteen of their machines, and only the most wild-eyed optimist would have foreseen that the automobile would be a ubiquitous middle-class good within twenty years.

Thank goodness for the unquenchable drive of entrepreneurs like Henry Ford. In 1876, at the age of thirteen, he saw a crude steam-powered horseless carriage moving itself down the street and was mesmerized. He would say later, "It was the engine which took me into automotive transportation."[2] Sixteen years later, in 1892, Ford produced his first automobile.[3] By 1903, he had incorporated the Ford Motor Company. By 1908, he had introduced the Model T to a public that had never imagined owning a car at all. And by 1911, he had prevailed in court over a cartel called the Association of Licensed Automobile Manufacturers, which had first dismissed Ford as an "unreliable upstart" and then tried to block him from producing his Model T.[4] Five years later, Ford Motor Company produced 585,000 Model T autos. Ford's compulsion to perfect his manufacturing processes never let up, and by 1921 his assembly-line system had produced a million vehicles.[5] Henry Ford had turned a plaything for the rich into a universal necessity.

In his dazzling book, *The Dao of Capital*, the investor Mark Spitznagel makes the essential point that "Ford Motor Company would not have prospered had the founder not committed to continuous long-term investment in improvements and roundabout production."[6] Translated, Ford's reinvestment of his profits in improvements to his manufacturing process made all the difference.

Imagine if today's U.S. corporate tax rates, which are among the highest in the world, had been in place at the dawn of the twentieth century.[7] It may be too much to suggest that none of us would ever have heard of Ford, but it's reasonable to presume that today's tax rates would have prevented Henry Ford from producing the Model T in the quantities and at the prices that ushered in the age of the automobile. Investment is how companies increase the quality of their product and improve the way they produce it. Profits make better processes and better products.

Just as the story of the Rolling Stones shows how high personal taxes on the rich hurt middle- and low-income earners, Ford's story reveals the harm of high corporate taxes. Politicians justify high corporate taxes on the grounds that corporations are big enough to take the hit. But setting aside for a moment the reality that corporations are owned by individuals, we mustn't ignore what profitable companies do with their profits. To understand this point, let's return to Henry Ford's story.

As Spitznagel writes, "When profits [for the Ford Motor Company] swelled, he paid well for labor, creating an uproar when he doubled the basic wage to $5.00 a day, which triggered a virtual stampede of job seekers."[8] The popular myth is that that Ford raised wages so his workers could buy his automobiles, but in fact he was responding to economic necessity.

Spitznagel has found that annual employee turnover within Ford had reached 370 percent in 1913. By "paying workers well, he effectively *lowered* his costs because higher wages reduced turnover and the need for constant training of new hires."[9] It has been said that capitalism, or the profit motive, makes us compassionate in our actions even if we don't feel compassionate in our hearts. Ford's concern with the profits that allowed him continuously to improve his business drove him to pay his workers more than the prevailing wage.

Fortunately for Ford—and for everyone who drives an automobile—he didn't face the exorbitant tax rates that corporations labor under today. Low corporate taxes allow companies both to reinvest in the known and to experiment with new ideas.

The French Connection won the Academy Award for Best Picture in 1971, made a star of Gene Hackman, turned the little-known documentary filmmaker William Friedkin into an A-list *auteur*, and introduced audiences to the big-screen excitement of a true high-speed car chase. But this film was almost not made. As Friedkin recalls in his memoir *The Friedkin Connection*, he and Phil D'Antoni "schlepped *The French Connection* around for two years.... We took it to every studio, and were rejected by all."[10]

With no serious bidders on the film, Friedkin eventually signed up for unemployment benefits. The very next day he received a call from an agent who told him that Dick Zanuck, head of Twentieth Century-Fox, had requested a meeting. Friedkin and D'Antoni went to see Zanuck, who told them, "I've got a million and a half dollars hidden away in my budget for the rest of the year. I'm on my way out. They're gonna fire me, but I've got a hunch about that *French Connection* script."[11] The rest, of course, is history.

George Gilder has observed, "It is the leap, not the look, that generates the crucial information."[12] How true. Economic growth is about taking risks, learning from them, and then using the information gleaned from experimentation to inform future economic activity. The extra one and a half million dollars that Twentieth Century Fox had lying around meant that one of the twentieth century's most important films could be made. Furthermore, the success of *The French Connection* informed Hollywood's subsequent endeavors and helped define filmmaking in the 1970s.

Friedkin's movie is merely the "seen," to quote the nineteenth-century French political economist Frédéric Bastiat. The "unseen" is the experimentation that never takes place because government is taxing away so much in corporate earnings. Profits are the reward for entrepreneurial creativity. American filmmakers—from Steven Spielberg, to Brad Bird (Pixar), to David Cameron—set the global standard for creativity, but we should never forget the films that are never made. How many exciting ideas never see the light of day because of the corporate taxes shackling the movie industry?

Filmmaking, of course, isn't the only business hemmed in by high tax rates, and it's certainly not the most important. Oil remains an essential economic input, yet profitable U.S. oil companies arguably suffer the greedy hand of government the most. ExxonMobil alone paid thirty-one billion in taxes on its profits in 2012, more than any other company in the United States.[13]

Oil companies have long been a favorite whipping boy of the political class, and it's politically easy to demand that "Big Oil" pay more of its fair share. But a large part of the energy industry's tax problem is that it is tied to the place where the oil and gas are. While Google can move its human assets from high-tax California to low-tax Texas, oil companies cannot move Prudhoe Bay from Alaska, with its 9 percent corporate tax rate, to Texas, where corporate profits are not taxed. They can't move the Bakken Shale out of North Dakota, with its 5.15 percent corporate tax, to South Dakota, where corporate profits once again are not taxed.[14] It's no surprise, then, that the list of the ten highest-taxed U.S. businesses includes three oil companies.[15]

Of even greater importance is what the world economy loses when an oil giant like ExxonMobil hands over so much precious capital to the federal government every year. ExxonMobil's profits and market valuation are certain signs that it is delivering enormous value to its shareholders and customers. Its executives have made it the most valuable of the numerous public oil companies in the United States, demonstrating unexcelled skill in deploying the capital allocated to them. Does anyone believe that John Boehner, Nancy Pelosi, Mitch McConnell, and Harry Reid are better allocators of the billions of dollars that ExxonMobil annually relinquishes to the government?

In spite of the predations of rapacious politicians, the oil industry is enjoying a renaissance of sorts. But we mustn't forget Bastiat's "unseen." How much better off would corporations in the energy industry—and by extension their shareholders—be without the self-righteous fleecing to which they must submit?

Is it possible that we've already forgotten what happened in 2008, when Congress used taxpayer dollars to bail out corporations that could no longer support themselves? The bailouts properly offended the electorate. This raises a question that goes to the heart of the corporate tax question: Do we prefer businesses that can suceed without taxpayer assistance, or would we like to continue saving the weak? The question answers itself.

Just as successful companies should be allowed to succeed, unsuccessful companies should be allowed to fail. The great Austrian School economist Ludwig von Mises wrote that the entrepreneur who fails to use his capital to the "best possible satisfaction of consumers" is "relegated to a place in which his ineptitude no longer hurts people's well-being."[16] Mises meant that businesses succeed because they fill an unmet need. If they fail, it is often because they have failed the consumer. In that case, bankruptcy is an economic good, because it relieves those the market has left for dead of any further capital to destroy.

The influential Austrian had a point. Inept corporations weaken society not only by failing to serve customers and shareholders but also by dissipating precious capital in the process. Politicians should keep this principle in mind the next time they are tempted to bail out failing businesses, even very big ones. The successful businesses that serve our myriad needs and desires while employing many of us should not labor under oppressive taxation. Just the same, government should get out of the way when companies fail because they do not meet our needs.

CHAPTER THREE

Government Spending Did Not Create the Internet, and Has Never Created a Job

Work expands so as to fill the time available for its completion.
—C. Northcote Parkinson, *Parkinson's Law*

84 *Charing Cross Road* was one of the better movies of 1987. Starring Anne Bancroft, Anthony Hopkins, and Judi Dench, the art house film chronicles a transatlantic friendship between two bibliophiles over twenty years.

What strikes the viewer today is the cumbersome way that people acquired out-of-print books in the mid-twentieth century. The prohibitive expense of an international telephone call required ordinary people to communicate by letter. So Helene Hanff (played by Bancroft), a customer in New York, writes to Frank Doel (played by Hopkins), a second-hand-book seller in London, about buying several volumes from him by mail and pays with a check.

From our perspective, the transaction seems intolerably slow. The absence of the internet, email, and cheap long distance telephone service made something as simple as purchasing a book a difficult endeavor.

Fast forward to the 2000s, and Hanff would not have to contact Doel at all. Instead, she would go to Amazon.com or the AbeBooks website, where she could search the inventories of second-hand booksellers from the entire English-speaking world and purchase the desired books with her credit card. Thanks to the visionary Jeff Bezos, *84 Charing Cross Road* is available on Amazon.com, but it no longer describes how we live.

Jeff Bezos has a net worth in the billions because the company he founded led online retailers in transforming the way people shop. The market has rewarded his creative genius so handsomely because exchanges that were once difficult and time-consuming now take place in a matter of minutes or even seconds.

What does any of this have to do with government spending? First of all, many people believe that government spending created the internet. In 2013, *Fortune* magazine's Allan Sloan wrote,

> Bezos's company, after all, is based on the Internet, which was created during the Cold War by a military research-and-development arm of the federal government, the Advanced Research Projects Agency. No Arpanet, no Internet. No Internet, no Amazon, no $25 billion personal fortune for Jeff Bezos.[1]

Absolutely false. Government by definition has no resources, as your annual income tax return demonstrates. Government can spend, and for that matter borrow, only to the extent that it can tax away wealth. Nor does government create jobs. The work government "creates" is a function of what it can tax away from workers' earnings or borrow based on that power to tax. All jobs—public or private—trace their origin to private sector productivity. The only wealth that politicians and bureaucrats have to invest was taken from someone else.

What about the internet? Government investment had a role in creating a crude and largely unusable version of the internet, and even that was accomplished only by taking something from the private sector first. It was private production by individuals motivated by profit that made the internet of today possible. Allan Sloan's paean to government investment notwithstanding, government can give only what is first taken away.

Not so in the private sector. We have already seen how Henry Ford's reinvestment of his profits made the automobile ubiquitous. Personal computers are an equally powerful example. In the 1970s, a personal computer cost over a million dollars. But thanks to people like Michael Dell, computers today are the low-cost rule across all income classes in the United States and much of the developed world. The proliferation of inexpensive smartphones created by entrepreneurs at BlackBerry and Apple shows how the profit motive has democratized access to information and communication on devices that fit in our pockets. And since you will usually enjoy a profit if you come up with ways to improve people's lives, capitalism provides in abundance.

The important question is not how much should government spend to create something as transformative and life-enhancing as the internet, but how much sooner would something as transformative and life-enhancing as the internet appear without the heavy spending of government? Government spending does not create jobs. It erects barriers to investment and therefore job creation.

Remember—entrepreneurs cannot be entrepreneurs without capital, whether it is their own savings, funds borrowed from family members, or investment from others. One of the best examples is Google. It's easy to forget that this omnipresent company was once neither large nor influential. Back in 1998, Jeff Bezos put $250,000 of his own money into the venture.[2] Google was eventually able to attract a great deal more investment, but it was Bezos's funds that made the company's early ascent possible. He was also an early investor in Twitter, a company so successful that its name, like Google's, has become a verb.[3]

Facebook has been instrumental in reuniting long lost friends and acquaintances, and it has become the way hundreds of millions of people announce life events, share their political views, or simply wish friends a happy birthday. It is a public company now worth billions of dollars, but at one time it was a tiny social media site meant to bring together college students at elite universities. Recognizing its potential early on, the billionaire Peter Thiel invested five hundred thousand dollars, laying the groundwork for the world's foremost social network to become infinitely more than its creators could have imagined.[4]

Then there is Apple, Inc., one of the most valuable companies in the world today. But when Steve Jobs returned in 1997, Apple was in serious trouble. Jobs eventually righted the ship, but it is not well known that Bill Gates put $150 million into the sagging technology firm when its future was dubious and other sources of credit were not interested.[5]

The point is elementary: entrepreneurial ideas need capital. Government doesn't provide that capital. It competes for it. Corporate taxes are a penalty on production. They take precious capital that could be invested in new products or improvements to existing ones.

Government spending acts like another tax on production. Government has money to spend because it first takes money in taxes or borrows it from the private sector, reducing the amount of investment capital available to those who need it. Government spending represents the extraction of limited funds that, if not consumed by politicians, might reach a future Microsoft or a company like Apple that is on the verge of huge technological advances.

Sadly, the government often wastes the money it takes from the private sector. It's a long and sad story, as we see if we go back to the Great Depression of the 1930s, when the conceit that government could spend society into prosperity became political orthodoxy in America.

Arthurdale is a largely forgotten town in West Virginia, but in the '30s it was the scene of an ambitious experiment by federal government. A state historical marker at the site reads: "Established 1933–34 under Federal Homestead Act, one of several model planned-communities nationwide, and a pet project of Eleanor Roosevelt, to assist unemployed through self-sufficient farming and handicrafts."[6]

Eleanor Roosevelt discovered the area that became Arthurdale in 1933. Author C. J. Maloney describes in his 2011 book *Back to the Land* how, upon seeing the destitution at Scots Run near Morgantown, "she demanded of her husband, President Franklin Delano Roosevelt, that something be done for them. The town of Arthurdale, West Virginia, created and sustained expressly on FDR's command, was that something."[7]

"Eleanor's Little Village" ultimately failed, as you would expect a government-planning experiment to do, but at least it left us some important lessons about government spending. One of these is about waste. Private homebuilders erect houses intending to sell them for more than it cost to build them. But there was no such market discipline in Arthurdale, where homes built by the federal government at an average cost of $16,600 each were sold for $750 to $1,249.[8] That's what happens when the party allocating capital faces no discipline from the marketplace. Private lenders generally don't tolerate the blatant waste of their money, and they would have quickly pulled their funds if a private construction company had been building those houses in Arthurdale.

The cost overruns in Arthurdale manifest how the federal government labored under no such market discipline. Why should it have? This is not to speak ill of those who work in government, but to say that the federal government has no private investors to please. Instead, it has the bottomless well of taxpayer dollars perpetually to draw from when funds are running short.

Government programs are about waste not because all government officials are crooks, inept, or both. The problem is that government programs are funded regardless of their effectiveness. Every day poorly run businesses fail. Just how many government programs does Congress shut down annually? Is it conceivable that the politicians who fund government programs have a better rate of success than private investors? The answer is obvious: of course not. Incentives matter. Administrators of government programs, enjoying endless funding, feel no urgency to adapt to new realities in the marketplace. Waste is the natural result of such an arrangement.

One response to complaints about "wasteful government spending" (a redundant phrase if ever there was one) is that government must invest where even the most intrepid of private investors will not. More to the point, government must play the role of the venture capitalist for projects that are seemingly too risky for even the boldest of investors—a plausible argument at first blush, yet it quickly succumbs to numerous contradictions. Although federal pay has recently eclipsed the wages of some private-sector work,[9] successful investors remain some of the richest people in the world. Warren Buffett tops this list, but a perusal of the Forbes 400 confirms that plenty of capital allocators would love to replace Buffett at the top. Net worth is a market signal, and it tells us that the most astute investors do not toil for the relatively puny salaries offered by the federal government.

The notion that private investors lack the nerve to put capital into the most perilous new ideas is belied by history. Recall the early days of the automobile. Investment in that contraption was the very definition of risky. Still, at the dawn of the automotive age, there were over two thousand automobile companies in the United States. Only 1 percent survived.[10]

The failure of formerly high-flying companies has been commonplace in the computer and technology industry for a long time. Yet investment in Silicon Valley continues to soar. Apologists for government investment would have us believe that investors will never wade into certain risky areas, but the truth is that the greater the risk, the greater the reward. Intrepid investors are to varying degrees attracted to the riskiest investment opportunities *precisely because* of the potential for outsized gains.

Governments, then, are not only experts at wasting limited capital but are also filled with individuals who are incapable of directing capital toward successful ideas. The good ones are earning billions in the private sector. The unconvinced should read the late Robert Bartley's essential 1992 book, *The Seven Fat Years*, in which he asks readers to "Rank in order the most likely recipient of capital from an industrial planning bureaucracy:

(A) Steve Jobs's garage.

(B) IBM

(C) A company in the district of the most powerful congressman."[11]

The obvious answer to Bartley's question shows why politicians who talk about government "investment" deserve our skepticism. The oft-repeated phrase "follow the money" is apt here in that government is rather conservative in the non-ideological sense. Steve Jobs, as is well known, was a college dropout who founded Apple in his garage. Apple today is a monument to American innovation, but garage start-ups are by the very adjective that describes them not the companies that politicians will migrate toward.

They tend to invest in the Solyndras of the world. The failed solar panel company received an infamous $535 million loan from the Department of Energy that taxpayers will ultimately swallow. Solyndra's biggest private backer was George Kaiser, a top donor to President Barack Obama and other Democratic Party causes.[12]

All of this matters a great deal in discussions about economic growth simply because a dollar is a dollar is a dollar. The "seen" of Arthurdale, Solyndra, and every other government "investment" is the funds taken from the citizenry in order to build houses or solar panels with little regard to cost or return on investment. The "unseen" is what profit-disciplined businesses might have done with the capital that the government has consumed.

How many Googles and Facebooks will never come to be because the federal government extracts so much money from its productive citizenry? What struggling companies might have been saved as Apple was if not for the federal government's spendthrift ways? These questions are painful to ponder. But they reveal the scope of the opportunities we will enjoy if we ever shrink Leviathan.

CHAPTER FOUR

It's the Spending, Stupid: Budget Deficits Really Don't Matter

The deficit is not a meaningless figure, only a grossly overrated one.
—Robert L. Bartley, *The Seven Fat Years*

In April 2013, Apple, Inc., easily floated a seventeen-billion-dollar debt offering. Investors eagerly lined up to buy the company's debt in what was the largest non-bank deal in history.[1] That Apple could take on so much debt surely surprised no one. The success of its offering reflected a broad market consensus that the technology colossus, one of the most valuable companies in the world thanks to its sleek iPhones and iPads, would have little problem repaying what it had borrowed. In 2011, Google successfully completed a three-billion-dollar debt offering.[2] The rate of interest that both companies had to pay on their debt was only slightly higher than the rates that the U.S. government has to pay when it borrows.

Why is it that the federal government can borrow so cheaply? The U.S. Treasury's debt is backed by the richest economy in the world—that's why. Whatever problems the United States faces, its private economy still claims some of the world's most economically dynamic individuals and companies. The enormous productivity of Americans makes it easy for the Treasury to borrow money at very low rates of interest, enabling the federal government to spend at a deficit. Because the government can tax those economically dynamic individuals and companies, investors know the Treasury is a good bet to repay the money it borrows.

It's easier to think about government debt if we take it down to the individual level. Let us say someone wins fifty thousand dollars during a lucky weekend in Las Vegas. When he announces his windfall to some friends, three of them ask if they can borrow the money. The first friend is a hard-working investment banker who earns two million dollars per year. He receives most of his pay at bonus time, much of the bonus is paid in company shares that can be sold only after one year. Short on cash in the near term, the banker promises to pay the money back once the share lock-up is lifted.

The second friend is a mid-level paper salesman. He earns a hundred thousand dollars in a good year, but in a volatile economy his pay some years dips to seventy-five thousand. And as the economy becomes increasingly paperless, he could lose his job at any time.

The third friend is a fun-loving free spirit who constantly tinkers with new business ideas. Too unorthodox to put on a suit each day and work in a corporate bureaucracy, this risk-taker has happened on an exciting new iPhone app and desperately needs capital to get it developed in time for meetings with some Sand Hill Road venture capital firms.

Logic dictates the investment banker is the best lending bet. With his high annual income, he could easily repay the fifty thousand dollars at year-end. Both parties know this is a low-risk loan. With plans in place to sell a quarter-million dollars' worth of bank shares when the lock-up ends, the banker merits a 3 percent rate of interest.

The paper salesman is a higher risk. Technology is making paper less necessary, as the lender knows. More worried about the salesman's creditworthiness, he would charge him 6 percent to borrow the fifty thousand.

The intense competition in the technology industry makes the developer of the next "killer app" the riskiest borrower. Yet it is precisely that risk that lets the lender charge a princely rate—say 12 percent—for the use of that money.

Ultimately, the owner of the fifty thousand dollars decides that each of his friends is a good bet relative to the interest he will pay, so he divides the money unequally among them on conservative grounds—$33,500 to the investment banker at 3 percent, ten thousand to the paper salesman at 6 percent, and sixty-five hundred to the high risk–high reward entrepreneur at 12 percent.

The question of government deficits is as basic as this story. The U.S. economy is the largest in the world, and the U.S. Treasury annually receives nearly three trillion dollars in tax revenues. It should be easy for the United States to run large deficits.

The United States is not the only nation that can float its debt with relative ease. The countries with the next-biggest budget deficits include Japan, England, China, and France.[3] It is not shocking that countries whose treasuries are showered with tax revenues can run up big deficits. More to the point, rich countries have no problem borrowing in debt markets made up of some of the most sophisticated investors in the world.

By contrast, poor countries are largely shut out of those same debt markets. Nicaragua and Honduras have almost no annual debt, while the perennial economic laggard Zimbabwe actually posts a budget surplus in some years. No reasonable investor would bet on governments in countries with such weak economies. It doesn't matter what their tax rates are because there is so little to tax.

Back to Apple and Google for a moment. Both of these private-sector companies operate far more effectively than the U.S. government, so why do they pay slightly more to borrow money? Because they might have a bad year, or years. But the federal government never has a bad year. Although its revenues rise and fall with the economy, they're always so abundant that investors view Treasury debt as riskless. Buyers of government debt are betting on the ability of the nation's private sector to generate the wealth necessary to pay back the money borrowed. Nosebleed government deficits, paradoxically, are a market signal that investors are confident about the economic future of the United States.

Just as the lucky gambler would lend the most at the lowest rate of interest to the investment banker, a smaller amount at a higher rate of interest to the salesman in a shaky industry, and the smallest amount at the highest rate of interest to the serial entrepreneur still aiming for the big score, sophisticated institutional investors allocate credit to companies and governments according to the risk involved. Those with the best prospects are able to borrow the most money at the cheapest price, and then those deemed the least creditworthy must pay seemingly usurious rates in order to attract lenders.

Yet even though sophisticated lenders the world over line up for the privilege of lending to the U.S. Treasury at the lowest interest rates in the world, we could fill several Rose Bowls with all the commentators who for decades have been predicting fiscal doom for the United States. What is even stranger is that many of these commentators would agree that markets are rather wise.

The British historian Niall Ferguson is a well-known right-of-center economic thinker who has written many excellent books on economic history. But writing about the U.S. budget deficit in October of 2013, Ferguson warned,

> [T]he fiscal position of the federal government is in fact much worse today than is commonly realized. As anyone can see who reads the most recent long-term budget outlook—published last month by the Congressional Budget Office, and almost entirely ignored by the media—the question is not if the United States will default but when and on which of its rapidly spiraling liabilities.[4]

The popular and market-friendly commentator Mark Steyn writes in his 2012 book *After America* that "the prevailing political realities of the United States do not allow for any meaningful course correction," and "without meaningful course correction, America is doomed."[5] *National Review*'s roving correspondent Kevin Williamson declares in his 2013 book, *The End Is Near and It's Going to Be Awesome*, that the United States' insurmountable budget deficits are driving us broke.

Ferguson, Steyn, and Williamson could all be right. But pessimists have been predicting disaster for America since before it was an independent country. And although each of these men would agree that markets in general are rather smart, implicit in the commentary from each is that the markets for debt are stupid. That seems unlikely to me. Excessive government spending unquestionably hurts growth, but debt markets are not exactly composed of people who majored in basket weaving. Buyers of government debt are just as careful as people who lend to individuals.

Even if Ferguson, Steyn, and Williamson know something that investors don't, worries about government debt still miss the forest for the trees. Government borrowing is, on its face, a problem since governments compete with entrepreneurs and companies for limited capital. But as I've pointed out in earlier chapters, a dollar is a dollar is a dollar.

Don't ever forget that we live in a global market. Whether the federal government borrows money or takes it in taxes isn't the point. Both actions reduce the amount of capital to which the private sector has access, and that hurts growth. Which is preferable, annual federal deficits of five hundred billion dollars on one trillion dollars in annual spending or a balanced budget of three trillion dollars? The economic logic says the former is better. What's important is the amount spent on an annual basis.

Indeed, it is of the utmost importance to reduce government expenditure in total. Entrepreneurs cannot be entrepreneurs without capital. If the federal government is consuming less of the capital stock, then the productive will have a bigger pool of capital to bid on.

Returning to the individual example earlier in this chapter, what if the guy in Vegas wins $100,000 instead of $50,000? The entrepreneur with visions of a world-changing app is now a more attractive borrower. With an extra fifty grand, it makes sense to risk a larger share of the total amount lent on a borrower who promises a bigger reward. Now he might lend fifty thousand to the banker,

$30,500 to the paper pusher, and $19,500 to the next great software developer.

You can see why government spending deserves more attention than deficits. Economic growth is about the leap, experimentation, and taking risks on new ideas. When government consumes more capital, investors will be more cautious about how they allocate what's left. Yet the riskiest ventures offer the greatest potential benefits to the economy. *Sports Illustrated*'s annual swimsuit edition, which brings in forty million dollars each year to Time, Inc., "began as a lark, a what-the-hell, nothing-else-is-working improvisation" back in the early 1960s.[6]

In 2002 the classic 1984 film *This Is Spinal Tap* was included in the U.S. National Film Registry, "which preserves films deemed 'culturally, historically or aesthetically significant.'" Christopher Guest, one of the film's creators, recounts that "we went around Hollywood showing our little movie, trying to get somebody to give us the money to finish it, and we were met with a resounding, 'We don't get this. What the hell are you doing?'" Eventually the legendary television producer Norman Lear provided the financing, and an eminently quotable movie was born.[7]

In 1986, Russell Maryland was a lightly recruited high school football player who, thanks to his dad's sending a tape to the University of Miami late in the recruiting process, was awarded the football power's final scholarship for that year. After his senior year for the Hurricanes, Maryland was the number-one pick in the NFL draft. He went on to win Super Bowls with the Dallas Cowboys and was inducted into the College Football Hall of Fame in 2012. Most college coaches overlooked him, but with an extra scholarship, the Miami Hurricanes took a winning risk.[8]

It's hard to achieve the big economic leaps if capital is scarce. The script for *The French Connection* lies idle, *This Is Spinal Tap* never gets made, *Sports Illustrated* doesn't take a risk on a swimsuit issue, and Russell Maryland's football career ends after high school. On the other hand, restrained government spending means there is more capital available, and a small amount of the bigger capital pool can go to the risk takers.

Excessive government spending is a real but unseen cost. The unseen is all the brilliant ideas that never get funded. To reduce the burden that is government spending is to increase the slice of capital that will migrate to the riskiest ideas, and by virtue of being risky, the ideas that can truly transform the economy. Because we want to live better, let's get to work on slashing federal outlays; deficits be damned. They really don't matter.

CHAPTER FIVE

Capital Gains Are the Elusive Jackpot That Drive Innovation

The prospect of capital gains provides an especially important incentive; it is the big jackpot that attracts entrepreneurial vigor.
—Robert L. Bartley, *The Seven Fat Years*

The Dallas Cowboys are the most valuable team in the National Football League.[1] Thanks to sponsorship and premium seating revenues of two hundred million dollars per year, along with a share of league television, licensing, and merchandizing revenues, the team can claim a net worth of over three billion dollars.

The owner, Jerry Jones, bought the Cowboys in February 1989 for $149 million. He quickly fired the legendary coach Tom Landry and hired his former University of Arkansas teammate Jimmy Johnson. Jones and Johnson proved an excellent team, at first anyway. By 1993 the Cowboys were Super Bowl champions. They won it again in 1994, and a third time in 1996, with Barry Switzer as head coach.

Jones's stupendous success may appear easy in hindsight, and his purchase of the team back in 1989 may seem a no-brainer. The NFL's annual revenues of ten billion dollars put it on par with several countries. The league gets five billion dollars a year for the rights to televise its games. It earns one to two billion dollars annually in sponsorships from companies like PepsiCo, two billion from ticket sales, and reportedly a billion more from licensing and merchandizing sales.[2] Considering what a cash machine the NFL is and what the Cowboys earn separately from their state-of-the-art AT&T Stadium, Jones would have been crazy not to buy the team when it was put up for sale in the late 1980s.

But just as the present is a flawed predictor of the future (remember when Mark McGwire, Tiger Woods, and Lance Armstrong were among the most popular athletes—and people—in the world?), it is often worthless in trying to understand the past. Jones's investment bankers at Salomon Brothers tried to convince him *not* to buy the Cowboys, warning him that he was risking his net worth on a lousy investment.

Jones bought the team from H. R. "Bum" Bright, who sold it because the Cowboys were a money loser. In 1988 the team had posted a 3–13 record and lost nine million dollars. More than ninety of the luxury suites in their old home, Texas Stadium, were empty, only one game in '88 had sold out, and attendance had declined 25 percent from 1984 to 1988.[3]

Roger Staubach famously quarterbacked "America's Team" to two Super Bowl wins in the 1970s, and by 1988 he was overseeing a successful commercial real estate firm. His name and sterling reputation would have opened up almost any rich man's door if he had tried to raise the capital to buy the team he knew better than almost anyone. But when the Cowboys' long-time president Tex Schramm encouraged him to assemble a group to buy the team, Staubach "soon dropped the project when he found little interest."[4] The fact is, the NFL and the Dallas Cowboys of 1988 were a far cry from the gold mine they are today. Jones risked his fortune on a business that was unattractive to the smart money three decades ago.

So what was Jones's initial reward for the risks he took? When he flew down to Austin to dismiss Landry, the livid coach told him, "You could have saved your gas."[5] Landry was venerated in Dallas. When Jones fired him, people started calling the Arkansan "Jethro" after Jethro Bodine, the *nouveau riche* rube of *Beverly Hillbillies* fame. Others called him "The Eighth Blunder of the World," and many cars in Dallas sported bumper stickers reading "Money Can't Buy Class, Mr. Jones," and "The Dallas Cowboys ... From One Bum to Another."[6]

Maybe Landry had a point and Jones could have handled the transition more gracefully. But the fruits of Jones's life's work were wrapped up in an acquisition that everyone thought was a bad idea. Jones famously promised that he would have a role in every aspect of the organization: "I intend to have an understanding of socks and jocks...."[7] But what he didn't mention—probably because of his unshakeable belief in himself and the restless energy that characterizes entrepreneurs—was the price of failure. The players and employees would still have their wages, but he could have ended up with a lot less.

Jones's story is useful in explaining the capital gains tax, the tax we impose on successful investments. If Jones sold the team today, he would owe the federal government several hundred million dollars for having revived a franchise that was losing both games and revenue when he bought it. In other words, the capital gains tax is the penalty the government places on his success. Jones did more than risk his capital. Like most entrepreneurs, he put in ungodly hours fixing what he had bought. His biographer, Jim Dent, describes him as "an adrenaline-charged blur of a man. He can accomplish more on two hours of sleep than most men can on a full night."[8] And after all that risk and work, the federal government will help itself to a substantial portion of the investment's upside.

A funny thing about the debate over the capital gains tax is that its supporters call the fruits of investment "unearned income." There is no mention of the work that went into acquiring that capital in the first place. Though Jones earned the bulk of his pre-Cowboys fortune in the energy business, he started at the age of nine, "greet[ing] customers at the family supermarket back in Arkansas. In college he sold shoes from the trunk of his car." Dent notes that Jones "has sold virtually everything under the sun, from chickens to real estate."[9]

The policy of taxing "unearned income" ignores the effort that goes into creating the wealth that can eventually become investment in commercial ventures like the Cowboys. Worse, it suggests that people like Jones passively invest their earnings with no regard to fixing what is broken—not that there's anything wrong with that, as I will explain in the next chapter. Every dollar of Jones's substantial fortune was earned, and he used those earnings to purchase and revitalize an unattractive property called the Dallas Cowboys. But what if Jones had faced a capital gains tax rate of 98 percent?

That's silly, you say. No politician would penalize investment success at such a confiscatory rate. Yet Great Britain taxed what the Rolling Stones' guitarist Keith Richards referred to as "so-called unearned income" at a rate of 98 percent in the 1970s. Richards concluded, reasonably enough, "that's the same as being told to leave the country."[10] Judging from Britain's feeble economic growth in the '70s, lots of other entrepreneurially minded subjects got the message and did just that.

Successful entrepreneurs are not rich because starting a business is easy or safe. They're rich because starting a business is difficult, and investing in a new business is the very definition of uncertainty. Capital gains taxes make it much more difficult for entrepreneurs to attract the capital they need. With a capital gains tax of 98 percent, you'd be a fool to invest in a new business no matter how promising it seemed.

The U.S. economy experienced problems similar to Great Britain's in the 1970s. The capital gains rate charged on investment returns then was 50 percent, and, unsurprisingly, investment in future business concepts nearly ground to a halt. The cost of investment was high (and the dollar was falling—a problem I'll discuss in detail later), and there was an average of only twenty-eight initial public offerings a year from 1974 to 1978.

A reduction of the capital gains rate to 25 percent in 1978 caused the number of IPOs to soar. The number increased to 103 in 1979, and in 1986, 953 companies were taken public.[11] Incentives, such as lowering the penalty on investment returns, clearly matter.

The capital gains rates that prevailed in the United States and Great Britain in the 1970s would have substantially increased Jerry Jones's risk in buying the Cowboys. Why would he buy a losing team and spend the money and effort necessary to turn it around if Uncle Sam was going to take half his profit if he ever sold it?

Here lies another contradiction within the conceit of "unearned income." With a capital gains tax of 50 to 98 percent, Jerry Jones probably wouldn't have bought the Cowboys. But if he had traveled the world and bought expensive cars instead, the tax system would have smiled on his behavior. A life of consumption rather than work and investment would have lowered his tax bill. Putting his life's earnings into the Cowboys, by contrast, would have generated a tax bill in the hundreds of millions of dollars, assuming he eventually sold the team.

But do entrepreneurs really worry about tax rates when they put money to work? Can't we assume that Steve Jobs and Jeff Bezos were so focused on revolutionizing computers, tablets, phones, and the way we shop for them that no amount of taxation would have deterred them? And when Jerry Jones bought the Dallas Cowboys, he declared, "I always wanted to be in the football business."[12]

Maybe so, but there are no entrepreneurs without capital. Someone somewhere must delay consumption in favor of savings and investment so that entrepreneurs can work their magic. Remember, people have choices when it comes to their money. At present, the tax on capital gains is 20 percent, but investors also have the option of buying municipal bonds issued by the cities in which they live. "Munis" have low volatility, so selling them usually produces small capital gains or losses. Even better, income from munis is exempt from both federal and state tax. If you think about it, you can see why IPOs practically disappeared in the '70s. Faced with high risk and high taxes if they invest in a business, savers will protect their wealth in largely tax-free investments like municipal bonds.

Steve Jobs and Jeff Bezos had to raise capital to start Apple and Amazon. More to the point, some investors delayed consumption in order to put their capital into Apple and Amazon. But if the capital gains rate had been 98 percent, à la Great Britain in the '70s, you probably wouldn't have a pocket-sized computer phone or the ability to shop for numerous goods online today.

Jerry Jones, of course, didn't have to raise capital to buy the Cowboys. He used his *own* money, so maybe the capital gains tax wouldn't have fazed him. Nevertheless, wealth is a function of savings and investment, so Jones made use of previous capital gains when he invested in his NFL team. And remember, he said he had always wanted to be in the football *business*. If Jones had faced 1970s-level capital gains taxes, the football business might have been far less appealing.

The NFL's collective success is largely the fruit of its ambitious owners' willingness to spend on front office workers, coaches, and players. It is often said that the genius of the NFL is its league-wide parity. Year after year, once down-on-their-luck teams become Super Bowl contenders. But if capital gains taxation promised a near-zero return for success on the field, owners would have little incentive to expend capital on the coaches or quarterbacks who represent the difference between mediocrity and hoisting the Lombardi Trophy. More realistically, the NFL of today would not exist if the capital gains rate were at levels that prevailed not too long ago. Why should anyone take risks to improve his organization if politicians will consume the majority of the rewards that might result?

Fortunately, capital gains taxes are much lower than in the 1970s. And for men like Jerry Jones, wealth is about "keeping score," so they continue to take big risks. Indeed, Jones's success taught other owners how to enhance the value of their teams. The Cowboys haven't won a Super Bowl since 1996, but Jones paved the way for businessmen like Robert Kraft, who bought the New England Patriots for $172 million in 1996 and took on an enormous amount of debt in the process.[13] Kraft's Patriots have reached the Super Bowl five times, winning three of them, and today they're regarded as the model franchise in the NFL. Under Kraft, the value of the Patriots has soared to $2.6 billion.[14] All the other NFL teams have benefitted from Jones's and Kraft's success.

Buying an NFL team was a big risk for Kraft—risk that was a source of friction with his late wife, Myra. She "went cuckoo on me when I got back" from buying the team, he acknowledges.[15] He probably wouldn't have purchased the Patriots if the capital gains rates of the '70s were in place in 1996. Without the possibility of turning his purchase into something far more valuable, Kraft had no reason to take on so much debt, and incur the wrath of his wife.

Some might respond that neither Kraft nor Jones intends to sell his team. That's not the point. If the capital gains rate had been 98 percent, or even 50 percent, Jones probably wouldn't have built the wealth he needed to buy the Cowboys, and Kraft would have been unable to attract the financing for his purchase. The NFL is a better and more prosperous league thanks to the arrival of owners like Kraft and Jones, but it is important to remember that other business sectors are no different. Investors have choices and make decisions that are shaped by incentives.

Failure is how we evolve economically. It provides information to entrepreneurs and frees up capital for more productive uses. But the possibility of failure makes investing risky. Investors who might risk their capital in the private sector know they might lose it all, and they face a 20 percent tax on whatever return they do get on their investment. Those same investors have the option of buying government bonds, and though the returns are small, they're reliable and, in the case of municipal bonds, tax-free.

Now, government performs certain functions that no one else can perform and which are necessary for a free economy—providing security and the rule of law, for example—but it produces no wealth.

Our tax code, nevertheless, puts entrepreneurs at an enormous disadvantage when they compete with the government for investors.

What have we lost with a tax code that gives government consumption preferential treatment over an investment in the next Steve Jobs? It's impossible to quantify, but since economic progress is the result of matching talent and ideas with capital in the private sector, it's horrifying to imagine what we're losing—cancer cures, advances in communication that would make the iPhone seem dull, and better transportation.

In a sane world politicians would abolish the capital gains tax altogether and raise the tax on income from government bonds. It won't happen any time soon, because politicians live to tax and borrow from our productivity in order to spend it. But make no mistake about the reduced standard of living that is the cost of squandering the people's money.

CHAPTER SIX

The Best Way to Spread the Wealth Around Is to Abolish the Estate Tax

Is the capital accumulated by the labor and abstinence of all former generations of no advantage to any but those who have succeeded to the legal ownership of part of it? And have we not inherited a mass of acquired knowledge, both scientific and empirical, due to the sagacity and industry of those who preceded us, the benefits of which are the common wealth of all?

—John Stuart Mill, *Principles of Political Economy*

Paris Hilton rocketed to fame and fortune in the early 2000s not because she won a Best Actress Oscar, started a successful software company, or created a successful hotel brand. She attained global renown and a big income for, well, being Paris Hilton.

The young, and sometimes the old, found themselves oddly attracted to the comely great-granddaughter of Conrad Hilton, the founder of the international chain of hotels that bear his name. Paris starred in the reality television show *The Simple Life*, and the release of a sex video perhaps surprisingly enhanced her personal brand.

While Miss Hilton can perhaps look forward to a large inheritance, her present notoriety nets her an annual income in the millions.

The attention lavished on Miss Hilton's every erratic (and erotic) move has aroused the interest of some sectors of the public in, of all things, the tax code—specifically, the estate tax, which they think should be increased to disinherit wastrels like her. But if the heiress's detractors considered the matter more carefully, they would come to the opposite conclusion.

Everyone knows that "you can't take it with you," but the federal government wants to make sure that you don't leave it behind either—at least not to your friends and loved ones. Uncle Sam therefore helps himself to 45 percent of your worldly goods if you die moderately well off. So why not spend with abandon before you die? Half of what you'd otherwise leave to your family will instead be shoveled into Leviathan's maw as soon as you're six feet under.

Politicians like to argue that wealth should not be concentrated in the hands of those who did not earn it. President Obama put the matter bluntly to "Joe the Plumber" during his 2008 campaign for president: Society is better off when politicians work to "spread the wealth."[1] Obama might have been a little too candid, and his advisers were probably horrified that he made his views so public. Nevertheless, President Obama revealed a deep misunderstanding about what happens when the government is not confiscating wealth.

The best way to "spread the wealth" around is to leave it in the hands of the wealthy. That sounds counterintuitive until you consider someone like Larry Ellison, the founder of Oracle, who can measure his wealth in the tens of billions. Ellison literally has more money than he can spend. That doesn't matter, though, because there is no such thing—short of stuffing it in the proverbial mattress—as idle money. When you deposit your money in the bank, the bank lends it out at a higher rate of interest than it pays you for the privilege of holding your deposit.

Us Weekly chronicles the affairs of the famous and the infamous, and Paris Hilton has been featured in the glossy innumerable times. One section of the magazine includes pictures of famous people doing things that regular people also do. Celebrities are just like everyone else, *Us Weekly* assures its readers. They pump their gas, they go to the store. They also have bank, money market, and brokerage accounts. Their accounts are quite a bit larger than yours and mine, but that's the point. The rich have a lot more money in savings.

Regardless of the size of one's account, however, no act of saving ever subtracts from demand or investment in job-creating businesses. One man's saving merely shifts consumption to someone else. Deposits in the bank are immediately lent to someone who needs the money to buy a car or pay college tuition. When Paris Hilton puts her money in a bank account, her fortune is redistributed to people who need that money for all manner of purchases, or a business start-up.

On the other hand, when Congress taxes away inherited wealth, money that would have been available to all at the market rate of interest falls under the control of legislators and an army of bureaucrats—the very characters the American public most despises.

The story does not end there. You've read it many times already, but it bears repeating—there are no companies or jobs without investment first. The ability to borrow and spend the money that Paris Hilton does not spend on private jets and clothes, along with the millions she will inherit, can become the seed of future Microsofts. This nation of entrepreneurs is brimming with ideas about how to get rich by creating products that everyone will enjoy. These ideas must match up with investment in order to help everyone. Imposing high taxes on the people who, by virtue of being rich, will provide the capital for these ideas doesn't just punish sybaritic heiresses—it punishes everyone.

To see what I'm talking about, let's revisit the 1970s. Back then, television was pretty bland. There were only three networks, a PBS channel, and, if you lived in a big city, a few more local stations. People called the television set the "idiot box" (the flat screen was decades into the future) because of the low-quality shows produced by a market with little competition. Americans were as sports-mad then as they are now, but the menu of televised sports was limited to what three networks decided to fit into their broadcasting schedules.

Enter Bill Rasmussen. A serial entrepreneur and master salesman, Rasmussen happened on the idea of buying transponder time on newly emerging cable satellites to create a twenty-four-hours-a-day, seven-days-a-week sports channel.[2] The new channel, originally named ESP-TV, evolved into the largest cable channel in the United States—the now much-loved ESPN.[3]

Entrepreneurs grow rich by solving problems or, as in the case of ESPN, providing something that people don't even know they want. And they often do this in the face of great skepticism. Today ESPN occupies a large campus in Bristol, Connecticut. But skepticism about the venture's prospects when it started back in 1979 confined it to an office the size of a living room. Rent was a hundred dollars per month, and the founders' "desks" were made from plywood nailed to old doors.[4]

When we think of the rich and successful, we usually focus on the "seen"—the big houses, palatial offices, and features in magazines like *Vanity Fair*. That's the end result. The "unseen" is what was there before all of the success. When Rasmussen announced the rollout of his cable sports channel to the *four* reporters who showed up at a Holiday Inn in Plainville, Connecticut, Bill Pennington, a future *New York Times* reporter, was "one of the people laughing. I thought, 'This is the stupidest thing I've ever heard.'"

Investors at the time apparently agreed. Michael Freeman, the author of *ESPN: The Uncensored History*, reports that "ESPN was hemorrhaging so much some at the network feared it wouldn't survive beyond 1980."[5] Rasmussen's son Scott emptied his bank account to come up with the ninety-one dollars for the incorporation fee, and Rasmussen himself took a $9,400 advance from his Visa card to pay the bills that were piling up.[6] The financial challenges were only beginning.

Even though Rasmussen was one of the first to appreciate the potential of satellites to reach television viewers, the cost of access to just one satellite was exorbitantly expensive for a cable network that was running on fumes. But entrepreneurs like Rasmussen have one thing in abundance—confidence in their idea. So in the absence of financing, Rasmussen cut a deal with RCA to rent one of its twenty-four-hours-a-day satellites for the then princely sum of thirty-five thousand dollars a month.[7] How he managed to honor that contract is a reminder of why trying to confiscate inherited wealth through the estate tax is so counterproductive.

John Paul Getty was the founder of an eponymous oil company. It was so successful that *Fortune* magazine named him the richest living American in 1957.[8] Getty died in 1976, leaving an estate valued in the billions. Stuart Evey was the man in charge of Getty Oil's non-oil investments.[9] The master salesman Bill Rasmussen found a believer in Evey, who was backed by the massive Getty estate. After much negotiation, Getty Oil invested ten million dollars in ESPN. Rasmussen's vision, which had attracted such ridicule, became a reality.

Proponents of the estate tax will scoff that ten million dollars was a pittance for Getty, and that successful businessmen pass plenty of wealth down to heirs. We need the estate tax, they say, to reduce the obscene concentration of wealth. It is a fair point, but the modest size of Getty's investment in ESPN is actually an argument for *abolishing* the estate tax.

Because ten million dollars meant so little to the Getty family, a brilliant cable network was created. ESPN, as Rasmussen's difficulty in finding backers showed, was the definition of a risky investment. It got funding because the Gettys had so much money that they were willing to take major risks with their substantial excess. If ESPN was funded with J. Paul Getty's chump change, how many more intriguing ideas could attract investment if rich people's estates weren't pillaged when they die?

Currently, estates worth five million dollars or less are untaxed, while estates larger than five million are taxed at the federal level of 45 percent. On its face, this system might seem fair. Since the vast majority of us will leave behind far less than five million dollars, our heirs will never have to worry about writing a big check to Uncle Sam. Only the really rich will have to deal with the IRS.

But it's not really fair at all. The non-rich don't benefit from the government's confiscation of large fortunes, and they're denied access to that money through the financial system to buy cars, build houses, and start businesses. A popular British television program shows what I mean. *Downton Abbey* chronicles the lives, loves, and drama of the aristocratic Crawley family at their Yorkshire estate in the early twentieth century.

When the series opens, Downton is in good financial shape thanks to the marriage twenty years earlier between the head of the family, the Earl of Grantham, to Cora, an American heiress. Marriage has long had an economic component that romantic Americans would perhaps rather not acknowledge. While the earl and countess appear happily married, it is understood that the marriage was, at least, initially, based on financial considerations. Cora had the money without the pedigree. Robert had the title but lacked the money to keep Downton Abbey in his distinguished family. The spouses were perfect complements to one another.

Among the series' many storylines is the persistent concern for how to keep Downton Abbey financially secure so that it can remain within the Crawley family. At end of the third season, the heir presumptive and co-owner of Downton, Matthew Crawley, dies, triggering the British death duties. In the fourth season, the Crawleys must figure out a way to pay the taxes without selling off some of the farmland on which the livelihood of many families depends.

I'll avoid a spoiler here, but let's just say that the Crawleys survive. After all, there wouldn't be much left of the series without Downton Abbey itself. The point is, *Downton Abbey* puts a human face on what happens when the taxman seizes a fortune meant for family. If part of the estate has to be sold off to appease His Majesty's Government, the families who have tended the land for generations will be dispossessed. Just as the non-rich suffer when the rich are taxed, it's the simple farming families of Downton who suffer the blow of a tax aimed at the wealthy Crawleys.

So who benefits from the breakup of an estate? To explore this question, let's come back to our side of the Atlantic. George Steinbrenner, the longtime owner of the New York Yankees, died in 2010, a year when the federal estate tax was briefly at zero thanks to a broad tax deal. By dying in 2010 rather than 2011, Steinbrenner saved his heirs from a six-hundred-million-dollar estate tax bill.[10] A running joke in 2010 was that old men with large fortunes should get on with dying if they were already ill. Imagine the savings!

This nation was founded by men so skeptical of government that they created one whose powers were almost solely geared to protecting the rights of individual citizens to live as they desired. It became the richest nation in the world because its constitution forbade excessive meddling by politicians in the lives of citizens. Yet by 2010, the citizens of what was the freest country in the world were reduced to hoping that certain family members would die in 2010 instead of 2011 so the government wouldn't seize half of what they left behind.

The incredulous might respond that a man savvy enough to build a fortune like George Steinbrenner's goes to great lengths to protect his wealth. Worst-case scenarios like selling off the Downton estate rarely come to pass because of skillful estate planning overseen by the nation's best lawyers. The skeptics would have a point, but a poor one. Yes, the rich are able to protect their life's work from the IRS with more or less success thanks to high-priced attorneys. But have the skeptics ever considered the economic waste involved? Estate lawyers have a real purpose in today's economy, but do not confuse what they do with actual wealth creation. At best, they are merely expensive facilitators of wealth preservation; facilitators who would have a far smaller role under a more rational tax code that didn't turn death into a taxable event. Indeed, the greedy hand of the political class has fostered the growth of professions that exist to prevent the *expropriation of wealth*.

The estate tax encourages the mistaken belief that a rich man's wealth helps others only when he is parted from it, either voluntarily or involuntarily. In 2010, Warren Buffett and Bill Gates, the two richest Americans, popularized the "Giving Pledge," a generous-sounding proposal for the super-rich to leave the majority of their wealth to "philanthropy" rather than future generations of their families. Buffett, Gates, and the others taking the Giving Pledge earned their money, so they have every right to dispose of it as they wish. If it makes them happiest to give it away to charity, then so be it. But it's worth remembering what Howard Kershner wrote in his 1971 book *Dividing the Wealth*: "the noblest charity is to show another how to avoid charity."[11] Without taking anything away from the undeniable good that comes from charity, the reality is that the greatest gift to bestow on anyone is a job. In free economies, those jobs are abundant.

The history of the twentieth century brutally revealed that the surest way to impoverish a country is for its government to plan everything centrally, including the distribution of wealth. Americans are some of the biggest givers to causes around the world, and they can give generously because they live in a country that, for all of its modern errors, remains economically free enough to produce enormous wealth.

Gates deserves cheers for trying to make a difference, but it was his brilliance in business that made his generosity possible. Gates, like all other successful entrepreneurs, attained his wealth because someone else delayed his own consumption—and yes, did *not* give to charity—making available to Gates the capital that allowed him to create Microsoft.

If Gates and Buffett earn adulation for giving much of their wealth away, we should also lionize those who hold on to every penny they have earned. When the rich "hoard" their wealth, it is loaned to those who need money for cars, clothes, and college tuition, not to mention the next generation of Bill Gateses, full of ideas but in need of the capital that will abound if some of society's richest keep most of their wealth intact so it can pass to future generations. More inherited wealth means more plentiful capital to seed the innovations of the future.

Sir Isaac Newton famously remarked, "If I have seen further it is by standing on the shoulders of giants." Only a microscopic portion of humanity will ever come into inherited money that is traceable to Rockefeller, Getty, Gates, or Hilton. Yet everyone will inherit the fruits of their commercial genius—better universities, hospitals, and museums; cures for disease; and most important of all, better economic opportunity. They are the giants on whose shoulders tomorrow's entrepreneurs will stand.

In his classic 1982 book, *The Economy in Mind*, the late Warren Brookes wisely observed, "Envy in reality is the single most impoverishing attitude of thought."[12] Envy is a waste of time, and when it becomes public policy it kills growth and jobs, hurting the envious more than the envied.

CHAPTER SEVEN

Wealth Inequality Is Beautiful

... it is the perception of inequality that induces people to take risks.
—Reuven Brenner, *History: The Human Gamble*

The *New York Times* may be the "paper of record," but *USA Today* bills itself as "The Nation's Newspaper." While the *Times* can claim news bureaus around the world and a highbrow readership, *USA Today* prints the news in an eminently readable format for the masses. More Americans rely on the ubiquitous *USA Today* for a snapshot of what is happening in news, business, and entertainment than on any other newspaper. And its sports page is arguably the best in the United States.

The late Al Neuharth rolled out *USA Today* in 1982 in the midst of a grinding recession. His timing might seem counterintuitive, but entrepreneurs see what others do not. They disrupt an existing market and provide goods that consumers perhaps did not even know they wanted. In short, entrepreneurs improve life.

Neuharth grew rich thanks to the success of *USA Today*. As he sometimes relayed to readers in his weekly column, his wealth allowed him to adopt many kids coming from poor backgrounds. Capitalism has a tendency to be compassionate.

"I was a poor German-Russian kid from South Dakota," Neuharth recalled. "My dad died when I was two."[1] He compensated for his lack of financial means with a rich spirit and a drive to do great things. Comparing himself with the talk-show host Larry King (who grew up poor in Brooklyn, and whose dad died when he was in grade school), Neuharth wrote, "Larry and I both knew we'd have to take some big risks if we wanted to make it big time. He gambled on a late-night radio talk show that he got syndicated nationally in 1978. It ultimately developed into CNN's *Larry King Live*. I gambled on *USA Today* in 1982. It became 'The Nation's Newspaper.'"[2]

Politicians and pundits often decry income inequality or the wealth gap, but their unhappiness is unfounded. Individual success that leads to wealth disparity often causes those who are not wealthy to take the risks necessary to attain riches. The success of King and Neuharth attests to economic freedom's sterling track record of improving the living conditions of those who are not rich.

Neuharth created a newspaper that democratized access to information, while King gambled on a show that brought the lives of the rich, famous, and erudite into America's living rooms. King ultimately thrived on CNN, a network founded by another restless entrepreneur, Ted Turner. A billionaire today, Turner's willingness to gamble on the once laughable idea of a twenty-four-hour news channel has further democratized access to knowledge of the world around us.

It was not long ago that J. K. Rowling was a divorced mother whose reduced circumstances forced her to live with her sister in Edinburgh, Scotland. In an interview with the *Daily Telegraph*, Rowling reflected on that impoverished period:

> I had no intention, no desire, to remain on benefits. It's the most soul-destroying thing. I don't want to dramatise, but there were nights when, though Jessica ate, I didn't. The suggestion that you would deliberately make yourself entitled … you'd have to be a complete idiot.
>
> I was a graduate, I had skills, I knew that my prospects long-term were good. It must be different for women who don't have that belief and end up in that poverty trap—it's the hopelessness of it, the loss of self-esteem. For me, at least, it was only six months. I was writing all the time, which really saved my sanity. As soon as Jessie was asleep, I'd reach for pen and paper.[3]

Impoverished financially but not in spirit, Rowling spent many days and nights writing what became the Harry Potter series. She gambled on her talent and created what is probably the most successful children's books franchise of all time.

Contemplating suicide because of mounting debts, a broken family, alcoholism, and a drug arrest, Dominick Dunne fled Beverly Hills in shame in the 1970s. He rented a room lacking a television or a telephone at Twin View Resorts in rural Oregon. He was finished as a movie producer, but Dunne gambled on a career as writer. His first movie script was roundly criticized, and his first book, *The Winners*, was a flop. Dunne wrote in his journal, "I have never believed in myself more than when I was writing my script. I was never happier with myself." With a burning desire to succeed despite his dire financial circumstances, Dunne persisted. He died in 2009 as one of the most popular criminal fiction writers in the world.[4]

Bernie Brillstein recounted his early difficulties in his autobiography, *Where Did I Go Right?* At the age of thirty-five, "I owed money, and I'd begun to believe that I might not make it in life."[5] The success of others in the entertainment industry and his own relative failure burdened him. With nothing to lose and desperate to prove himself, Brillstein started his own talent management company. His firm had a role in everything from *Saturday Night Live* to *The Muppet Show* and *Ghostbusters*. More recently, Brillstein's firm was behind *The Sopranos*. Inequality in hypercompetitive Hollywood (the subtitle of his book is *You're No One in Hollywood Unless Someone Wants You Dead*) fueled his creative fire.

Michael Bloomberg was let go by the investment bank Salomon Brothers in 1981, although his severance package included ten million dollars.[6] By any measure, including the massive fortunes of today, Bloomberg was very rich. He could have retired to a life of ease. But he was eager for something more in life, including business success that would rate a *New York Times* obituary. So the "unemployed" Bloomberg got to work on creating his own market and global news organization, what is now Bloomberg LP. His gamble on the news terminals now deemed essential on Wall Street and beyond has made him one of the richest men in the richest city in the world—a city he served as mayor from 2002 until 2013 and which will benefit from his charitable endeavors long into the future.

Inequality is highly visible, so opportunistic politicians thunder against it. What you hear less about is the fire that inequality lights under the rest of us. The achievements of others can spark a constructive form of envy. As the economist Reuven Brenner explains, "the more envious one is, the more one is willing to gamble."[7] Even better, the successful gambles that make some people wealthier than everyone else produce abundance for all, actually reducing the "lifestyle gap."

The modern age of commercial computing began in 1964 with the introduction of the IBM System/360, the most basic version of which cost over a million dollars.[8] Only the wealthiest could afford a computer that consumers of modest means today would scoff at for its limited speed and features. The prohibitive price of those early computers is a reminder of the value added by an entrepreneur. The successful envision what most do not. Indeed, what is evident to them is a problem in need of a solution, at which point they get to work.

When Michael Dell started his company in 1984, Apple was making waves with its Apple II, but personal computers were still rare. They were an expensive hobby for techies. Dell concluded that computers could be sold to the masses more cheaply by eliminating expensive retail showrooms. He's a billionaire today because he figured out how to mass-produce a product that only the rich had been able to enjoy. What was once a slow, elephantine, million-dollar, internet-less machine is now used by people of all income classes. Dell's story is one of many reminders that luxury is a historical concept. The rich get that way because they turn obscure luxuries into common commodities.

As recently as the 1970s, owning a telephone was impossible.[9] You *rented* your phone from Ma Bell, which charged you for the "luxury" of placing a call to a friend one block away. Handheld cellphones? They didn't exist in the 1970s. But by 1983, Motorola had introduced the DynaTAC 8000X, the "brick" made famous in Oliver Stone's 1987 film *Wall Street*. It couldn't fit in your pocket, its battery charge lasted thirty minutes, and it lacked the text, e-mail, and television capabilities that animate today's mobile phones.[10] A phone like Gordon Gekko's would set you back $3,995, not including the monthly service and long-distance calls, which were hundreds of dollars more. The early mobile phones were therefore rare and usually seen only in the stomping grounds of the rich and famous. Fortunately, profits—or at least the possibility of profits—attract imitators. Motorola began the cellphone revolution, but soon enough other technology companies and service providers entered the market to serve a global population eager to have connection from anywhere.

Some readers remember calling home to check messages left on bulky answering machines that have gone the way of the payphone, or literally *waiting by the phone* for a call from a client, boss, or future spouse. Younger readers may not comprehend the relative deprivation that was the norm for so long. Nowadays we look askance at cellphones with only a call function. Email, internet access, movies, and even the ability to watch your favorite sports team—live—are features we expect on our "smart" phones, which are both functional and affordable.

A mid-level Apple iPhone that retails for several hundred dollars (or less if the purchaser enters a contract with a wireless provider) has thirty-two gigabytes of flash memory, which would have cost the consumer *$1.44 million* as recently as 1991. Taking into account all its other features, an iPhone that the whole world uses today would have cost over *three million dollars* the year before Bill Clinton was elected president.[11] The proliferation of low-cost cellphones that dial call almost anywhere for a nominal fee is the result of entrepreneurs being matched with capital—entrepreneurs whose success increased the wealth gap. Far from being socially destructive, a rising wealth gap signals the democratization of goods previously enjoyed only by the wealthy. Capitalism is about turning scarcity into abundance, and wealth inequality is an important corollary to that truth. As the billions of the late Steve Jobs attest, wealth inequality is a welcome signal that lifestyle inequality (as opposed to income inequality) is waning.

It's the same story with movies. It has long been the rule that filmmakers who desire consideration for Academy Awards must screen their films for at least one week in New York and Los Angeles. Blockbusters of the *Superman* variety have always enjoyed wide release, but as recently as the 2000s, people in out-of-the-way places were out of luck when it came to viewing most of Hollywood's fare. A film like *84 Charing Cross Road* would make it only into the "art houses," concentrated in the biggest cities. VCRs and video rental stores like Blockbuster mitigated the problem of distance, but even then the most rural among us had limited, not to mention inconvenient (remember "late fees"?), access to the wonders of film.

Entrepreneurial genius sometimes appears in the strangest of ways. It was not the movie industry that discovered a way to broaden access to its art but a technology firm from Silicon Valley. Reed Hastings and Netflix solved the problem of inconvenient and understocked video stores and abolished late fees. The replacement of video cassettes with DVDs allowed easy distribution of films through the mail, so a Netflix customer in Montana suddenly had as easy access to obscure films as any cineaste in Manhattan.

DVDs by mail removed the barrier of geography, but that was not the end of the matter. Hastings, mindful that the next innovation would do to Netflix what Netflix had done to Blockbuster, saw time as a barrier to enjoying Hollywood's abundance. Instant access to a film, he saw, would be even better than DVDs by mail. Netflix subscribers can now watch movies when they want through streaming video over the internet. Hastings is now rich. So are the innovators who have enhanced the capacity and speed of the internet, making streaming video possible. Should I resent them because they have more money than I do, or should I be grateful for the economic system that allowed them to enrich my life and the lives of millions of other people?

A perusal of the annual Forbes 400 list of the world's richest people shows a highly descriptive trend. America's greatest fortunes are largely a monetary sign of entrepreneurial activity that made life better. Patrick Soon-Shiong, a 400 member, is a manufacturer of an anti-cancer drug. The list includes heirs to great fortunes such as the Waltons of Walmart fame, and the mere existence of their wealth means everyone else has greater access to the funds necessary to build their own fortunes (see chapter six). The Waltons are worth billions today because Sam Walton democratized access to all manner of consumer goods, and in doing so, gave Americans a "raise" every time they shopped in one of his stores.

The fortune created by John D. Rockefeller (1839–1937) is arguably the most famous in the United States, and his heirs are among the Forbes 400 to this day. In the mid-nineteenth century, the Biblical admonition that "night cometh, when no man can work," was still literally accurate. Rockefeller started selling kerosene at low cost to families whose houses went dark when the sun set. He made his initial fortune by eliminating this discomfort.[12] He later applied his entrepreneurial genius to gasoline. Before anyone decries his grand riches, do not forget that Henry Ford's mass-produced automobile was possible only because Standard Oil made gasoline broadly accessible.

Some might concede that wealth inequality reduces lifestyle inequality but object that entrepreneurs and their heirs aren't the only ones in the Forbes 400. What about the billionaires who are on the list not for creating anything but for simply "moving money around" on Wall Street? That's an understandable objection, but it's shortsighted.

The hedge fund manager John Paulson made billions in 2008 when the mortgage securities on which he had purchased insurance went bust. Thanks to his bet against the housing market, Paulson's net worth skyrocketed, so some concluded that his fortune was made on the backs of hapless homeowners whipsawed by a collapsing housing market.

Yet behind every mortgage is a saver. People can borrow money to purchase a home only insofar as rich and poor alike are delaying consumption in favor of saving. In a certain sense, the truly "hapless" characters in the drama of 2008 were the prudent savers. People who bought what they could not otherwise afford used the savings of the prudent.

Whatever the motives of the borrowers who went bust, the reality is that the world has limited capital. When some of it is destroyed, the broader economy is harmed by the mal-investment. Everyone sees the empty houses that no one wants to buy, but no one sees the venture that might have been the next FedEx but dies from lack of investment because so much seed capital flowed into home construction and mortgages.

Paulson sensed that something was amiss, and the markets rewarded his astuteness with a fortune. Yet whatever he earned is a small fraction of what his mortgage call meant for the broader economy. His successful investments saved a great deal more capital from being consumed by a housing sector that no longer needed it. There are many fathers of the financial disaster of 2008, but Paulson's billions were a powerful signal to investors to look elsewhere when committing capital. Investors do not grow rich by blindly buying and selling. Rather, they anticipate where capital will achieve its highest return. Paulson signaled to investors where capital would vanish if it were deployed. Economic growth is weakened when capital is used sub-optimally, or in the case of housing in the 2000s, destroyed. Rich investors like Paulson take the initial intrepid risks that provide everyone else with information about where to place their money.

The movers of money and credit do the economy a great service for the market signals they provide. But their importance does not end there. Investors are always looking for positive returns, and some achieve them by reviving what is debilitated. Mitt Romney was one of these investors. He earned his fortune as the head of Bain Capital, a private equity firm.

During the Republican presidential debate in 2012, Romney chided his opponent Newt Gingrich for taking consulting fees from Fannie Mae, a notorious recipient of a government bailout. Gingrich responded, "If Governor Romney would like to give back all the money he has earned from bankrupting companies and laying off employees during his years at Bain Capital, then I'd be glad to listen to him."[13] Gingrich's derogatory description of how private equity firms make money is hardly unique, but it's also highly incorrect.

Private equity's best and brightest don't become wealthy by buying up successful companies and selling them a few years down the line. That does occur, but the old investment axiom "buy low, sell high" still applies. The real profits in private equity result from the purchase and revitalization of companies near death or already in bankruptcy.

Investors can earn a nice return from buying shares of the companies in the Dow Jones Industrial Average, and it's easy to buy an index fund that invests only in those "blue chips." Investors are doing something very different with private equity. Leaving aside the safety of diversification, they pay large fees to private equity firms to join their investments in seriously ill companies. It's very risky, but if the private equity firm is able to nurse a company back to health, the returns can be enormous.

Are there layoffs at these sick companies? Of course. They've been run, almost by definition, by bloated and ineffective management. Before its merger with United Airlines, Continental Airlines was an industry-wide joke. Its hapless management once instituted a flight from Houston's Intercontinental Airport (Continental was based in Houston) forty-five miles down the road to Houston's Hobby Airport. Enter David Bonderman and Jim Coulter of the private equity firm Texas Pacific Group. They bought Continental in the 1990s and ultimately made ten times their money on their investment—not because Continental was healthy, but because it looked as bad as the inedible food it served its passengers.[14]

Whether it is John Paulson entering into investments that save vast sums of capital from destruction, Warren Buffett investing in well-run companies in order to achieve a long-term positive return, or private equity executives like Bonderman seeking outsize returns by resuscitating dying companies, the investors disparaged for "moving money around" deserve accolades. Their great wealth is a certain signal that they are wisely deploying the capital that is the lifeblood of economic growth.

But in spite of the undeniable wealth creation going on all around us, many complain that economic opportunity today is limited. Pundits and economists produce all manner of statistics supposedly proving that the poor and middle class have no clear path to improvement. Statistics, however, can and do obscure reality. In any country, immigration is as good an indication as any of opportunity. The migration of millions of human beings to the United States, legally and illegally, is a powerful market indicator of the possibility of upward mobility in this country. If not, the world's tired, poor, and huddled masses would go elsewhere.

The other common complaint concerns the growing wealth of the "1 percent" versus the "99 percent." Pundits and economists have recently feasted on studies showing outsize income gains of 31.4 percent for the 1 percent from 2009 through 2012. Again, however, statistics can mislead. The Cato Institute's Alan Reynolds found that the top earners experienced a 36.3 percent *decline* in real income from 2007 through 2009. The demonized 1 percent were earning quite a bit less in 2012 than they were in 2007.[15]

It's fruitless to get bogged down in statistical duels. The important thing is to understand that growing income among the top earners is a sign that enterprise is being rewarded and technology is advancing. In a sane world, a decline in wealth inequality would be cause for worry, because it would signal reduced opportunity for the ambitious and a stagnating standard of living for everyone else.

The anxiety that people feel because of inequality of wealth is actually an implicit endorsement of free-market capitalism. To understand this paradox, consider that the 2014 NBA Champion San Antonio Spurs beat a Miami Heat team led by LeBron James, Dwyane Wade, and Chris Bosh. Of the eight players on the Spurs who averaged more than 20 minutes a game in the 2013–14 season, only two attended a big name basketball factory from a BCS conference, and only one was drafted higher than 15th.

Even better, consider that in Super Bowl XLVIII (Seattle Seahawks 43, Denver Broncos 8) there were as many players on the field who had played college football at Portland State (DeShawn Head, Julius Thomas) as had played at college football "blue bloods" Alabama,

Auburn, Louisiana State, and Ohio State combined. These four traditional powers could claim only two alumni on the two rosters: James Carpenter from Alabama and Trindon Holliday from Louisiana State.[16]

The NFL is nothing if not a meritocracy, and its teams will go to great lengths to find the most talented players, regardless of pedigree. In a multi-billion-dollar business catering to fickle fans with numerous choices about how to occupy their Sundays, selecting players on the basis of anything other than ability to play will produce a losing team that hemorrhages money and attendance each year.

Russell Wilson, the starting quarterback for the Seahawks, was instrumental in their Super Bowl victory. Thanks to his diminutive-by-NFL-standards height of five feet, eleven inches, Wilson was selected in the third round of 2012 draft. The Seahawks had also signed Matt Flynn to an expensive free agent contract, reflecting management's initial view that Wilson was not ready for the NFL. But in a meritocracy, where teams, coaches, and owners are judged by wins and losses, Wilson won the starter's role in the preseason before the 2012 season.

Connections of the political type do not apply to the NFL. Wilson proved the better player ahead of his rookie year, and despite the relatively low expectations that followed him into the league, he became the starting QB. In 2012, he led the Seahawks to the playoffs and was named Rookie of the Year. One year later, he hoisted the Lombardi Trophy.

Soon enough Wilson will have a new contract that makes him the highest paid player on the Seahawks and one of the highest paid in the league. And none of his teammates will begrudge him that salary. They know that however good the rest of the team is, they're unlikely to win it all without a top-flight quarterback. Quarterbacks are like CEOs—the good ones are hard to find, and they therefore command a big salary. That's why inequality of wealth is never a problem in a purely capitalist, meritocratic system. Those who contribute the most are paid the most, and rarely is anyone bothered.

Super Bowl XLVIII is also a reminder that wealth and success are hardly static. All the talk about the 1 percent and "concentration of wealth" ignores the capitalistic truth that each year's team picture is never the same as the year before. And just as change at the top is a constant in professional sports, so it is in the rest of the economy. The vast majority of the 2013 Forbes 400 were not in the original list in 1982. Facebook's CEO, Mark Zuckerberg, wasn't even born yet.

The coach who led the Seahawks to the lopsided victory in Super Bowl XLVIII, Pete Carroll, was out of football altogether in 2000. He had been fired as head coach of the New England Patriots in 1999. Five years earlier he had been fired as head coach of the New York Jets after one season. If you had predicted that Pete Carroll would be the winning coach in the Super Bowl thirteen years down the road, you'd have been laughed out of the room.

Carroll's story proves that nothing is forever in a merit-based system, and the past does not predict the future. Hired by the University of Southern California as head coach in 2001, Carroll had the Trojans ranked number four in his second season and won national titles in 2003 and 2004. His wilted reputation revived, he was offered the head coaching job at Seattle in 2009. Four years later, his Seahawks won the Super Bowl.[17]

Inequality of income and wealth simply *does not matter* in a capitalist society. Immense wealth creation by an ever-changing 1 percent improves life for everyone and is non-discriminatory. The 1 percent club is always open for new members.

Every football fan knows the anguish of a star player's going down with a knee injury, wiping out the entire team's prospects for the season. What if a surgeon came up with a way to quickly cure shredded knees, getting injured players back on the field in a week? If that surgeon became a billionaire, would football fans bemoan his contribution to wealth inequality? This scenario is not as far-fetched as you might think. In the Civil War, men suffering gunshot wounds to the abdomen or chest were left to die. A fractured hip was a death sentence. The odds of death from a broken femur were three to one. Cancer? Forget about it.[18] Capitalism has an impressive track record of making the impossible possible. As medicine advances, it is not unrealistic to bet on doctors' eventually making a torn ACL yesterday's problem. Will society be worse off if the physician who achieves that breakthrough is enriched for it? What about the scientist who finds a cure for cancer?

Income inequality in a capitalist system is truly beautiful. It provides the incentive for creative people to gamble on new ideas, and it turns luxuries into common goods. Income inequality nurses sick companies back to health. It rewards hard work, talent, and achievement regardless of pedigree. And it's a signal that some of the world's worst problems will disappear in our lifetimes.

CHAPTER EIGHT

Savers Are an Economy's Most Valuable Benefactors

Capitals are increased by parsimony, and diminished by prodigality and misconduct.
—**Adam Smith**, *The Wealth of Nations*

Peter Bogdanovich, best known for the films he directed in the early 1970s, surely merits mention in any discussion of the most venerated "auteurs" from that period, which included Francis Ford Coppola, William Friedkin, and George Lucas. Among his films were *The Last Picture Show*, *Paper Moon*, and *Daisy Miller*. Bogdanovich's conquests weren't limited to film. He enjoyed a close friendship with the legendary Orson Welles, conducted a very public romance with Cybill Shepherd, the beautiful star of *The Last Picture Show*, and carried on an affair with the *Playboy* playmate Dorothy

Stratten (until she was murdered by her estranged husband). As the saying goes, Bogdanovich "had it all."

But in 1985, with only $21.37 in the bank, he filed for bankruptcy.[1] The principle cause of his financial catastrophe was his purchase of the rights to *They All Laughed*, the movie in which he was directing Stratten when their affair began. As he explained in the *Wall Street Journal* in 2014, "I spent $5 million of my own money buying back the film from the studio and distributing it myself. In retrospect, this move was crazy. It's nearly impossible to distribute a film on your own, and I lost my shirt."[2]

Yet, the purchase of *They All Laughed* was not the sole cause of his financial troubles. Prodigality was also a major problem. Reports indicated monthly expenses of two hundred thousand dollars with only seventy-five thousand in monthly income. Those expenses included sixteen thousand dollars per month for lawyers, more than fifteen thousand dollars in agent and management fees, two thousand dollars for transportation, and a thousand dollars for laundry.[3] Bogdanovich spent his way to the poorhouse.

With its grand tradition as a college football powerhouse, the University of Texas boasts a long line of gridiron luminaries—players like Bobby Layne, Earl Campbell, and Ricky Williams. But the greatest of them all is surely Vince Young. In the early 2000s, this Longhorn quarterback almost single-handedly revived a team and a program that were wandering in the wilderness. Young carried his team to a thrilling 38–37 victory over the Michigan Wolverines in the 2005 Rose Bowl. One year later, back in the Rose Bowl, Young dismantled number-one USC's defense in a 41–38 win that gave Texas its first national championship since 1970. It was arguably the greatest individual performance in the hundred-year history of the storied bowl game.

After his emergence from that game as the best quarterback in college football, Young was the third player taken in the pro draft. Unlike most quarterbacks, who take a few years to adjust to the advanced defenses of the NFL, Young was a star in his first season with the Tennessee Titans, winning the 2006 Rookie of the Year award. Then his star began to dim. He slumped in his sophomore season, throwing nine touchdown passes versus seventeen interceptions, and the Titans cut him by the 2010 preseason. Young joined the Philadelphia Eagles for one season and then migrated to the Buffalo Bills, who cut him before the season began.[4] In 2013, he signed a contract with the Green Bay Packers, but they too released him during the preseason.[5] His fortune turned even more dismal in 2014. Just seven years after signing a twenty-six-million dollar contract with the Titans, Young filed for bankruptcy (though the filing would later be reversed). While spending two hundred thousand dollars per month, he took out a loan of $1.8 million during the 2011 NFL lockout. His expenses included a three-hundred-thousand-dollar birthday party. On top of everything else, he is supporting four children conceived with four different women.[6]

The sad stories of Bogdanovich and Young exemplify the fallacy, embraced by too many economists and reporters in the financial press, that consumer spending is the cause of economic growth. Just before becoming chairman of the Federal Reserve, Janet Yellen defended the Fed's program of quantitative easing in an interview with *Time*: "Our policy is aimed at holding down long-term interest rates, which supports the recovery by encouraging spending."[7] A few days later, the *Wall Street Journal* chimed in: "A slowdown in U.S. income growth could short-circuit the *surge in consumer spending that propelled the economic recovery in recent months*" (emphasis added).[8]

Yellen and other believers in spending our way to prosperity are correct that individuals produce in order to consume, but they ignore the importance of production. To state the obvious, production precedes consumption. If you doubt me, ask yourself how you are able to consume. You can consume because you have a job that allows you to or because you can borrow from other producers willing to shift their consumptive power to you. Despite what you read in the newspapers or hear on CNBC, people trade products for products. In order to consume, they must produce first.

Most economists and financial reporters would have viewed Peter Bogdanovich's and Vince Young's conspicuous consumption as an economic plus. Spending millions with abandon, each of these guys was a one-man "stimulus" machine. The problem is that the U.S. economy is a collection of individuals, and individuals who spend their entire paychecks—or worse, go into debt to spend even more—are self-destructive. If a person is going to spend profligately and take on debt in the process, he had better have a secure source of income for the foreseeable future. If he doesn't, then he's headed for bankruptcy, just like Bogdanovich and Young.

People who live beyond their means eventually run out of means. Big spenders become beggars dependent on the kindness of strangers. Sooner or later the profligate have to ask for help from the very people economists see as the bad guys—savers. What Yellen and the others miss is that you cannot elevate consumption and debt unless a lot of people are aggressively saving. Short of printing money without regard to production (more on that in a later chapter), there is no credit without saving first. The two go together.

In chapter six I explained why saving money is the best way to redistribute it. One billionaire's miserly stockpiling of his wealth represents small business loans for thousands of entrepreneurs with potentially economy-changing ideas that need capital. When anyone—rich, middle class, or poor—saves his income rather than spending it, he expands the credit available for people to remodel a kitchen, buy a car, or best of all, start or expand a business. For an entrepreneur to turn his vision into reality, he must have either substantial savings of his own or access to the savings of others.

Let's consider the basic economic principles with a simple example. When you pay twenty dollars to the Domino's deliveryman you're not really exchanging *money* for a pizza. You're trading a portion of your work as a construction worker, salesman, or investment banker for the product on offer from Domino's. We trade products for products; money is merely the accepted measure used to complete the exchange. Our production is our demand. Or better yet, to demand or consume anything in the marketplace, we must supply something first, and investment enables supply.

The critical role of investment becomes clear if we follow the story of a computer salesman earning seventy-five thousand dollars a year. He takes home forty-five thousand dollars in disposable income after taxes. The average economist would say that this salesman will stimulate the economy most if he spends all of that forty-five thousand on rent, restaurants, clothes, vacations, and other consumer goods. Heavy consumption, according to the conventional wisdom, boosts economic growth by making money rapidly circulate from one set of hands to others.

But our salesman knows that living on the edge is scary. A layoff could strike any day, so it's best to stash some of that money. Even better, he realizes that much of his day is wasted driving around looking for the offices of potential customers, so he invests in a GPS navigation system that leads to a 20 percent increase in sales—an income boost of fifty thousand dollars.

Our salesman then discerns that too much of his day is spent on paperwork, not to mention cold-calling potential customers. He realizes that paying an assistant thirty-five thousand dollars a year, while expensive in the near term, will free him up for more of the person-to-person meetings necessary to close big deals. That thirty-five-thousand-dollar investment leads to two hundred thousand dollars of additional income over time.

As he learns more about the business and the specific needs of the customer base, the salesman realizes that with a two-hundred-thousand-dollar loan he could start his own business selling computers manufactured to his specifications overseas. The initial outlay would be large, but with much of the existing client base wedded to him and his attention to service, taking on debt and spending some savings in the near term could lead to a seven-figure income down the line.

This story of the enterprising computer salesman is simplified, but it demonstrates the wonders of saving. Consumption depends on production, and re-investment of profit often increases production. As John Stuart Mill said, profits are "the remuneration of abstinence."[9]

Imagine if Henry Ford had been a prodigal spender who blew the profits from Ford Motor Company on booze, women, and toys. More than a few owners of the two thousand-plus U.S. car companies[10] in the early twentieth century probably did just that. Maybe his talent was so prodigious that it could have kept him flying high anyway. But what made Ford an entrepreneur for the history books was religiously reinvesting his company's profits in the perfection of his manufacturing systems. Delaying consumption in favor of investment allowed Ford to mass produce cars with ever greater efficiency, and America's consumption of those cars grew at the same pace. If today's establishment economists had been around in Ford's day, they would have bewailed his parsimony.

Having become enormously wealthy thanks to his company's success, Ford could have settled back into tight-fisted retirement. And as far as the well-being of the broader economy was concerned, that would have been fine. Unless he stuffed his profits under a mattress, Ford's "hoarded" savings would have migrated to others, including entrepreneurs seeking funds for new businesses.

The relentlessly ambitious Steve Jobs could have retired and thrown as many three-hundred-thousand-dollar birthday parties as he liked. He would have won the applause of the economics profession for it. But the "unseen" in that scenario would have been the wealth and jobs he never would have created if he had pursued a life of conspicuous consumption.

Investment is the only wealth multiplier. As Adam Smith wrote, "It is by means of an additional capital only, that the undertaker of any work can either provide his workmen with better machinery, or make a more proper distribution of employment among them."[11] Increase investment, expand output, and watch wealth increase over the long term. In consuming their income, Young and Bogdanovich stripped themselves of wealth and the economy of the capital to create more of it.

Americans are actually great savers. The vast wealth on deposit in this country belies the frequent reports to the contrary. But we're inclined to misunderstand the nature of the biggest purchase most of us make—housing. It's common to consider your house an "investment." It's not. Housing is a consumptive good. The purchase of a home will not make you more efficient. It won't lead to software or healthcare innovations that make businesses more efficient, cure cancer, or open up foreign markets. The purchase of a house consumes capital.

Looking back on the housing boom of the 2000s, it is no surprise that it coincided with a rather dormant market for shares in initial public offerings. The 1980s and '90s were marked by the IPOs of Microsoft, IBM, and Cisco (to name but three), while Google was the only high-flier issue that made much noise amid the rush to housing in the 2000s. With housing the place to be, entrepreneurs in need of investment suffered a capital deficit. In short, capital consumption rose at the expense of the capital formation that drives economic growth.

Janet Yellen, in that interview with *Time*, seemed unconcerned about housing's eating up too much capital. Eager to justify the Fed's allocation of capital toward treasuries and mortgage bonds that would drive down interest rates, Yellen explained that "part of the [economic stimulus] comes through higher houses and stock prices, which causes people with homes and stocks to spend more, which causes jobs to be created throughout the economy and income to go up throughout the economy."[12]

Yellen was forgetting her Adam Smith, and John Stuart Mill for that matter. Never mind that stock markets were much healthier and unemployment much lower in the '80s and '90s, when the Fed was not aggressively trying to push interest rates down. Any central bank policy meant to stimulate home buying will retard economic growth because the purchase of a house takes money out of capital markets for business. Stimulating consumption, of housing or anything else, decreases investment in production. That increased production would, in turn, increase wages. Henry Ford could pay his employees an industry-leading wage because his continuous reinvestment in manufacturing enhancements rendered the labor of his workers enormously productive.

With economists, politicians, and advertisers pushing consumption as a patriotic duty, it's easy to forget that thrift and temperance were once considered bedrock American virtues. "Buy what thou hast no need of, and ere long thou shalt sell thy necessaries," warned Benjamin Franklin in Poor Richard's Almanack. In *Dividing the Wealth*, Howard Kershner invites us to come back to our senses: "The man who accepts the responsibility of denying himself the pleasure of current consumption in order to save and accumulate capital is the real hero and patriot who is conferring vast blessings upon his fellows."[13]

CHAPTER NINE

Job Creation Requires Perpetual Job Destruction

The progress of civilization has meant the reduction of employment, not its increase.

—**Henry Hazlitt**, *Economics in One Lesson*

Economic growth in Las Vegas has been one of the few constants over the past several decades. A housing correction after 2008 slowed its ascent somewhat, but population growth has held steady for the city. In the 1950s alone, the city's population tripled.[1] By the new millennium, 1,500 people were migrating to the resort and gambling town every week.[2] Clark County, the home of Las Vegas, has seen its population grow more than twenty times since the mid-twentieth century. No other U.S. county comes close to that growth rate.[3]

Some arrivals have been retirees eager to enjoy the city's plenteous entertainment and no state income tax. But the main driver of this decades-long influx of human capital into Vegas has been the high paying jobs offered by casino resorts such as the Desert Inn, Sahara Hotel, and the Sands. In keeping with Alexis de Tocqueville's observation in the nineteenth century that Americans are "restless amid abundance,"[4] they headed for Las Vegas and its plentiful jobs in the twentieth century.

And yet the three legendary hotels I just mentioned—symbols of the city's glory days—no longer exist. The site of the Desert Inn is now occupied by the Wynn and its sister hotel Encore. The SLS Las Vegas stands where the Sahara once shimmered. And the Sands has been replaced by the Venetian and Palazzo. The destruction of these once-great casino resorts contains a lesson about job creation.

There are no sacred cows in Las Vegas. When a casino loses its luster, and its profitability along with it, Nevadans don't run to Washington seeking a bailout. They bulldoze the joint. The destruction of a hotel ends a lot of jobs—that's the "seen." The "unseen" is what comes next: the replacement of a failure with a new and better idea. It's that constant renewal that has made Las Vegas a job-creating machine. New, more profitable casinos attract more investment, creating more jobs. It's Sin City's virtuous circle.

The opposite of Las Vegas is Detroit, whose population shrank 25 percent from 2000 to 2010.[5] Remember those two thousand carmakers from the early twentieth century? Imagine the burden on taxpayers if we had done bailouts in those days. And what would propping up failures have done to survivors like General Motors, Ford, and Chrysler? The successful companies that became the Big Three would have been forced to compete with companies kept alive with capital extracted from the citizenry.

But here we are today, with both General Motors and Chrysler owing their existence to the taxpayers. In their anxiety to save jobs in Detroit, politicians are propping up the Motown equivalent of the Desert Inn. The "seen" is the thousands of jobs preserved by the bailouts of GM and Chrysler in 2008 and 2009. The "unseen" is how much more vibrant Detroit would be today without government's false compassion. Successful carmakers like Toyota, Honda, and Volkswagen could have purchased the valuable assets of GM and Chrysler and managed them better. Some of the eager migrants to Las Vegas, Silicon Valley, and Austin might have opted instead for Detroit. The Motor City's stratospheric unemployment rate is tragic testimony that the surest way to suffocate new jobs is to prop up the losers of the past.

Workers follow economic growth, and economic growth takes place in cities and towns unshackled from the past. Las Vegas has had its struggles in the last few years, but its history suggests that it will weather these difficulties because its entrepreneurs are constantly replacing the dead or moribund with new businesses. Tourists return to the Entertainment Capital because there's always something new to see. About the only thing that draws tourists to the remains of Detroit, on the other hand, is the same voyeuristic instinct that makes people stop to gawk at a car wreck.[6]

A well-run business *never* runs out of money. If short on cash, a properly managed business can always find private investors willing to back its management. The management of GM and Chrysler lost the trust of investors. Bankruptcy would have brought in new owners who could raise the funds necessary to keep the companies in operation and possibly expand their payrolls.

A classic example of such restructuring comes out of Silicon Valley. Steve Jobs recalled that when he returned to Apple in September

1997, "We were less than ninety days from being insolvent."[7] But with Jobs in control, the threat of insolvency vanished with a $150 million investment from Microsoft.[8]

The turnaround entailed a painful first step: Jobs laid off over three thousand Apple employees.[9] That was a lot of livelihoods lost and families uprooted. But shedding labor that was not contributing to profits was unquestionably necessary. A year after the company had reckoned with insolvency, Apple was on the rise. Speaking at San Francisco MacWorld in 1998, Jobs urged his audience to "Think Profit." They did, and Apple's profit of $309 million that year allowed it to attract the investment necessary to start hiring again.[10]

John Doerr, the head of the venture capital firm Kleiner Perkins Caufield Byers, responded to the change at Apple by establishing an iFund backed by two hundred million dollars to finance new "apps" for Apple products. By June 2011 Apple had paid out two and half billion dollars to the developers of the products that stock its App Store.[11]

Jobs's willingness to destroy unproductive jobs led to far more new jobs down the road. Recall Enrico Moretti's finding that Apple is responsible for sixty thousand jobs in the Cupertino area, many of them *outside* the technology field.

The town of Ann Arbor, Michigan, was the headquarters of the now defunct bookseller Borders, which closed 399 stores and laid off 10,700 workers in 2011.[12] That's a lot of lost jobs, but as Henry Hazlitt recognized, economic progress is often a function of destroying work. If job-creation were our sole economic aim, we could achieve it in a perversely simple way. Millions of jobs would appear tomorrow if we banned computers, ATMs, and tractors. Businesses would have to hire legions of typists and clerks, banks would have to add tellers, and scores of men with shovels would be needed for every idled tractor. Of course, most of us would be condemned to a life of drudgery. Everyone would have a job, but it would be back-breaking. Even worse, abolishing "job killers" like the computer would abolish profits. Investment capital would flee to other countries, and we'd all be working for pennies.

There were many reasons for the fall of Borders, including management errors, but it is safe to say the rise of the internet is high on the list. Amazon.com might have killed Borders, but it now employs more than thirty-three thousand people.[13] Of course, Amazon's effect on Borders is only a small part of the internet story. For the longest time American Airlines operated a walk-up ticket office in the Drake Hotel in Chicago as well as similar offices around the country. The ability to buy tickets online has rendered those offices and the jobs of the people who staffed them obsolete. More broadly, the ability of travelers to book flights, hotels, and rental cars on Expedia.com and other internet travel sites has nearly wiped out travel agents.

It is hard to quantify, but the internet has probably destroyed more jobs than any innovation in history. But the jobs the internet takes it gives back in abundance. Moretti estimates that "the number of jobs in the Internet sector has grown by 634 percent over the past decade [2002–2012], or more than two hundred times the growth rates of the overall number of jobs in the rest of the economy during the same period."[14]

An obvious response to assurances that the internet makes more jobs than it kills is that not everyone has the tech savvy to work in Silicon Valley. Fair enough, but returning to Moretti's earlier point, technology multiplies jobs in abundance for all skill levels. Well-paid tech workers in Silicon Valley, Seattle, Boston, and Austin need the services of lawyers, doctors, roofers, and yoga instructors.

Okay, but what about all those high-wage manufacturing jobs, the foundation of the American middle class, that technology has killed off? Even here, the long-term story is undeniably good.

It is hard to imagine today, but in the 1970s the *Economist* referred to Seattle as the "city of despair." In the "Boeing Bust" of 1967–1971, the city's largest employer shed more than sixty thousand jobs. A billboard near the entrance to the airport read, "Will the last person leaving SEATTLE—Turn out the lights."[15]

As luck would have it, Bill Gates and Paul Allen grew up in Seattle. Though they originally incorporated Microsoft in Albuquerque, New Mexico, the desire to return home ultimately won out. All those job-killing computers animated by Microsoft's products made a lot of clerical workers obsolete. But while Boeing has more manufacturing workers in Seattle than Microsoft has employees, the aviation giant creates fewer local jobs than Microsoft does.[16] In short, technological advances surely destroyed quite a few manufacturing jobs, but there has been a net gain in the end.

Not everyone can get one of the lucrative jobs at Microsoft (average annual compensation: $170,000),[17] but a city filled with high-earning techies is a magnet for lots of other workers—high-skilled and low—in other fields. And a prosperous Microsoft made Seattle an attractive location for other tech firms, like Amazon, to put down roots.

Seattle was once a Detroit-like crumbling monument to manufacturing's once glamorous past. Seattle booms today and employs workers of all stripes because backbreaking assembly-line jobs left the city. They went overseas, and Americans increased the value of their toil in jobs created by what is now called the "new economy."

The irony is that the rise of Detroit itself a century ago led to plenty of job destruction, in the United States and around the world.

Horse-drawn carriages and buggy whips quickly became obsolete. That was the "seen"—the kind of "seen" that today's politicians and commentators focus on, the loss of jobs caused by innovation. The "unseen" was the jobs created by the automobile industry. More broadly, businesses could expand the size of their markets because trucks (like trains before them) enabled them to ship goods to more distant locales.

It is hard to quantify, but the mass production of the automobile destroyed numerous jobs in the early twentieth century. But far from forcing Americans into breadlines, that destruction cleared the way for better jobs, much as the internet today is replacing jobs it has eliminated with enhanced employment possibilities.

Naysayers point to dying cities like Detroit as evidence of the harm of job destruction. But the real lesson of such cities is the danger of worshipping particular kinds of jobs for their own sake rather than maximizing profits, even at the short-term expense of employment. Steve Jobs's principle, "Think Profit," is what attracts vital investment. Detroit did not implode because of bad luck or heartless "robber barons" (a robber baron by the name of Henry Ford largely created Detroit, after all). Job creators abandoned a once-prosperous city because it chose to remain in the past. Detroit is jobless today because supposedly compassionate politicians tried to maintain the status quo—a sure path to destitution.

Henry Hazlitt pointed out a simple truth that is easily forgotten: It is only in poor countries that everyone must work. Rich countries are constantly obliterating work. In his 1946 classic *Economics in One Lesson*, Hazlitt wrote that wealth-enhancing technological advances allowed the United States to eliminate child labor and work for the aged.[18] Thanks to the wealth and higher-paying jobs created by job destruction, children don't have to work in factories or fields and the elderly aren't forced to work until death. Conversely, work is the constant for everyone in impoverished countries such as Haiti or Bangladesh. Technology and free trade mean more and more Americans get to do the work they love, while work for survival is the norm in poor countries. It is job destruction that has allowed kids to be kids and the old to retire and play with their grandchildren.

The progress of job creation through job destruction does not make losing your job less agonizing. I write from experience—it is a terrible feeling to be laid off. Yet getting laid off is not cause for despair. Good often comes from losing your job. Buddy Ryan and the Philadelphia Eagles drafted Cris Carter out of Ohio State in 1987. Carter had talent, but in 1990 Ryan released him with the memorable quip, "All he does is catch touchdowns."[19]

Twenty-three years later, at his NFL Hall of Fame induction ceremony, Carter tearfully thanked Ryan for cutting him. He described his release as "the best thing that ever happened to me."[20] Carter had a substance abuse problem, and the loss of his job with the Eagles was the wake-up call that he needed. Thanks to Ryan's fatherly tough love, the immature wide out got straight and finished his sixteen-year NFL career with over thirteen thousand receiving yards and 130 touchdowns.

Steve Jobs was famously fired by Apple in 1984. The loss of the company he had founded forced him to look inward. He returned to Apple in 1997 with far more knowledge about how to run a business. In chapter seven, I shared the story of Pete Carroll, who converted his two NFL firings into lessons that propelled him to the heights of football glory. You can lose a job for all sorts of reasons, but the experience will leave you permanently scarred only if you ignore the causes. No one likes to be fired, but failure need not be permanent. Unemployment is harsh but it is not forever.

* * *

We are conditioned to think of unemployment as kind of like the weather: the unavoidable result of vast, impersonal forces. Like a drought or a persistent heat wave, you just have to endure it. It's part of the natural order. And yet unemployment is *wholly unnatural* for anyone who wants to work. It is the result of specific government policies. To understand what I mean, open your local newspaper and look at the advertisements. The February 14, 2014, issue of the *Washington Post*, for example, carries an ad from Cyprus Air offering "Safe, Clean, Gas Fireplaces" for 80 percent off. A sale at Bloomingdales offers 50 percent off of your second item. A four-day sale at Annapolis Lighting features a 40 percent discount on everything in the store.

The obvious lesson is that when retailers have inventory that they're struggling to sell, they lower prices to levels that bring in buyers. Every market good has a price, and "clearance sales" are the way that businesses clear unsold inventory. It's the same with labor. Unemployment reflects a failure of the price workers are charging for their labor to match the demands of their market.

Let's go back to the NFL for a moment. In August 2012 the Washington Redskins cut a star tight end, Chris Cooley, even though he had set a franchise record for tight ends of 423 receptions in his eight years with the team.[21] Cooley's contract gave him a star's salary, but Fred Davis had replaced him as a starter. Though he rejoined the Redskins after Davis suffered an injury, Cooley retired for good in 2013. If Cooley had wanted to continue playing in the NFL, he could have done so at the prevailing salary for backup tight ends. He chose not to. Employment in the "real world" is no different. The problem arises when government steps in to soften the blow of unemployment.

In his brilliant 1949 book, *Economics and the Public Welfare*, Benjamin Anderson wittily observed that "any country can have heavy unemployment if it is willing and able to pay for it."[22] His point was that labor, much like gas fireplaces and lamps, has a price. Just as Bloomingdale's will be stuck with its inventory until it brings its prices down to a level that will attract buyers, workers will remain unemployed if "generous" government transfer payments prevent them from adjusting their wage demands to market realities.

We see this today in unemployment benefits that have been extended to ninety-nine weeks. Employees are a cost that businesses must bear: they hire workers if they feel the addition of new employees will boost profits. But every dollar the unemployed receive from the government is an extra dollar that employers must offer to lure workers back into the workplace.

Politicians justify the payment of jobless benefits by pointing to slow economic growth. But those benefits exacerbate the very economic illness they say they are trying to cure. Jobless benefits make it more expensive for businesses to hire workers, because workers must compare the benefit of a new job with the "earnings" they will lose if they stop receiving an unemployment check. Some will choose the relative leisure of unemployment over work that might not pay much more. For others the unemployment check will allow them to hold out for a more desirable job. When government bids up the price of able-bodied labor, it's harder for business to make a profit, the economy suffers from reduced production, and workers are consigned to the indignity of living at the expense of others. Rich countries are their own worst enemies when it comes to healing a weak economy.

In recent years, government has increased hiring costs in ways beyond simple unemployment benefits. In 2010, President Barack

Obama signed the Affordable Care Act, mandating that businesses with fifty or more employees offer healthcare insurance. Ostensibly, Obamacare is a work of governmental compassion, but it imposes a substantial cost on struggling businesses. By making it even more expensive to hire a worker, Obamacare has increased the country's unsold labor inventory.

Too many politicians, commentators, and voters don't understand how work, while the norm, can become scarce when government policy raises the price of hiring. Of course, the biggest barriers to hiring are efforts to "save" jobs through subsidies to dying or failed businesses. Emotion writes too much economy-sapping legislation.

In a free economy, capital migrates to talented entrepreneurs eager to pursue profitable opportunities. Innovations like the automobile, computer, and online retail services destroy jobs, but the process leads to better, higher-paying jobs. The lesson, as always, is to let market forces work. Yes, to create jobs in abundance, we must allow the free marketplace to regularly annihilate them.

CHAPTER TEN

Conclusion: Bulldoze the U.S. Tax Code

Yet history shows, time and again, that punishing the entrepreneurs and businesses that create jobs and capital is a sure route to economic devastation, while lowering taxes—not with one-shot reductions that politicians like, but by substantially cutting rates—is always the best economic stimulus.

—Steve Forbes and Elizabeth Ames, *How Capitalism Will Save Us*

In May 2012, shortly before Facebook's IPO, the social networking site's Brazilian-born co-founder, Eduardo Saverin, renounced his U.S. citizenship and moved to Singapore, hoping, many assumed, to avoid enormous capital gains taxes. Singapore has no capital gains tax.

Saverin was widely denounced for his decision. Senator Charles Schumer was so incensed by the young billionaire's "despicable" act that he introduced legislation to impose a 30 percent tax on investments of expatriots.[1] Schumer's bill, which was not enacted, also would have banished Saverin from the United States for life. Though it was highly questionable whether Saverin could shield much of his Facebook gains by renouncing his citizenship, the prospect that he might made him a "traitor" in the eyes of politicians and the media. But from a purely economic standpoint, the reduction of his tax bill benefited the U.S. economy. His actions were undeniably good for economic growth.

As I explained in chapter six, when the rich hold onto their wealth, everyone else has access to it. Saverin might place his wealth with J. P. Morgan, Goldman Sachs, or one of the other financial institutions that invest the wealth of the superrich. They earn their fee by putting the money to work, so any bounty from Facebook's IPO that the taxman didn't get would quickly reach an existing business eager for growth capital or a new business seeking start-up funds.

But what if Saverin converted his wealth into Singapore dollars? What good would it do the United States then? Such a conversion would require an exchange with an individual or institution that wanted his U.S. dollars. In that case, the buyer of Saverin's dollars would have to put them to work or in a bank, and the result would be essentially the same as if Singapore's newest tycoon had banked or invested those dollars himself.

Instead of moving to Singapore, Saverin could have stayed put and written a massive check to the federal government. But then the private economy, where all wealth is created, would have had reduced access to the capital necessary to grow. At a micro-level, average people in need of credit would have had less to draw on.

Some might argue that the federal government could invest the money. Unfortunately, government—regardless of who's running it—is not in the position to act like a business. In the private sector, businesses face collapse if investors lose faith in their management.

Government faces no such discipline. The ceaseless flow of taxpayer dollars into the treasury allows it to continue spending regardless of the results. The judgment of the market is silenced.

An even bigger problem is the talent mismatch. The former senator Trent Lott once obnoxiously observed, "Washington is where the money is. That's what generally keeps people here."[2] But while staffers, senators, congressmen, and high-level bureaucrats can make fortunes in Washington's version of the private sector after leaving the government, the *real* money is made outside of Washington. Anyone who knows how to invest is not working in government. Investment success is hard enough to achieve in the market-disciplined private sector. Moreover, the best capital allocators earn a fortune by directing capital to its highest use. While government work pays well by most standards, and people coming out of government can earn at the "1 percent" level in Washington, the true financial geniuses would never settle for Trent Lott's mere millions, let alone the relatively meager salaries paid to even the highest level federal employees.

Saverin did the economically reasonable thing by shielding as much of his wealth as he could from the black hole of government. I would go even further, however, and argue that in sacrificing his American citizenship to keep tens of millions of dollars of life-giving capital in the private sector, he acted heroically. We'll never know how many people owe their jobs—perhaps their whole careers—to his decision, but you can bet that Eduardo Saverin would be a hero to them.

Senator Schumer might be interested in banishing people who think they can make better use of their fortunes than he can, but the United States was founded by men suspicious of government power and the politicians who wield it. The Constitution was not written haphazardly, but conceived by wise men with an eye on constraining the powers of politicians, including the powers of the Founding Fathers themselves. Congress and the president are empowered to protect the individual rights of citizens. Beyond that, the Constitution grants the political class only a few explicitly defined governing powers. Any powers not specifically delegated to the federal government, says the Tenth Amendment, are reserved to the states or the people.

What happened to the Founders' vision? A federal government exercising limited powers—providing for the common defense, coining money, and other basic functions focused on preserving individual freedoms—would have no need of massive annual collections from the taxpayers. Schumer's fury at being deprived of Eduardo Saverin's millions suggests that the federal government has grown well beyond its constitutional limits. That's why I say that if Saverin succeeded in keeping all those millions out of the hands of a power-hungry political class, he's one of freedom's heroes.

* * *

There is no excuse for today's federal tax system. It obstructs wealth-creation and jobs. The only interests it serves well are those of the political class. When they debate among themselves about the proper level of taxation, it's clear that they think the federal government can tax at any level they want.

Many people were enraged when it was revealed in May 2013 that the federal government's taxing authority, the Internal Revenue Service, was playing favorites with tax-exempt organizations. Specifically, groups seen as hostile to big government (and therefore to its feeding mechanism, the IRS) were subjected to heightened scrutiny that amounted to harassment. In some cases, IRS officials leaked confidential information about disfavored groups to their political opponents. In response to this scandal, many have called for the reform of the IRS, but they miss the point. The IRS is politicized no matter which party is in power. No reform will change human nature. The real disgrace is that Americans—whose country was founded on individual freedom—cower before the political creation that is the IRS every April 15. The real disgrace is a tax code that is a monument to social engineering. The tax code rewards some groups for being "non-profit," some for buying a house with debt, and others for having children.

The reasonable response to the monstrosity that is our tax code is the flat tax that Steve Forbes has so articulately proposed. A flat tax would make the IRS largely irrelevant and would take away the club that lets fallible politicians tell us how to live. A flat tax would abolish the myriad deductions that define the tax system. It would eliminate taxes on capital gains, corporations, dividends, and estates—all of which amount to quadruple taxation of individuals' earnings.

The downside to a flat tax is that it might work too well. In a country filled with some of the most productive, entrepreneurial people on earth, the stimulation of growth could *increase* the federal government's already abundant revenues. All that additional money in the treasury might fuel the government's uncontrolled growth.

Now, the federal government has a necessary role in protecting citizens from foreign intruders, administering justice, and protecting property rights. It needs revenue, but not nearly as much as it receives. The best tax, therefore, might be a tax on consumption rather than income—what some call the Fair Tax. The first reason for such a tax is that in a free country, citizens should not have to prove their income to the federal government. Adopting a consumption tax and abolishing all other taxes and deductions would end the IRS altogether.

Second, even a flat income tax still puts a price on work. A sensible tax system would make work "free" while taxing consumption. Some will suggest that such a tax would penalize retailers, but people produce in order to consume. The wants of human beings are unlimited, so a light tax on consumption would have a negligible effect on consumption.

Third, even if a consumption tax did have a noticeable effect on spending, society would be better off. To return to my refrain, there are no companies, no start-ups, and no jobs without savings and investment first. If people avoid consumption, their savings will supply the credit to the innovators of tomorrow. All the products we enjoy today are the result of past savings, and a small national tax on consumption would free up enormous amounts of capital to fund the next Steve Jobs.

Fourth, a consumption tax would be blind. It would be hard for politicians to impose a graduated consumption tax with an eye on playing favorites. Instead, we'd all be equal before the tax law, as we should be.

Fifth, and perhaps most critical, a consumption tax is the only way citizens can starve the federal government. Theoretically, a consumption tax, unlike a flat income tax, would give citizens the power to pay the government less some years. This is particularly important when people are unhappy with the federal government, but it's also important when we citizens are having a difficult year such that we're consuming less. If we're struggling, so should the government struggle through reduced revenue intake.

We don't know for certain why Eduardo Saverin renounced his U.S. citizenship, and really it is none of our business. If he did it with taxes in mind, the problem is not with Saverin but with the tax code that drove such an entrepreneur from our shores. It is time to bulldoze this obnoxious affront to the free society that our Founding Fathers established at such great cost over two centuries ago.

PART II

Regulation

CHAPTER ELEVEN

Appalachian State Almost Never Beats Michigan, and Government Regulation Almost Never Works

If you are good, 49 percent of your decisions will be wrong. Even if you are great, something just short of a majority will be losers.
—**Nick Kokonas** on trading, *Life, on the Line*

On September 1, 2007, Division 1-AA Appalachian State beat the fifth-ranked Michigan Wolverines football team 34–32 in Ann Arbor. The result stunned not just the college football world but everyone with even a passing interest in sports.

ESPN's Pat Forde wrote, "These are the kinds of things that don't normally happen in college football, where the chasm between the have and have-not is wider than in any other sport."[1] Indeed, since the partition of college football's Division 1 in the late 1970s, never had a 1-AA team beaten a 1-A team that was ranked in the top twenty-five, let alone one that was ranked in the top five.[2] Michigan is a football factory. It has produced some of the NFL's best players, including the New England Patriots quarterback Tom Brady, number-one NFL draft pick Jake Long, and future Hall of Fame defensive back Charles Woodson. Appalachian State can claim only a handful of NFL players—eight as of 2013[3]—none of them stars.

Yes, every once in a while, Appalachian State beats Michigan—but it's pretty darn rare. On the day that Appalachian State "shocked the world," Louisville and Boise State beat their 1-AA opponents 73–10 and 56–7, respectively, while the Florida Gators smashed Western Kentucky 49–3.[4] And there's a lesson here about government regulation of business. The conceit of regulation is that bureaucrats of below-average talent have the knowledge, insight, and skill to oversee the talented and to catch their errors before they do themselves. In other words, government regulation assumes that Appalachian State is going to beat Michigan every time.

The mismatches that define the early weeks of each college football season are like the mismatches that define regulation. The best high school football players aspire to play for teams such as the Texas Longhorns and Miami Hurricanes, and the best financial, medical, and business minds migrate toward J. P. Morgan, Merck, and Coca-Cola. Those with talent generally seek employment with other talented people, where the work is stimulating and the compensation high. It is unlikely that the best and brightest will settle for a federal regulatory agency and its relatively low pay. A great analytical mind will probably go to Goldman Sachs rather than Goldman Sachs's regulator, the Securities and Exchange Commission. So "victories" for lightly talented regulators—catching problems ahead of the experts in the private sector—are about as rare as Appalachian State victories over Michigan.

The problem of mismatched talent is aggravated by perverse incentives. The more capable regulators can be tempted to go easy on the businesses they oversee in the hope of eventual employment with them, where the pay is better. This is part of what the Nobel laureate economist George Stigler called "regulatory capture"—regulated interests' exercising decisive influence over their regulators. Apart from regulatory capture, regulation doesn't work because of the talent mismatch and the inability of even the best businesses and investors to see reliably into the future.

John Allison retired as CEO of BB&T Bank in 2009 after transforming a small bank with four billion dollars in assets into a global financial institution with $152 billion in assets. In *The Financial Crisis and the Free Market Cure* (2013), Allison observes, "Financial services is a very highly regulated industry, probably the most regulated industry in the world."[5] Yet the oversight of the Federal Deposit Insurance Corporation, the Office of the Comptroller of the Currency, the Federal Reserve, the SEC, and other agencies did not prevent the banking industry from plunging into crisis in 2008. As consumers backed by generous bank loans rushed into housing, writes the *Wall Street Journal*'s Gregory Zuckerman, "Rather than rein it all in, regulators gave the market encouragement, thrilled that a record 69 percent of Americans owned their own homes, up from 64 percent a decade earlier."[6]

Known as the "Maestro" in the early 2000s because of his allegedly skilled chairmanship of the Federal Reserve, Alan Greenspan told a convention of community bankers in 2004 that "a national severe price distortion [in housing] seems most unlikely."[7] In June 2007, Greenspan's successor at the Fed, Ben Bernanke, asserted, "We will follow developments in the subprime market closely. However, at this point, the troubles in the subprime sector seem unlikely to seriously spill over to the broader economy or the financial system."[8]

While the Federal Reserve is responsible for regulating banks and keeping an eye on their health, its blindness to the looming problems inside those same banks did not surprise Allison, who recalls, "In my career, the Fed has a 100 percent error rate in predicting and reacting to important economic turns."[9] Indeed—how surprising is it that the salary-men at the Fed fail to detect a crisis before the multimillion dollar earners in the banking industry do?

It may be obvious that regulators are not up to their task, but working for the government means never having to say you're sorry. "One of the most remarkable things about Washington," observes American Enterprise Institute senior fellow Peter Wallison, "is the fact that poor performance by regulators is regularly rewarded with more funds and broader powers, both conferred by a grateful (and apparently forgetful) Congress."[10]

The market sees to it that poorly run businesses are starved of capital so that they cannot waste any more of it. Government, by contrast, devotes more human and financial resources to what isn't working. It's as if Western Kentucky, after that thrashing by Florida, poured millions of dollars into its football facilities on the assumption that a better weight room might produce a different result next time. There might be some improvement, but the Gators are still going to have their way with the Hilltoppers 99 percent of the time. Government regulators almost always arrive late to the scene of the accident regardless of how many billions of tax dollars Congress appropriates to them. As they say in sports, you can't coach speed or height.

Human beings—even the smartest and most experienced—are seriously limited in their ability to see the future. Even the best stock, bond, and commodity traders lose money on *slightly less than half* of their trades. If the best, most handsomely compensated market traders are wrong about the future 49 percent of the time, the low-paid bureaucrats regulating them haven't a chance. What Samuel Johnson said about second marriages applies to regulation: it represents the triumph of hope over experience.

So does the failure of government financial regulation leave us exposed to the wolves of Wall Street? No. There are effective regulators in the marketplace, but they don't work for the federal government. One of them is the hedge fund manager John Paulson.

Paulson famously earned billions in 2007 and 2008 for betting against the home mortgages that banks were so feverishly issuing to voracious borrowers. He is hailed as a genius now, but Paulson was not always so highly regarded. Although white-shoe investment banks like Morgan Stanley and Goldman Sachs were happy to earn commissions on his trades, Paulson was, according to those who handled his trading account at Goldman, "a third-rate hedge fund guy who didn't know what he was talking about."[11] A trader at Morgan Stanley who executed the trades by which Paulson intended to profit from a housing correction thought, "This guy is nuts."[12] The people who handled his trades thought the insurance against mortgage defaults he was buying was the equivalent of earthquake insurance that would never be paid out.[13]

The payoff can be enormous when so many on Wall Street, or on Main Street, do not agree with you. Paulson saw what others did not: the mortgage market was headed for a correction. And if you're as smart about the markets as he is, you don't squander your talent as a salaried government regulator. You stay in the market yourself and make billions. Yet Paulson's trades, and his eventual success, served banks and other financial institutions more effectively than the regulators who show up after the damage is done. The profits he made from buying insurance on mortgages were a signal to banks that they were far too exposed to housing and the underlying debt that propped it up. They didn't take him seriously at first when some banks went under or were bailed out. But nothing grabs the attention of others like success, and Paulson's billions surely saved banks from much bigger mistakes. Even better, Paulson "regulated" away many greater errors by savers and investors, without whom there are no mortgages. Paulson's foresight provided those savers and investors with explicit market signals telling them to cease committing capital to housing.

Credit default swaps (CDSs) achieved much the same result. Without getting into a highly technical explanation of CDSs, it's enough to say here that they are merely a market measure of the creditworthiness of financial institutions and businesses. The large market for credit default swaps indicated what this chapter has made plain, that investors knew well that they couldn't rely on regulators to ensure the financial health of the banks they vainly presumed to oversee. CDSs were the logical market response. They are market regulation personified.

Along the same lines, the ratings agencies of the private sector are in the business of appraising the quality of all manner of bonds. But as "Vinny" in Michael Lewis's 2010 book *The Big Short* observes, "The ratings agency people were all like government employees."[14] The people employed to rate the quality of mortgages that gave so much life to the housing market were almost totally unable to comprehend the markets they were supposed to analyze. As Robert Bartley explained in *The Seven Fat Years*, no rational person would "believe that an individual bond rater could outguess the collective decisions of the market; if he could, he'd be rich and not have to work in such a stodgy place."[15]

Those who should know better finger CDSs as the "cause" of the 2008 financial crisis. Such an obtuse suggestion is the equivalent of a Michigan fan blaming the scoreboard for the Wolverines' loss to Appalachian State in 2007. Back in the real world, CDSs then and now are simply the market's view at any given moment of the ability of businesses to pay their debts. Because bureaucrats and ratings agencies are so poor at foretelling problems in the financial sector, markets have created instruments to do what regulators cannot.

Our financial regulatory system asks the impossible of those who administer it. Rarely do regulators detect banking problems before those in the business do. So markets devise financial instruments that reflect the informed wisdom of the marketplace. The idea that these instruments caused a "financial crisis" is the height of naiveté, as we'll see in a later chapter. The troubles of 2008 in the heavily regulated banking industry provide more evidence that all the money and resources put into federal oversight are wasted. We're asking people of average talent to forecast the future more accurately than the most gifted financial minds can do.

* * *

Finance may be too complicated for regulation, but what about consumer products, or the drug industry?

It would be hard to find a better-known consumer product in the world than Coca-Cola. But not everyone would "like to buy the world a Coke." Critics warn of the "Coca-Colonization" of the world,[16] fearing that the powerful brand is a tool for imposing American cultural norms on other parts of the world. They can relax. The history of Coca-Cola shows how quickly a great brand can get into serious trouble.

On April 23, 1985, Coca-Cola rolled out "New Coke." The company's legendary CEO Roberto Goizueta billed it as "smoother, rounder yet bolder." Coke's historically loyal customers didn't agree with him, however. Soon enough stories fizzled up about cases of the original drink selling for thirty dollars, and a Hollywood producer was said to have put a hundred cases in a wine cellar for safe keeping.[17]

What was arguably the world's most powerful brand was brought to its knees by a customer base that didn't like New Coke. Within two months, New Coke was being pulled from the shelves. "We did not understand the deep emotions of so many of our customers for Coca-Cola," explained the company's president, Donald Keough.[18] So much for the irresistible market power of the corporate colonizer. "Coca-Cola Classic" was sheepishly restored to an angry, and relieved, public.

In 1957 Ford Motor Company announced to America, "The Edsel is Coming!"[19] It is said that the Edsel came with new gadgetry that helped define the future of the automobile, but the buying public was not impressed with the car's looks, and it got a reputation for shoddy workmanship. The Edsel became a cautionary tale about corporate hubris. It's another example of how customers themselves regulate companies with their wallets.

The actors Kevin Costner, Sylvester Stallone, and Ben Affleck all have Academy Awards for Best Picture on their resumés (*Dances With Wolves*, *Rocky*, and *Argo*), but when they were bad, audiences let them know it. No one stood in line for *The Postman*, *Tango & Cash*, or *Gigli*. Customer preference is an effective and costless regulator.

Without government's watchful regulatory eye, wouldn't pharmaceutical firms sicken, maim, or kill their customers? And yet here too, upon examination, the case for regulation doesn't hold up. You have the same talent mismatch that undermines financial regulation. There's a great deal of money to be made in the pharmaceutical industry, so the talent is concentrated on the business side of the regulatory fence.

But the case for pharmaceutical regulation is most seriously challenged by a simple question: How many successful, multi-billion-dollar businesses got that way by killing or maiming their customers? Even if the employees of pharmaceutical firms were completely indifferent to the safety of their products, their companies would not stay in business for long. Successful businesses reach large markets through positive word of mouth. Without the Food and Drug Administration, the incentives for Merck, Pfizer, Eli Lilly, and others to produce life-enhancing drugs with limited side effects would be just as strong as it is with federal regulation if not more.

If Pfizer sold a faulty drug in a world without the FDA, the failure—which could lead to bankruptcy—would be its own. Regulation, on the other hand, has the potential to create a false sense of security. If the federal government puts its stamp of approval on something, maybe it's safe. Or maybe it's honest (remember Madoff Securities in 2008?). As always we have the less talented overseeing the more talented. Regulation to some degree relieves us of responsibility for our own lives, and as the Madoff debacle reminds us, the consequences can be disastrous.

Apart from pharmaceutical firms' overwhelming self-interest in the safety and efficacy of their products, the market supplies other "regulators" that make the FDA superfluous. Many drugs require a doctor's prescription, and it's a fair bet that most people have more faith in their doctor's judgment about a particular drug than in that of the salaried bureaucrats at the FDA. The next level of regulation inherent in the market is pharmacies, which have a powerful incentive to ensure that the medicines they sell to their customers are safe and effective.

Federal drug regulation is as costly as it is unnecessary. The heaviest cost is the cures that reach the market too late or not at all because the FDA looms as a barrier. You won't hear about it from the drug companies themselves, which are loath to speak ill of the regulatory masters who can make their job even more difficult and expensive. Another reason for their silence is that the FDA protects the established pharmaceutical firms from competition. If you doubt it, you need only discover a cure for cancer. Unless you're willing to sell your discovery to one of the big drug companies, the odds of your ever bringing it to the market are quite slim.

The problems with our system of drug regulation were dramatized in the film *Dallas Buyers Club*, set in 1985, when an AIDS diagnosis was tantamount to a death sentence. At the time, the FDA was supervising trials of the drug AZT—which the film argues did more harm than good—but was blocking imports and trials of other potential cures. "Regulated to death" is perhaps an apt description of what happens when governments expropriate the role of the marketplace in the area of health.

* * *

Surely air travel is a field in which the risks are so serious that public safety demands robust government regulation. After all, when a commercial aircraft goes down, hardly anyone walks away. But it was none other than the arch-liberal Senator Edward M. Kennedy, in a televised debate with Eastern Airlines' president, Frank Borman, who asserted on March 1, 1978, that "the problems of our economy have occurred, not as an outgrowth of laissez-faire, unbridled competition. They have occurred under the guidance of federal agencies, and under the umbrella of federal regulations."[20] Kennedy argued, correctly, for more airline competition, while Borman defended "the orderly regulated marketplace."[21] The Kennedy-Borman debate revealed that regulations often exist to protect markets for established businesses. No supporter of big business, Kennedy was arguing for the competition that airline deregulation would bring—competition that would make air travel more accessible to the common man.

Most people don't realize that big carriers such as American Airlines were largely a creation of the federal government. As T. A. Heppenheimer reported in his 1995 book, *Turbulent Skies*, the federal government took "the lead in promoting the growth of this nation's airlines," and its reason for doing so was to help the U.S. Postal Service move mail more quickly around the country.[22] Given the federal government's role in creating the industry, it is no surprise that the same government heavily planned fares and routes. It is also unsurprising that U.S. airlines have suffered substantial losses and bankruptcies over the many decades of commercial flight. Airline executives have been heard to joke that they wish someone had shot down the Wright Brothers so that air travel had never been discovered. But we didn't need the government to invent commercial air travel for us. And if we had left it up to the market, how much more advanced, comfortable, and punctual would the airlines be today?

The idea that there would be more plane crashes without the Federal Aviation Administration is hard to take seriously. In a wholly unregulated market, an airline with a poor reputation for safety would be out of business quickly. In the age of terrorism, airlines competing for passengers would have all the incentives they need to make sure no one boarded with a bomb, and they'd probably assure their passengers' safety a lot more graciously and efficiently than the TSA does.

Ted Kennedy ultimately got his way, and airline routes and fares were eventually deregulated. But as the federal government's still prominent presence at airport gates and in control towers attests, Uncle Sam's involvement is heavy enough to ensure that the wonder of air travel is a nuisance many would prefer to avoid.

* * *

As we've seen, one of the problems with regulation is the mismatch in talent between regulators and the regulated, but regulation creates another problem related to talent. Big profits generate the big pay packages that attract the most talented people to an industry. Government regulation squeezes profits in the target industry, encouraging the best people to work elsewhere. The biggest problem in the heavily regulated financial, transportation, and pharmaceutical sectors is that there *are not enough* billionaires in each.

It's a truism in the banking sector that "for a well-run bank, any capital requirement is too much, and for a poorly run bank, no capital requirement is high enough." But since *all* banks are required to maintain certain capital cushions, the well-run banks are penalized with lower profits than they would have otherwise.

Banks need a capital cushion for times when depositors rush in to get their cash. Those cushions deter bank runs. But if cash on hand is what consumers want so they can sleep at night, then banks will honor their customers' wishes with or without regulations requiring them to keep cash on hand. Warren Brookes wrote long ago, "Businesses, like people, seldom if ever fail solely because of a lack of money."[23] A well-run financial institution would never fail because of a lack of cash because it would never lack the collateral necessary to borrow money at times of high customer withdrawal.

In short, capital requirements foisted on banks are worse than superfluous. They harm the healthiest institutions (and, by extension, well-qualified borrowers), and by reducing profits they make it harder for those banks to attract the people who would run them best. The reward for this is more frequent bank failures, which are, unfortunately, covered by the taxpayers. The "seen" here is highly paid bankers who are sometimes foolishly bailed out, but the "unseen" may well be the loss of more talented bankers who would be less likely to fail in the first place.

We should expect lower-quality executives to migrate to heavily regulated industries such as airlines and Big Pharma. The contrast with Silicon Valley is stark. James Ostrowski pointed out some years ago, "What is perhaps the country's most important industry—the computer industry—is almost entirely unregulated, governed only by the Darwinian laws of laissez-faire economics."[24] Is it any surprise then that Silicon Valley is littered with billionaires?

In markets where people are free, and even encouraged to fail, they are equally free to earn as much money as the free markets will allow. In unregulated Silicon Valley, no one props up failures, and the many successes are not forced to subsidize the mistakes of the failures. Instead, bankrupt ideas are replaced by better ones in a frenzy of fortune-making. Imagine if there were an FDA-style regulatory agency that had to approve the entrance of new social networks? Friendster and MySpace might be subsidized at the expense of

Facebook. Without such regulation, an entrepreneur with a better sense of the market might one day topple Facebook.

As we marvel at the success that freedom from regulation, low barriers to entry, and unlimited profits have brought to Silicon Valley, we have to wonder what the airline and pharmaceutical industries would be like in a similar environment. Better yet, what would Steve Jobs, Jeff Bezos, or Sergey Brin have accomplished with an airline or a drug company? What comfortable, efficient, and affordable travel, what cures might we enjoy today? What is the "unseen" that regulation has deprived us of?

As Warren Brookes observed, it's generally not lack of money that causes businesses to fail. "They fail," he said, "because of lack of ability, judgment, wisdom, ideas, organization, and leadership. When these qualities are present, money is seldom a problem."[25] And government regulation helps to ensure that industries most in need of that kind of leadership are least likely to attract it.

The damage that government regulation does to the American economy is all the more appalling when you consider how expensive it is for businesses to comply with the mandates of their regulatory masters. Wayne Crews, a vice president of the Competitive Enterprise Institute, estimates that the annual cost of regulatory compliance is two *trillion* dollars.[26] And Crews would almost certainly agree that the number underestimates the actual economic costs involved. Economic growth is about production first and foremost, and regulation cripples our ability to produce.

Since the government can shut a company down or indict its management on a moment's notice, businesses must expend great sums at the expense of profits and growth in order to stay on their regulators' good side. Though BB&T was quite well capitalized amid the 2008 financial meltdown, regulators made it clear to John Allison that if he refused to accept bailout money that the bank did not need, BB&T would soon receive attention from "very concerned" regulators with the power to shut it down.[27]

Regulators are worse than worthless in banking and finance. They're wholly superfluous in other areas of commerce such as drinks, cars, and entertainment. When it comes to our healthcare regulation, there's probably a death toll. And because regulation saps the profits that attract the skilled, the costs to the economy as a whole are incalculably large.

Our best estimates of the expense of regulation capture only a fraction of the actual costs. Regulations are an expensive, growth-sapping burden that leave us with reduced innovation. The regulatory state has convinced its citizens that it is the only thing standing between them and the law of the jungle. The truth, as we have seen, is quite the opposite. It's time to scrap the whole misbegotten system, in which the blind lead the sighted and the mediocre drive out the talented.

CHAPTER TWELVE

Antitrust Laws: The Neutering of the Near-Term Excellent

Competition is supposed to reward firms that innovate first, that build integrated systems, and that expand before their rivals do.
—Dominick T. Armentano, *Antitrust: The Case for Repeal*

Irving G. Thalberg was one of the most successful movie producers ever. He oversaw the production of four hundred films, and under his stewardship Metro-Goldwyn-Mayer became Hollywood's most prestigious studio. A testimony to his lasting influence on the film industry is the Irving G. Thalberg Memorial Award, which the Academy of Motion Picture Arts and Sciences bestows on the "creative producers whose bodies of work reflect a consistently high quality of motion picture production."

As brilliant a producer as he was, however, Thalberg still had blind spots. He famously told Louis B. Mayer, "Forget it, Louis, no Civil War picture ever made a nickel."[1] The Civil War picture in question was *Gone with the Wind.* MGM passed up the chance to produce a film adaptation of Margaret Mitchell's bestseller, which became, by most measures, the top grossing movie of all time.[2]

Thalberg wasn't the only Hollywood genius with regrets. *The Godfather*, the twenty-third-highest grossing film of all time[3] and universally regarded as a classic, was almost never made. Paramount Pictures' senior vice president Robert Evans had a terrible time convincing the studio to take on the film adaptation of Mario Puzo's bestselling novel. A Paramount executive, Peter Bart, told Evans, "They're scared of it, Bob...it's that simple. It's still a spaghetti gangster film. It's never worked yet."[4] And Marlon Brando was almost passed up for the role of Vito Corleone. Dino de Laurentiis told Charles Bluhdorn, the CEO of Paramount's parent company, Gulf & Western, "If Brando plays the Don, forget opening the film in Italy. They will laugh him off the screen." Worse, the word from Gulf & Western headquarters to Evans was: "Will not finance Brando in title role. Do not respond. Case closed."[5] Once again, the smartest people in the business couldn't predict the future.

What television show has a more secure place in the pantheon of American entertainment than *Monday Night Football*? But the chairman of CBS, William S. Paley—one of the great visionaries of his industry—rejected a proposal for a Monday evening professional football broadcast in the late 1960s.[6] When ABC eventually picked up *MNF*, Anheuser-Busch declined the opportunity to be a sponsor. So Miller Brewing ultimately bought exclusive rights as *MNF*'s beer advertiser for five million dollars.[7] *MNF* became a cultural phenomenon, of course, and turned Miller beer into a national favorite. Unhappy Anheuser-Busch executives came back to ABC and told them "they would pay whatever it took to get into the show." Miller, however, had the rights locked up.[8]

O. J. Simpson eventually became a fixture on *MNF* as a commentator, selected because he was "instantly, inescapably likeable."[9] The former football star, once famous for running through airports for a rental car, was considered for the lead role in the 1984 film *The Terminator*. In one of history's little ironies, the part went to Arnold Schwarzenegger because the studio brass decided that "[p]eople wouldn't have believed a nice guy like O. J. playing the part of a ruthless killer."[10]

When David Chase shopped his idea for a TV series about a mobster and his family, ABC, CBS, and NBC all turned him down. HBO picked it up, and *The Sopranos* became the foundation of the cable network's enormously successful television series business.[11] Not that HBO has been infallible either. Though it green-lighted *The Sopranos*, HBO turned down *Mad Men*, to AMC's profit,[12] as well as *Breaking Bad*.

A co-founder of Carlyle Group, the billionaire David Rubenstein passed up a chance to be an early investor in Facebook.[13] Twenty-six teams passed on the quarterback Dan Marino before the Miami Dolphins took him in the 1983 NFL Draft. Todd Blackledge, Tony Eason, and Ken O'Brien—all drafted before Marino—never amounted to much in the pros.[14] In 2000, the quarterback guru Bill Walsh chose Hofstra's Giovanni Carmazzi in the third round, overlooking Tom Brady, who lasted until the sixth round.[15]

History, then, is crowded with experts making mistakes about the future, but what does that have to do with antitrust laws? A lot. Antitrust regulation is based on the power of government lawyers to see into the future. They are able, it is supposed, to discern which businesses will wield too much power. Because of this clairvoyance, antitrust lawyers are authorized to break up successful businesses, force combining firms to shed valuable business lines before merging, and penalize companies for charging too much or too little for their products.

The problem, as with other forms of regulation, is one of talent. If you're skilled at forecasting the future, you don't toil for a federal salary. You work in the private sector, and if you're good, you earn many times what you'd earn policing companies from the nation's capital. If Irving Thalberg could not see the potential of *Gone with the Wind*, and if William Paley dismissed *Monday Night Football*, who really thinks that government lawyers can tell which businesses will possess too much power down the line?

* * *

In 2010, Blockbuster Video filed for bankruptcy. But once upon a time, Blockbuster reigned as the largest video rental chain, with sixty thousand employees and over nine thousand stores.[16] How quickly things change.

In 2005, Blockbuster abandoned its plan to purchase its competitor Hollywood Video after antitrust officials at the Federal Trade Commission leaked their plan to block the deal.[17] The FTC predicted that a merger between Blockbuster and Hollywood Video would concentrate too much market power in one company, giving it the ability to raise prices on consumers. Hollywood Video ultimately paired up with another competitor, Movie Gallery, only to cease operations in 2010 when Movie Gallery filed for bankruptcy.[18]

It wasn't competition from other video chains that bankrupted Blockbuster but an unexpected change in the video rental industry. Antitrust officials who blocked the ability of Blockbuster to combine with a rival missed the "disrupter," Reed Hastings.

In 1997, Hastings failed to return a copy of *Apollo 13* to his local Blockbuster on time, and he was assessed a forty-dollar late fee.

Hastings sensed an opportunity and founded Netflix in Los Gatos, California, two years later.[19] Netflix offered two major improvements on the Blockbuster model. First, geography no longer bound customers to a retail location. They could select DVDs or videos online and receive them by mail, often within a day, thanks to a network of warehouses around the country. Second, customers could keep their movies for as long as they desired. Netflix charged a flat monthly fee based on how many DVDs a customer wanted at a time, removing a great deal of unease—and expense—from the movie renting. Yet, despite these improvements, Netflix was in trouble by 2000. Blockbuster could have purchased Netflix then for fifty million dollars but passed on the opportunity.[20]

While antitrust officials focused their energies on the possibility that Blockbuster might grow too powerful through the acquisition of other retail chains, tiny Netflix entered the DVD rental business and took over the market. The biggest names in video rental have long since vanished, while an outsider that the FTC knew little about managed to change the business completely.

Netflix is a hot stock today. But Reed Hastings is well aware of how he caught once powerful Blockbuster flatfooted. For his next innovation, he introduced online streaming video services to eliminate waiting for a DVD to arrive in the mail. Someday another entrepreneur may well make Netflix's model obsolete, and it is a fair bet that antitrust officials will not see the business disruption coming.

Indeed, a merger between Blockbuster and Hollywood Video might have allowed the firm to compete with Netflix, but thanks to the hubris of antitrust regulators, we'll never know. Instead, investors—who would give anything to possess the talent that antitrust regulators purport to have—get to watch new video entrants such as Roku, Apple TV, and Amazon Prime compete with Netflix. Meanwhile, Netflix has moved into movie production. So far its output is limited, but both *House of Cards* and *Orange Is the New Black* have received popular and critical acclaim. If Netflix does to Hollywood's studio model what it did to Blockbuster's video rental model, it will again make a mockery of the very idea of antitrust regulation. If Netflix chooses to buy a movie studio, will antitrust officials allow them to? One can only hope.

Federal regulators would not allow Blockbuster to purchase Hollywood Video, but on occasion they are a bit more "generous." Of course, there's a catch. Regulators allow companies to merge if they weaken themselves in the process. On November 12, 2013, the Department of Justice approved the merger of American Airlines and US Airways. However, the approval depended on the combined company's forfeiting gates at some of the most heavily trafficked airports around the United States. Specifically, the two carriers sold access to coveted gates at Reagan National in Washington, D.C., and LaGuardia in New York for $425 million.[21] The two airlines merged in order to become more competitive, but ended up less so.

Forced divestiture of assets is the norm in mergers today. It also defies the basic economic logic of allowing the shareholders who own companies to combine them in ways that will maximize shareholder returns. But bureaucracies, ever in search of a purpose, have seemingly found one in forcing companies to neuter themselves before a merger. All this is based on the naïve presumption that tomorrow's commercial outlook will mirror today's. The problem is that it rarely does.

In 2000, America Online (AOL) announced a merger with the media giant Time Warner. AOL's market capitalization was double that of Time Warner's,[22] and the internet darling appeared unstoppable.

"AOL everywhere" was its tagline. The columnist Norman Solomon warned of the "servitude" to which consumers would be reduced by the supposed power of the combined entity.[23] Taking its cue from the handwringing media, the Federal Trade Commission took a year to approve the deal.[24]

In April 2002, the merged company announced a fifty-four-billion-dollar loss; a year later the loss was ninety-nine billion. By September 2003, the once dominant AOL had become obsolete in the constantly evolving communications field, and Time Warner dropped AOL from its name.[25] Ted Turner, the founder of CNN and the largest individual shareholder of the combined company, lost 80 percent of his net worth, or eight billion dollars, on a deal so stupendously misconceived that it has inspired two books—*Fools Rush In* and *There Must Be a Pony in Here Somewhere*—chronicling the debacle.[26]

Nearly fourteen years after the announcement of the failed AOL/Time Warner combination, the cable operator Comcast announced a plan to purchase Time Warner for forty-five billion dollars. The antitrust Chicken Littles began flapping about on cue. *Business Insider* warned, "Comcast's $45 Billion Purchase of Time Warner Cable Is Trouble," while the *Arizona Daily Star* fretted, "Many fear Comcast–Time Warner Cable merger spells monopoly."[27] Time Warner's previous megamerger had been an object lesson in the perils of predicting monopolies, but the confidence of the antitrust faithful in the forecasting talents of federal regulators was unshaken.

Competition can arise from unexpected places. Blockbuster never imagined that Netflix, which it scorned to acquire at a bargain price, would bring about its demise. If Borders had foreseen that Amazon would trump Barnes & Noble as its main competitor, it would have entered into internet book sales alongside Jeff Bezos.

Antitrust regulators, out of fear of Comcast's acquiring monopoly powers, will surely make Comcast jump through hoops to acquire Time Warner.

Mergers are ultimately about survival. Companies must adjust to an uncertain future business climate, and restraining the ability of larger businesses to act in the best interest of shareholders is counterproductive. Antitrust regulation does not foster competition so much as it reduces successful companies to sitting ducks.

Blockage of mergers also robs the economy of essential information that makes growth possible. If the future were obvious, then everyone would be a billionaire. Since it's not, antitrust regulators should leave businesses free to compete without restraint. Some will succeed and others will fail, but that is the point. Speedier judgments by the market allow quicker allocation of limited capital to new ideas.

New markets are constantly appearing, but antitrust regulators can react only to yesterday's marketplace. Microsoft manufactures software and Dell makes computers, but a combination of the two would never get past antitrust lawyers. Nor is there any chance for a merger between television networks such as ABC and NBC. Microsoft was late to the internet search engine game, so Google is far more popular than Microsoft's Bing. Microsoft saved Apple from bankruptcy in the late 1990s, but the iPod easily crushed the Microsoft Zune. Apple also beat Dell to the market with tablets, which might eventually replace desktop computers. ABC and NBC claim lots of viewers and content, but as the "binge-watching" of Netflix's *House of Cards* reveals, sources of content that do not require a television promise to grow further. Federal bureaucrats can't possibly anticipate the developments in these markets, and it's laughable for them to try.

Then there is the issue of waste. Henry Hazlitt wisely observed that "one occupation can expand *only at the expense of all other occupations*."[28] In short, it is impossible to do everything. But if Microsoft and Dell were to combine operations, some of their limited resources would be freed up to work on new product lines. How would such a merger end up? We simply don't know—see AOL/Time Warner.

Antitrust policy is notoriously inconsistent. Antitrust regulators from the Department of Justice kept Microsoft in their crosshairs in the late 1990s. If the software giant had charged for access to the Internet Explorer browser built into its Windows software, it would have certainly faced federal lawsuits for using its "monopoly" software power to gouge customers. Yet bundling Explorer into Windows for free was deemed "predatory." Today, Microsoft's Internet Explorer is losing market share to Mozilla Firefox and Google Chrome, showing that all the antitrust fuss was about nothing.

Antitrust regulation is animated by the fear of monopoly. If businesses grow too large or attain too much market share, they will raise their prices. That concern seems plausible at first glance, but it is divorced from observable realities. With its iPod, iPhone, and iPad—products that were unique upon their introduction—Apple created monopolies out of thin air. But instead of raising the prices of these devices, Apple has been feverishly cutting them. The reason for this is basic: profits attract imitators and innovators.

Businesses that attain a monopoly—and monopolies are ephemeral in a market economy—do not maintain their market share by gouging customers. Rather, they aggressively seek production enhancements that will allow them to continue reducing prices so they can possess as much of the market as possible amid the entry of new firms in search of the profits. Apple is acting in its own interest when it cuts prices or bundles products.

The most famous "monopolist" was John D. Rockefeller, who started selling kerosene in 1870, bringing light into otherwise dark evenings. His Standard Oil Company had 4 percent of the kerosene market in 1870. By 1890, its share of the market amounted to 85 percent. If the logic of antitrust regulation were valid, the price of kerosene would have risen with Rockefeller's market share. In fact kerosene prices fell from thirty cents per gallon in 1869 to nine cents in 1880 and 5.9 cents by 1897.[29] Companies do not grow successful by jacking up prices. Instead, they aggressively search for production efficiencies that *increase profits* amid *constantly falling prices*. Rockefeller grew wealthier by meeting market needs—for kerosene first, and later for the fuel oil that powered increasingly ubiquitous cars. While he was meeting consumer needs, Rockefeller did not deter competitors. In 1911, the year that Standard Oil was ruled an "illegal monopoly," there were roughly 147 oil refineries in business to compete against Rockefeller. Just as, a century later, antitrust regulators would pursue Microsoft at the very moment new firms were eroding its dominance, they went after Standard Oil when it was producing only about 9 percent of America's oil supply.[30]

Government regulators—you can count on it—are always late to presumed "problems" that are invariably fixed by market competition. Once again, if regulators could predict markets, they surely wouldn't be working as regulators.

The history of General Motors is a fine example of the absurdity underlying monopolistic assumptions. In 1952, John Kenneth Galbraith asserted, "The decisions of General Motors on power, design, price, model changes, production schedules, and the myriad other details concerning its automobiles are final. There is no appeal; the career or reputation of no authority is at stake." In 1976, two American Motors executives warned that if GM's growth was not halted, "they might find themselves selling the whole market." If "they wanted to wipe out everybody by 1980, the only one who could stop them is the government."[31]

The federal government did not stop GM. It did not need to. The once "invincible" automaker found itself in such poor condition by 2008 that it had to beg the federal government for a bailout. General Motors was once highly profitable, but profits attract imitators and innovators if markets are largely free. The exciting "disruption" that felled GM is at work in other industries. In time, industry leaders like Apple, Netflix, and Amazon will be knocked from their perches. Market forces will do what antitrust regulators cannot do.

Skeptics should consult the classic book *In Search of Excellence.* Written in 1982 and describing the best practices of forty-three top U.S. businesses, it flew off of bookstore shelves upon release. Everyone wanted to know what the best businesses did in order to stay on top. Yet within two years, fourteen of those businesses were in serious financial trouble.[32] Antitrust is ultimately about using government force to make the excellent less excellent. It is an obstacle to economic evolution. History shows that competition in the marketplace makes the work of antitrust lawyers superfluous.

We should ask ourselves a couple of important, and provocative, questions. Which is preferable: weak companies like GM and Citigroup, which need taxpayer support to stay in business, or strong companies like Microsoft and IBM, which can survive on their own? If markets excel at humbling the powerful, then antitrust attorneys are unnecessary. And what's not to like about monopoly profits? Isn't the pursuit of monopoly profits a good reason to go into business in the first place? Achieving a monopoly suggests that a business has identified and abundantly met a market need.

Consumers confer market share on businesses. If a company enjoys a large share of the market, it's because it best serves consumers' needs. Businesses grow large because consumer demand for what they offer is large. But large companies can falter, ensuring a rapidly changing picture of the most successful companies.

That's what is so great about monopoly profits. The profits signal to the ambitious the wealth they can earn by entering previously unknown markets. Without monopoly profits, investors, entrepreneurs, and businesses have no idea where capital will be most rewarded. So when antitrust regulators neuter the successful pioneers, they leave the markets in the dark, and we're left with the blind leading the blind.

CHAPTER THIRTEEN

Conclusion: Don't Dismiss College Dropouts Delivering Alternative Weeklies

These Google guys, they want to be billionaires and rock stars and go to conferences and all that. Let us see if they still want to run the business in two to three years.

—**Bill Gates** on Google, 2003[1]

Back in the 1970s, Roland Swenson dropped out of the University of Texas "to pursue a degree in rock 'n' roll." Austin is littered with musically inclined twenty-somethings. Yet by the age of thirty-one, Swenson was seemingly still stuck in his twenties as a proofreader and a deliveryman for one of those "alternative weekly" newspapers so popular with the college-aged.[2] Most people grow up and grow out of the college lifestyle, but Swenson remained. Nothing about his career choices in his first thirty-one years signaled future success.

But people can surprise. In 1994, Kurt Warner was bagging groceries at a store in Iowa for $5.50 an hour after the Green Bay Packers cut him. Warner never gave up on being a quarterback, and the pursuit of his dream took him through the Arena Football League and NFL Europe, both now defunct. But his exploits in the minor leagues of professional football soon caught the eye of the St. Louis Rams, who eventually signed him. By 2000, Warner was the MVP of the NFL and had led the Rams to the franchise's lone Super Bowl victory.[3]

In the late 1990s into the 2000s, Katherine Stockett was a functionary at various New York City magazine brands (I know, we were and still are friends) until she moved with her husband to Atlanta in 2003. She was a pretty, well liked, and witty woman, but no one I knew thought she was marked for global renown. When she wrote a novel about social tension in pre–civil rights movement Mississippi, she received, as she put it to me in an e-mail, over "SIXTY—6-0—rejections. From agents." But, her persistence paid off. *The Help* became a bestseller, and the movie adaptation was a smash at the box office.

Back to Swenson: in 1986 he convinced his bosses to stage a music festival that they called South by Southwest, known nowadays as SXSW. Although it drew seven hundred attendees in its first year, it now draws more than seventy thousand, and Austin's restaurants, bars, and hotels are packed each March for the nine-day festival, one of the biggest musical events in the country.

These stories are a reminder that not only is the future almost impossible to predict, but it is difficult to know who will shape it. Antitrust presumes the opposite of that truth—that what lies ahead is knowable.

If it is extraordinarily hard to tell which seemingly average people will one day receive global acclaim, it is just as hard to tell which of today's success stories will become yesterday's news. Antitrust laws are rooted in the fallacy that the present predicts the future. Swenson, Warner, and Stockett are living rebuttals to that foolish idea.

Antitrust law attempts to regulate the normal workings of a market in which an incalculable number of decisions are being made every moment. Any such enterprise must collapse under the weight of its myriad contradictions. "No one knows anything," as they say.

Mark Zuckerberg was a student at Phillips Exeter Academy in 2000 and the billionaire founder of Facebook by 2010. In creating the world's largest social network, Zuckerberg left some giant business conglomerates in his wake, including MySpace, a social network owned by media behemoth News Corp.

In a twist befitting the social media giant, Facebook purchased the messaging company WhatsApp for nineteen billion dollars in 2014. WhatsApp's co-founder Jan Koum is a Ukrainian immigrant who, upon arriving with his mother in Mountain View, California, at the age of sixteen, lived on government assistance, including food stamps.[4] As the *Wall Street Journal*'s L. Gordon Crovitz noted, WhatsApp was "a company few regulators had heard of."[5] Business moves fast, changes direction with great speed, and proves how exceedingly difficult it is to tell who will next rise to prominence.

Regulation is the economic equivalent of presuming the slower defensive backs of Appalachian State can regularly cover the much faster wide receivers of the University of Michigan. Actually, that is an understatement. Regulation presumes the coach of Appalachian State knows exactly where the ball will go on each down. Not many coaches know that, and if they did, they'd still need the dazzlingly talented players capable of covering the opposing receivers.

Just as Michigan will score with painful regularity on Appalachian State, so will the more talented in the world of commerce almost always remain several steps ahead of those who presume to watch over them. Even those who honestly feel Goldman Sachs, Coke, and Pfizer need government supervision need to recognize some incontrovertible truths. Powerful companies are already subject to the best regulators of all, competition and consumers. Moreover, those who aspire to the role of government regulator rarely have the skills necessary for even a passable job in the private sector.

Former BB&T Bank CEO John Allison likes to make the point that "while government *can't* make us all equal, it *can* make us all small." Indeed, government regulation and hostility to profit have left the talented exceedingly poor throughout the centuries. China has seen both the horrors of government-decreed equality and the staggering increase in wealth that occurs when government steps aside.

Regulation does not just routinely fail; it *cannot* work. What it can do, however, is weaken businesses by forcing them to pour their human and financial resources into compliance with government rules and regulations rather than let shareholders and customers profit. We must scrap the regulatory state not because we want business to run roughshod over the citizenry (it can't), but precisely because we want business to train its full focus on serving the citizenry.

PART III

Trade

CHAPTER FOURTEEN

"Trade Deficits" Are Our Rewards for Going to Work Each Day

In fact, international transactions are always in balance, by definition.

—Robert L. Bartley, *The Seven Fat Years*

The late British writer Geoffrey Bocca had a diverse body of work that included a biography of Winston Churchill, a book on hedonistic living in Europe called *Bikini Beach: The Wicked Riviera*, and even one about a modern U.S. tragedy, *The Assassination of J. F. K.*

Bocca also spent time in Moscow in the decades before communism's collapse. The result was a fascinating book about his experiences in Soviet Russia titled *The Moscow Scene*. If you want a keen sense of the drudgery and poverty that define societies almost totally bereft of markets, property rights, and trade, Bocca's book is a good place to start.

His description of a trip to a restaurant in *The Moscow Scene* is particularly telling:

> I had scarcely sat down when a young blond thug in the black suit and clip-on bow tie of a *maître d'hotel* swooped and handed me a greasy menu, the pages almost disintegrating from use. I knew the menu by heart. It has not been changed in a quarter of a century at least. What I had in mind to begin with was borscht. But the headwaiter, who was pushing caviar tonight, took the menu out of my hands and turned to the caviar page.[1]

And thus began an argument between customer and waiter that would shock most anyone used to restaurants in societies defined by markets. Bocca wanted borscht, but the surly waiter kept demanding that he order caviar. After conferring with a colleague and questioning whether to serve Bocca at all, the waiter instructed him to order Chicken Kiev despite Bocca's desire for beef fillet as his entrée. Bocca described his waiter's bearing as that of a reform school graduate, which he might well have been, since waiting tables was about the lowest form of employment in that dystopian society.[2]

Bocca never got the meal he asked for, but the description of his visit speaks volumes about the wonders of trade. Indeed, at the table next to him was an attractive couple. They had brought two windshield wipers into the restaurant with them, curiously enough. The wipers were a powerful status symbol in Moscow. They indicated that you had a car, and wipers left on a car were prime targets for thieves.[3]

In capitalist and even in mixed economies, people produce in order to consume. But in the USSR, to the extent that a Soviet worker produced anything of value, there was nothing to buy in return for his production. The Soviets had small "trade surpluses," which economists celebrate, but no "trade deficits," which economists decry. They did not have trade deficits because there was nothing to buy. The shelves at state-run stores were nearly bare.

In the 1970s, Americans faced long gas lines created by federal controls on petroleum prices, but life here was paradise compared with life in the Soviet Union, where there were lines *for everything*. As Hedrick Smith put it in his eye-opening 1976 book about life in the Soviet Union, *The Russians*, "Imagine [the lines for gas] across the board, all the time, and you realize that Soviet shopping is like a year-round Christmas rush."[4]

Americans wore jeans in the '70s for a rugged, somewhat faux-impoverished look. In the Soviet Union jeans were a sign of wealth, selling on the black market for $106 a pair (a lot of money back then).[5] The satirist P. J. O'Rourke suggests that horrifically tailored "Bulgarian blue jeans" did more to end the Cold War than anything else.

The funny thing is, Russians were great savers. Smith was privy to estimates that savings rose from ninety-one billion rubles in 1975 to 165 billion by 1981.[6] But without functioning markets, there was no redistribution from savers to entrepreneurs. Russians couldn't do anything with their savings, so there was no reward for discipline and prudence. The most they could hope for was a chance to go shopping abroad.

The British diplomat Nigel Bloomfield explained to Smith that Russians, outside their own bleak country, "were like coiled springs, leaping at the department store cornucopias of the West." Rather than touring, "Russians came back incredibly laden with new dresses, slacks, shoes, shirts, radios, the whole kit."[7] Soviets clamored for trips abroad not just to breathe relatively freely, but also to shop. They could sell the goods they brought home at large markups to less privileged Soviet citizens long on rubles but with nowhere to spend them.

For a brilliant dramatization of the plight of Soviet consumers you need look no further than Robin Williams's 1984 film *Moscow on the Hudson*, about a Russian musician who defects to the United States at Bloomingdale's in Manhattan. Early in the movie he walks through a grocery store lined with shelves stocked with all manner of goods. Used to the empty store shelves that were the rule in the Soviet Union, the visitor is so confused that he faints.

The *Wall Street Journal*'s Mary Anastasia O'Grady has described a similar situation in Latin America. Writing about the need for a Central American Free Trade agreement in 2005, she offered an insight about imports that frequently eludes credentialed economists who focus on the harm of foreign goods' reaching U.S. shores. Imports are good, O'Grady insisted, and free trade agreements meant to include Central American countries would help "Centrals gain access to imports."[8] Thinking back to various Russian examples, "imports," whether from the city down the road or the country on the other side of the world, are the purpose of work. People produce *so that* they can consume.

But there aren't many goods for the relatively impoverished citizens of Central America to buy in exchange for their labor. They remedy this with help from relatives lucky enough to live in the United States, who bring American abundance with them on their trips back home. As O'Grady described flights to Central America:

> Forget about "carry-on" luggage on flights to Tegucigalpa, San Pedro Sula, or Managua. On these routes it's "haul-on" baggage. Passengers, big and small, drag overstuffed grips and twine-tied bundles the size of refrigerators down the airplane aisle. Strangers come together to collectively hoist grandma's loot into overhead compartments, with much grunting and sweating.[9]

The citizens of Hong Kong, by contrast, suffer none of this deprivation. Founded as a British colony in 1842 after the Treaty of Nanking, Hong Kong was called a "barren rock" because of its almost complete lack of natural mineral resources (oil, copper, tin, etc.) and farmable land. Despite its lack of "natural wealth," Hong Kong is one of the richest places in the world thanks to its wildly ambitious people.[10]

Hong Kong is completely dependent on imports for its oil, food, and appliances. Yet it thrives precisely *because* its inhabitants import these things from other countries. In Hong Kong's almost totally free market, nearly every product in the world can reach consumers tax-free. Americans traveling abroad roam the aisles of "duty free" stores at airports in order to buy things tax-free. The whole island of Hong Kong is "duty free," and its extraordinarily productive inhabitants exchange the fruits of their labor for the world's abundance.

A rich society of productive people with infinite wants, Hong Kong has a massive "trade deficit." Economists decry "trade deficits," yet Hong Kong is a monument to their wonders. What explains this apparent riddle? First, *countries* do not trade. *Individuals* do. A country's economy is just a collection of individuals. The United States has the biggest economy on earth and runs a massive annual "trade deficit," but then the "United States" does not trade. The individuals who live in the United States trade. They enjoy one of the highest average incomes in the world and are consequently voracious consumers.

Economics is about the individual. If we take the idea of "trade deficits" down to the individual level, we can see that what sounds economically destabilizing is really beneficial. In my case, I run trade "surpluses" with my various employers—*Forbes*, RealClearMarkets, and Toreador Research & Trading. They buy more from me (my labor) than I do from them. But I then take that "surplus" (my salary) and spend it on housing, clothes, and food. I run a trade *deficit* with my landlord, my clothier, and my grocery store. Do I worry that in my commercial relations with my grocery store, I do all the buying and the store does all the selling? Of course not. My trade deficit is actually my reward for producing. Some people like to save their surpluses, but as we've seen, no act of saving ever subtracts from overall consumption. Saving merely shifts consumptive powers to others through bank deposits that are lent out, or savings go to businesses eager to grow through loans from those same banks, or for that matter, money market accounts, brokerage accounts, etc. Either way, surpluses and deficits balance.

Let's take this analysis up a level from the individual. New York City is easily one of our richest cities. It's the home of more billionaires than any other city on earth. As Ken Auletta wrote long ago, "For those with talent, this city is the final test."[11] And New York City runs large trade "deficits" because its citizens need to "import" much of what they consume, from all over the United States and the world. Once upon a time, the city was filled with factories, but the manufacturers departed long ago. Today those factories are luxurious lofts and restaurants for wealthy New Yorkers.

Silicon Valley rivals New York when it comes to billionaires, and trade deficits too. Although people buy products from Apple, Intel, and Oracle, the factories that manufacture those products are in foreign countries. Despite this apparent lack of production, the denizens of Silicon Valley, like their counterparts in New York and Hong Kong, do not go without. Why is this? Newspaper headlines regularly feature scary articles bemoaning trade deficits, yet rich people run massive trade deficits. What's the explanation? The answer to this seeming riddle is quite simple.

Importing shoes from Italy, televisions from Japan, and bananas from Guatemala is called "trade," but selling stock in American companies to foreigners is called "foreign investment." This explains the worthless accounting abstraction that is the trade "deficit." There is really no such thing. To simplify—we can buy those shoes, televisions, and bananas from overseas because a massive amount of foreign investment flows into the United States every day to buy shares in our innovative companies. We export shares in our world-leading companies, and in return for those shares we import things that the rest of the world produces. The trade balances.

This explains the beauty of free trade. The Silicon Valley technologist does not have to worry about designing suits, nor does the financier in New York or Hong Kong. They leave that work to the Savile Row tailor in London, and their ability to "outsource" the design of their suits means they can maximize their time spent on designing software. Moreover, the New York and Hong Kong financiers can spend their time on finding the financing necessary to bring the software designer's vision to the marketplace.

Investment follows talent, so it's no surprise that rich places run trade "deficits." But a "deficit" in trade is a sign that investors put a high value on the work being done in Silicon Valley, New York, and Hong Kong. They can "import" a lot precisely because they "export" shares of the companies they own or work for.

A little common sense is in order when we're talking about trade. The streets of New York are home to shops and boutiques selling the most famous brands in the world, but the store windows are boarded up in downtown Detroit. Producers of goods and services do not ship their products to New York because it is impoverished but because it is not.

As Robert Bartley put it in *The Seven Fat Years*, "The mystery is why we even collect these figures [about trade deficits]; if we kept similar statistics for Manhattan Island, Park Avenue could lay awake at night worrying about its trade deficit."[12] Exactly. Nashville residents do not pay any mind to their trade "balance" with Seattle, and their trade "balance" with Shanghai is no more important. All trade balances. Trade "deficits" with producers from near and far away are the reward for everyone's productivity.

CHAPTER FIFTEEN

Comparative Advantage: Could LeBron James Play in the NFL?

... we must never lose sight of this maxim, that products are always bought ultimately with products. It is most for our advantage to employ our productive powers, not in those branches in which foreigners excel us, but in those which we excel in ourselves; and with the product to purchase of others.
—**Jean-Baptiste Say,** *A Treatise on Political Economy*

Cleveland Cavaliers forward LeBron James is currently the best basketball player in the world. A nine-time NBA All-Star, four-time league MVP, two-time Olympic gold medalist, and two-time NBA champion, James is the Michael Jordan of his era. Looking back even further, he is the Oscar Robertson or Elgin Baylor of the modern NBA.

At six feet eight inches and 250 pounds, James has the size, coordination, and jumping ability that would make him a successful NFL receiver. Indeed, more than a few professional football players have gone on record as saying that James could play, and perhaps even star, in the NFL right now.[1] Tight end is most often mentioned as his ideal position. But if James were to "take his talents" to the NFL, he would violate the economic principle of comparative advantage. James might be able to play in the NFL, but he would do so at the expense of his reign as the world's best basketball player.

From an earnings standpoint alone, it is a lousy idea. The Patriots' tight end Rob Gronkowski, one of the best at his position in the NFL, is paid roughly nine million dollars per year for his services.[2] James—who some say is underpaid—earns $19 million per year on account of his being the best.[3] Of course, a comparison with Gronkowski assumes that James would rank as a top tight end. The twenty-fifth-highest paid tight end is the Detroit Lions' Brandon Pettigrew, pulling in $1.2 million,[4] and many others earn even less.

If James were to split his time between the two sports, his total annual pay would probably decline, even with salaries from two teams. No NBA team will give a big contract to a player putting his body at major risk each NFL season. Moreover, professional football and basketball players generally use the off-season to refresh their tired legs. James's body would be worn down for each new NBA season even if he emerged from the sixteen-game NFL season uninjured.

The idea of James's playing in the NFL is even worse when you take into account his outside income. He reportedly earns another forty million dollars per year for product endorsements from Nike, Coca-Cola, Samsung, and McDonald's.[5] He commands these kinds of fees because he's the world's best basketball player. He wouldn't be if he were also playing football.

On the other hand there's Tony Gonzalez, who retired from the NFL after the 2013 season. A fourteen-time Pro Bowl tight end for the Kansas City Chiefs and Atlanta Falcons, Gonzalez is a nearly certain first-ballot pick for the NFL's Hall of Fame in 2019.

Gonzalez played college football for the Cal Bears, and he also starred on the basketball team. He could have played in the NBA, where he probably would have been an average player. The salary for the average NBA player, by the way, is not shabby—$5.15 million.[6] Assuming a long career in the NBA, even as a backup, Gonzalez would have done well. But he was better at football. His last contract with the Falcons was fourteen million dollars for two years.[7]

Gonzalez's salary as a player, like LeBron James's, is only part of the story. As soon as he retired, CBS signed Gonzalez as a commentator on *NFL Today*. Being one of the best tight ends ever will pay dividends long after Gonzalez's playing career has ended.

There have been two-sport stars at the professional level, but they're the exception. Bo Jackson played running back for the Oakland Raiders and center field for the Kansas City Royals. A hip flexor injury incurred while playing for the Raiders ended his sports career early, however—one of many reasons why James will most likely never attempt to play football.

The most famous athlete to go the two-sport route was Michael Jordan, whose story is the perfect parable about comparative advantage. Jordan might have been the best basketball player of all time. But after having won his third straight NBA title with the Chicago Bulls in 1993, he shocked everyone by retiring. Out of basketball for the 1993–1994 season, Jordan signed with a minor league baseball team, the Birmingham Barons. In 127 games, he batted .202, hit three home runs, struck out 114 times, and committed eleven errors on the field.[8]

Achieving those pedestrian statistics was not easy. Only a very accomplished athlete could switch careers late in life and hit .202.

But in terms of comparative advantage, Jordan's decision to play baseball was quite the blunder. To play for the Barons, Jordan had to give up his standing as the best basketball player in the world.

Ordinary people also run into the exigencies of comparative advantage. I am lousy with my hands and have never grown so much as a simple plant, so I would perish quickly if I had to construct my own housing or grow my own food. But even if I knew how to do those things, the laws of comparative advantage would still demand that I "outsource" the production of my housing and food to others. That's because economics is about tradeoffs. If I spent the day farming, it would be at the expense of what I do best, writing and editing. Almost everything we have—from a simple pencil to an ultra high definition television—is the result of cooperation among individuals with complementary talents.

Although one plus one equals two in arithmetic, one person working in accord with his comparative advantage plus another person working in accord with his comparative advantage can equal three or four or a hundred. That's what happened when Steve Jobs and Steve Wozniak started working together in a garage in the 1970s. Though they probably never uttered the phrase "comparative advantage," Jobs was the idea guy, while Wozniak was the computer programming wizard.

As Wozniak recounted to Jobs's biographer, Walter Isaacson, he didn't know his computer ideas were marketable, let alone *how* to market them.[9] "Woz designed a great machine," the public relations expert Regis McKenna told Isaacson, "but it would be sitting in hobby shops today were it not for Steve Jobs."[10] Neither of these two geniuses was worth much alone, but the division of labor that defines comparative advantage enabled the duo to build a company that changed the world.[11]

One of Jobs's early products after his return to Apple in the late 1990s was the iPod, which along with the iTunes Store transformed how the world consumes music. But as Jobs learned from his work at animator Pixar, "Tech companies don't understand creativity," while "music companies are completely clueless about technology."[12] The people at Apple (especially Jobs himself) may have loved music, but they never could have created it. The leading lights of the music business may have loved technology, but as the rise of Napster and other forms of digital piracy revealed, they didn't understand it. By their collaboration, however, Apple and the music industry forged a new audio era.

Jobs's charisma was the stuff of legend. No one in Apple's sales force could sell the company's products as well as he could. Yet despite the near certainty that Jobs could have sold far more merchandise at their flagship store on Manhattan's Fifth Avenue than the store's entire sales force combined, his true comparative advantage lay in conceiving appealing products at Apple's headquarters in Cupertino, California.

The beauty—and challenge—of comparative advantage is that it requires people to focus on what they are the very best at, even if it means leaving to others work that they could do better themselves. Perhaps LeBron James could have been an excellent tight end, but catching passes in the NFL would have prevented him from being the world's best basketball player.

Free markets allow people to experiment with various kinds of work till they find their comparative advantage. Free trade lets the same thing happen at the national level. One country, producing something better than other countries can do, can trade its work product for the goods and services it doesn't have. Our production is our consumption, or, as Jean-Baptiste Say put it, "Products are always bought with products." Just as LeBron James's power to consume is maximized by his choice of basketball as a career, our power to consume is greatest when we're doing what we're comparatively best at. In the next chapter we'll explore how the principle of comparative advantage applies to our fellow workers around the world.

CHAPTER SIXTEEN

"Outsourcing" Is Great for Workers, and as Old as the Pencil

Every man-made thing you see is something that no one person could possibly make alone.
—Donald J. Boudreaux, *Globalization*

In 1958, Leonard Read, the founder of the Foundation for Economic Education, wrote *I, Pencil*. Brilliant in its rather complicated simplicity, Read's book explained to millions of readers how something as prosaic as the pencil is the result of cooperation among people across the country and the world.

Read's pencil was manufactured in San Leandro, California, from wood cut by loggers in Oregon. The graphite core originated in Ceylon, and it could be sharpened into a smooth point fit for writing because of candelilla wax from Mexico. In other words, without "outsourcing," there would be no pencil.

For many people, "globalization" connotes the loss of jobs to distant lands. But you might as well fret that a Nike office in New York harms the company's hometown of Beaverton, Oregon. It's no different when Nike farms out work to London or Shanghai.

The production of goods and services has always been a global endeavor, as the pencil reveals. The more cooperation there is around the world, the more people can achieve the work specialization that is the source of wealth. Everyone becomes an expert outsourcer.

In the previous chapter I noted that if I had to rely on my own efforts to feed, clothe, and house myself, I wouldn't be long for this world, and my reliance on the skills of others is hardly unique. David Beckham, a world-renowned soccer player, is as talented a fellow as you'll find, but imagine the unsightly outcome if he didn't let someone else cut his hair. To meet the needs of daily life, he outsources as much as I do. Thanks to a market-based economic system, we all do.

Businesses that "outsource" work to the advertising partnership down the street, to a satellite office across the country, or to a factory on the other side of the world are simply doing what individuals do but on a bigger scale.

When you pull a five-dollar bill out of your pocket to buy a newspaper and a magazine in the morning, you are employing people here and in other lands. Businesses are doing as we do when they expand their operations globally. In short, "outsourcing" is the application of comparative advantage.

Nike employs four times more workers in Vietnam than it does in the United States.[1] The embrace of capitalism by a once murderous communist regime has benefited Vietnamese workers. Those who used to walk to Nike factories now ride on scooters, and an increasing number of them can afford cars.[2] The rising wealth of the Vietnamese, moreover, is good for Nike.

Nike employs eight thousand workers in suburban Portland. But if its founder, Phil Knight, had ignored comparative advantage and insisted on manufacturing his products in the United States, it's likely that there would be no Nike today. Jobs come from investment, and investors seek profits. If Nike had done the equivalent of my growing my own food, it wouldn't employ those eight thousand people in Oregon today, let alone offer the Vietnamese a way out of grinding poverty.

Don't forget that Nike's economic effect on Portland alone is not limited to those eight thousand jobs. Portland's Wieden+Kennedy is one of the largest independently owned advertising firms in the world, and it was the Nike account in its early days that propelled the firm's ascent. Indeed, Portland is booming because of businesses whose success is connected to the eight thousand high-paying jobs at Nike.

Enrico Moretti writes, "If you buy an iPhone online, it is shipped directly to you from Shenzen [China]. Incredibly, when it reaches the American consumer, only one American worker has physically touched the final product: the UPS delivery guy."[3] This may sound unsettling at first, but it's actually encouraging. In *The Elephant and the Dragon*, Robyn Meredith reports that "Chinese factory workers, whether making light bulbs, talking toys, or tennis shoes, earn each day about what Americans pay for a latte at Starbucks."[4] That low manufacturing cost shows that the physical assembly of an iPhone is the easy part of production. It's good news that Americans don't have to do that kind of work anymore. On the other hand, Moretti reminds us, the "majority of the iPhone's value comes from the original idea, its unique engineering, and its beautiful industrial design."[5] Just as a hungry individual orders a pizza from Domino's to gain an extra hour for productive work, Apple outsources the manufacture of iPhones to factories overseas so that its employees here are free to develop its next generation of products.

That's great for all those highly skilled techies in Silicon Valley, but what about the unskilled American workers who could never get a job like that? The answer, as we saw in chapter nine, is that Apple's job-creating impact extends beyond the twelve thousand people employed at its Cupertino headquarters to the sixty thousand other jobs that, by Moretti's calculation, are attributable to them.[6] The high returns that Apple's designers and marketers achieve for the company's investors, moreover, lead to even more jobs throughout the American economy.

People understandably focus on jobs. But if we forbade companies to outsource manufacturing to places where it can be done less expensively than in the United States, we would provoke the flight of investment capital from this country. Such a policy would wipe out many successful companies and millions of jobs.

Businesses have got to be able to save on labor costs through automation or offshore production in order to keep up with their competitors overseas. Nike and Apple, because of their success, have foreign companies like Adidas and Samsung nipping at their heels. If Nike and Apple don't squeeze as much profit out of every sale as they can, Adidas and Samsung will. The fall of Nike or Apple to foreign competition would hurt far more Americans than robots and foreign workers are supposedly hurting now.

Of course, that won't happen, because the genius of Apple and Nike is not in their plants and equipment but in the workers who show up at their headquarters every day to design the phones, computers, and sporting apparel that so many enjoy. If the American political class were ever to blunt their ability to operate profitably, each firm could set itself up outside this country rather quickly. Each would receive a warm welcome from foreign countries desperate for the stream of investment that follows success.

It is often said that outsourcing is a "race to the bottom," in which foreign countries long on "cheap labor" will hollow out the U.S. economy. But here is the dirty little secret about "cheap labor": *It's rather expensive.* Cheap labor is a sign of low productivity. Yet investment always seeks high returns. If the investors who create all the jobs were interested only in low labor costs, then New York, Hong Kong, and San Francisco would be empty.

Moretti notes, "Companies appear to locate in absolutely the worst places: they pick very expensive areas—the Bostons, San Franciscos, and New Yorks of the world. With sky-high wages and office rents, these are among the costliest places in America to operate a business."[7] But it is more costly for businesses to stay far from talent reservoirs. Expensive but highly productive labor is ultimately a better deal than low-cost workers who are not very productive. American workers' high wages are an advantage for them. Wages are high precisely because investors value their productivity. Silicon Valley is one of the most expensive places in the world, and it is filled with workers who cost a great deal to employ. Despite this, it attracts more than a third of all venture capital investment.[8]

"Outsourcing" is something everyone does constantly, but when a business does it, it becomes a dirty word. Since profits attract job-creating investment, however, outsourcing has made far more jobs than it has destroyed.

It never hurts to apply some common sense to any subject. Today, Manhattan has luxury apartment buildings that were once factories. Silicon Valley is thriving because companies make a point of leaving their manufacturing work to overseas workers in much the same way that Jennifer Aniston leaves the styling of her hair to Chris

McMillan. Detroit and Flint, Michigan, on the other hand, are crumbling cities that cling to factory work that pays a pittance. The race to the bottom does not happen in cities and countries that embrace outsourcing. But it has already happened in the cities and states that have avoided it.

CHAPTER SEVENTEEN

"Energy Independence" Would Be Economically Crippling; "Global Warming" Is a Crippling Theory

[Napoleon] did not realize until it was too late that the only closed political economy is the world economy. Britain could not be starved into submission by blockade unless she were totally cut off from the world. As long as Britain could trade with any nation outside France, it was thus trading indirectly with France.

—**Jude Wanniski**, *The Way the World Works*

Many years ago, while flipping through the television channels late at night, I stopped on HBO's *Real Time* hosted by Bill Maher. No real fan of the show, or Maher's politics, I nevertheless put down the clicker and watched a bit. Maher is not entirely devoid of insight. That night he used a photo of the Cuban dictator Fidel Castro wearing an Adidas track suit to make the point that embargoes are worthless as economic punishment for miscreant countries and their leaders.

American politicians can pass a law against exporting goods to Cuba,* but Cuban consumers (a very small category of persons, comprising Castro and a few other high-ranking figures) can buy U.S. goods from countries that trade with American businesses. Adidas is not an American brand, but Castro might well have been wearing Nike, which he could have bought from any country other than the United States where Nike sells its apparel—which is to say, almost any other country. There is no accounting for the final destination of any exported product.

Unfortunately for Cuba, an end of the U.S. embargo would not change much. People trade products for products, and the rulers of that ailing island, by severely limiting property rights, give their people little incentive to produce. Slavery, apart from its inherent immorality, is a bad economic idea, because if people cannot keep the fruits of their work or investment, they won't work or invest. In chapter one we saw that taxes are a price placed on work. In Cuba, work is almost 100 percent penalized. Cubans, therefore, lack products of their own to exchange for American goods. Lifting our trade embargo with Cuba, therefore, would have no effect without a liberalization of the island's economy.

What about those internationally venerated Cuban cigars? Couldn't they trade those with us? It's a good point, but as a visit to any cigar bar in this country reveals, the Cubans already export their cigars to the United States. There are laws against this export, but the Cubans do not necessarily send them here directly. American cigar aficionados buy Cuban cigars from merchants in other countries that do not have a trade embargo on the island nation. Again,

* As this book goes to press, there is an encouraging movement toward normalizing trade relations with Cuba.

there's no accounting for the final destination of any good. Americans can obtain Cuban cigars as readily as if they were manufactured in Winston-Salem, North Carolina.

Thousands of miles east of impoverished Cuba is another troubled region, the Middle East. There Israel sits, a tiny sliver of land within missile shot of many of its surrounding enemies. With their rich oil deposits, some of these enemies are not lacking in the material resources to "push the Jews into the sea."

Israel has historically been fuel "dependent," but it might be sitting atop billions of barrels of oil that innovations in drilling will make accessible for the first time.[1] Many are encouraging Israel to find that oil in the hope that vast new reserves might drive down the price of oil to the detriment of its hostile neighbors. But the economics of comparative advantage dictate that Israel should *leave the oil in the ground*. Retrieving it would be economically crippling.

Oil is by no means expensive today. Instead, the dollar has been cheap. The price of oil has always been tied to the dollar. In 1971 when the dollar's price was fixed at 1/35 of an ounce of gold, an ounce of gold (that is, thirty-five dollars) bought fifteen barrels of oil at $2.30 a barrel. Ten years later, when the dollar was worth 1/480 of an ounce of gold, that same gold ounce still bought fifteen barrels of oil, now at thirty-two dollars a barrel.[2] Oil is priced in dollars, and when the dollar weakens, the prices of gold and oil rise. In 2014, with the dollar worth 1/1379 of an ounce of gold, an ounce of the yellow metal still buys fourteen barrels of oil.

Movements in the price of crude have little to do with supply and plenty to do with the value of the dollar. Flooding the market with Israeli oil, therefore, would not destabilize its hostile neighbors. The United States is the only country that can substantially affect the price of oil. It would have to pursue a stronger dollar, and in fact the dollar has strengthened considerably since 2013, giving us much lower fuel costs, as one would predict.

Others will argue that Israel should produce oil in order to achieve "energy security." That is one of the main arguments traditionally made by proponents of "energy independence," who seek to have a secure supply of fuel in times of conflict. But history shows that this policy is an affront to basic economics. During the mid-nineteenth century, fears of a food embargo arose in Great Britain. Free trade, the argument went, might decimate British agriculture. The Corn Laws were meant to ensure a food supply for the kingdom's troops and people in times of war. The problem with that argument, however, was that since 1810 Britain had been at war with nearly every European power, and it still managed to import 1,491,000 quarters of wheat from the countries it had been fighting.[3]

The economics of the matter had not changed a century later. During World War I, the Royal Navy imposed a blockade on Germany, hoping to frustrate American trade with the Central Powers. U.S. exports to Germany plummeted, but exports to Sweden and other Scandinavian countries suddenly soared.[4] Germany could not trade with American producers directly, so it traded with them indirectly through countries that maintained normal trading relations with the belligerent nation.

In the late 1930s, when troubles arose between the United States and Japan, America restricted the sale of oil and steel to Japan. Modern history books assert that the need for oil and steel forced Japan into war with the United States. In truth, Japan had no trouble importing either commodity. It imported steel and oil from non-U.S.

sources, including fuel from Shell Oil that was sourced in the Dutch East Indies.[5]

The most famous embargo of all was in 1973, when Arab countries refused to sell oil to the United States and the Netherlands. As Jerry Taylor and Peter Van Doren, scholars at the Cato Institute, have pointed out, "oil that was exported [by Arab countries] to Europe was simply resold to the United States or ended up displacing non-OPEC oil that was diverted to the U.S. market. Saudi oil minister Sheik Yamani conceded afterwards that the 1973 embargo 'did not imply that we could reduce imports to the United States.... [T]he world is really just one market. So the embargo was more symbolic than anything else.'"[6]

But isn't the oil shock of 1973–1974, in which the price of gasoline rose by 120 percent from October to March, a matter of historical record? That's a good question, and Robert Bartley answered it in *The Seven Fat Years*: "The real shock was that the dollar was depreciating against oil, against gold, against foreign currencies and against nearly everything else."[7] The price of commodities across the board—from wheat, to meat, to soybeans—went up as the dollar fell. In short, the oil shocks were dollar shocks, and they would have occurred exactly as they did even without an Arab oil embargo.

Now let's apply these lessons about embargoes to Israel. If Israel went to war with every single oil-producing country in the Middle East, and if those enemies embargoed the sale of oil to Israel, Israel would still consume fuel as though the oil had bubbled up in Tel Aviv. Trade embargoes defy basic economics, and as long as *somebody* is willing to trade with Israel, it will get the oil it needs. But defying comparative advantage would harm the country's long-term economic health.

The problem with the oil industry is that, contrary to what most people think, oil exploration is not very profitable. Mark Perry, an economist at the American Enterprise Institute, has calculated that the energy sector ranks 112th among all industries in profit margins.[8] Now, Israel boasts the highest density of technology start-ups in the world. There are more Israeli companies listed on the NASDAQ exchange than from the whole of Europe. Venture capital investments in Israel are 2.5 times greater, per capita, than in the United States.[9] That's a pretty powerful economic signal that Israel's comparative advantage lies in technology. Israel is the LeBron James of technology. Diverting its resources from tech to oil would be like James leaving basketball to play football. He could probably make a nice living as an NFL tight end, but he'd make nowhere near what he makes as the best basketball player in the world. That doesn't mean private investors shouldn't be free to invest in oil exploration in Israel, but it suggests that some sort of organized national effort to achieve "energy independence" would be misguided. As Cato Institute president John Allison regularly observes, the consumers have all the power. As long as there is demand for oil in Israel (or the United States or anywhere else), it will reach that country at the market price. Oil producers need the world's consumption far more than Israelis need their oil.

If we apply this same analysis of comparative advantage to the United States, we reach the same conclusion—energy independence should not be our national priority. But since oil is priced in dollars, some worry about the dollars flowing out of our country to buy oil. The destination of those dollars, however, doesn't make any difference. They will end up where they will achieve a return—that is to say, the United States and other countries that use the dollar as the medium of exchange and investment. What's important is that they will often return as investments in profitable ideas.

The electronics and computer equipment sectors, in which American and Israeli companies shine, enjoy profits per dollar of sales of 14.5 cents (U.S.) and 13.7 cents (Israel). Microsoft earns twenty-seven cents on every dollar of sales. In the oil industry that figure is 8.3 cents.[10] Internet businesses enjoy profit margins of 23 percent, which dwarf the 6.1 percent average of the oil industry.[11] The most productive sector of the American and Israeli economies is technology. A politically driven national quest for the false god of "energy independence" would be the equivalent of LeBron James's splitting his time between basketball and football—unnecessary and counterproductive. Financial, human, and physical capital would be pushed into a sector with relatively low profits at the expense of pursuing higher profits elsewhere. All of this effort would be expended to produce a commodity that will always be available in abundance at the market price.

Oil companies, moreover, are sitting ducks for the depredations of tax-happy politicians, further diminishing their appeal as investments. As I mentioned earlier, ExxonMobil paid thirty-one billion dollars in taxes on its profits in 2012, more than any other company in the United States.[12] Of the ten most taxed U.S. companies, three—ExxonMobil, Chevron, and ConocoPhillips—are oil companies.[13] Google's, Nike's, and Apple's most important assets are the people who show up for work each day, and if taxation ever became too onerous, all three companies could move without missing a beat. Who would notice if the GooglePlex moved to Bermuda? But the most important asset of oil companies is oil in the ground, which *cannot be moved*. ExxonMobil can't move Prudhoe Bay or the Bakken

Shale. Precisely because oil is immovable, profits from its sale are easy for politicians to tax.

Someone might object here that, however nice it would be to follow our comparative advantage, we have got to have oil, and our access to it is seriously unreliable. Most of the world's oil, warns Peter Maass in *Crude World: The Violent Twilight of Oil*, "is now in the hands of state-controlled companies like Saudi Aramco, Gazprom, Petroleos de Venezuela, National Iranian Oil Company, and China National Petroleum Corporation."[14] These are the world's bad guys, and they could cut us off any time they choose.

That's not going to happen, however. Governments need revenue because politicians, whatever their country, exist to spend. It is naïve to think that these global thugs will shut off a major source of revenue. No matter what happens, the oil will flow.

The United States should treat oil as what it is—a commodity that will reach us in abundance no matter where it is drilled. "Energy independence" is an appealing slogan, but neither the laws of economics nor the lessons of history suggest that it makes any sense.

* * *

If you take your cue from the popular media, it doesn't make any difference to you whether our oil comes from Saudi Arabia or North Dakota, Venezuela or the Permian Basin. Our most urgent task is curtailing our consumption of oil and other fossil fuels, not finding more of them, because of the looming catastrophe of "global warming."

I'm no scientist, but I can read market signals as well as anyone else. Those signals are the product of all available information, and they strongly suggest that all the worry about "global warming" is overdone.

The *Wall Street Journal*'s weekly "Mansion" section is a chronicle of the amazing evolution of high-end real estate. In November 2013 the stories included "Miami House Not Yet Built Hits the Market for $40 Million," "Los Angeles Estate on 48 Acres Reduces Its Price to $34.995 Million," "Manhattan Townhouse Brings In $26 Million to Prominent Chinese Buyer," and "A House in the Hamptons Lists For $38 Million." Where people are buying property and at what price are market signals pregnant with information.

The prophets of climatic catastrophe say ocean levels are going to rise more than four feet by 2100 because of unchecked global warming, swamping coastal cities like New York. Perhaps. But no matter how much the United States reduces its own carbon emissions, the rising economies of Asia will more than make up for our reductions. And I say, *good for them*. It is obnoxious for rich Americans to dictate economy-sapping environmental policy to Chinese and Indians striving to live as we do in the West. In any case, the "tragedy of the commons" will prevent a coordinated response to climate change.

And yet coastal properties in the United States continue to fetch enormous prices. Even more troublesome for climate alarmists is that the most expensive coastal communities—places like Malibu, Manhattan, and the Hamptons—are filled with people who say they believe in man-made global warming. Ted Danson owns property in Martha's Vineyard, as does the environmental activist Laurie David. Al Gore has a palazzo a mile inland from Montecito, California. Global warming's most famous advocates apparently don't take their cause all that seriously. Rome is burning while the fire-safety activists fiddle. The market, meanwhile, says the "science" predicting catastrophe is nonsense.

If the markets are wrong about climate change, they will adjust as they always do. If there is one thing that capitalism is indisputably best at, it is providing in abundance. Capitalism and the markets are saying right now that there is no need to invest in wind, solar, and electric cars. If they are proved incorrect, market-driven price signals will lure profit-seeking investors into a green space that they currently will not enter—at least not with their own money.

Implicit in global warming "science" is the assumption that people do not, and will not, adjust to changes. But they do, and they will adjust to rising sea levels if they come to pass. Otherwise, beachfront property would be dropping in value every year in anticipation of the looming cataclysm. Market signals are mocking the presumption that politicians should act on the theory of global warming.

On the other hand, China—one of the worst environmental offenders—is funneling substantial investment into measures intended to ward off the menace of global warming. Market signals say they're wasting their time and money. But if the markets are wrong and the climate alarmists are right, we'll know where to buy the products and services to deal with the environmental changes. Just as we import bananas from Guatemala, shoes from Italy, and televisions from Japan, we'll be able to import green solutions from China. Until then, let others around the world expend taxpayer money on a theory in defiance of the markets. The American economy needs freedom from environmental regulations and an end to tax handouts that subsidize wind turbines and electric cars at the expense of economic growth.

CHAPTER EIGHTEEN

Conclusion: Free Trade Is the Path to Knowledge, Liberty, World Peace, and Big Raises

When goods don't cross borders, soldiers will.
—Attributed to Frédéric Bastiat

In May 2005, Chef Grant Achatz opened Alinea in Chicago, where he sought to "redefine fine dining in America." It is a high-concept kind of restaurant, with cooking stations that look more like a science lab than a traditional kitchen. The modernist cuisine, I confess, is well beyond my taste and comprehension.

But within two years of its opening, the notoriously tough food critic Ruth Reichl and *Gourmet* magazine ranked Alinea the best restaurant in the United States.[1] Achatz was already an accomplished chef before his co-creation with investor Nick Kokonas, but with the *Gourmet* ranking, Achatz had truly arrived.

What is perhaps less well known among gourmets and the merely gluttonous alike is that America's best chef grew up in St. Clair, Michigan, "flipping eggs at my parents' diner."[2] Of course, it is not about where you start. His boyhood friends laughed at his culinary dreams, but Achatz always told himself that someday he was "going to own a great restaurant, a famous one."[3] He has succeeded.

Just as Henry Ford did not wake up one day and start manufacturing cars, Achatz wasn't born a world-renowned chef. Graduating from the Culinary Institute of America at twenty-one, he went to work for the late great Chef Charlie Trotter and then for Chef Thomas Keller of the famous French Laundry in California's wine country. One day, Keller approached him about going over to Spain in order to learn from Ferran Adrià, chef at elBulli, then widely viewed as the best restaurant in the world.

Achatz was twenty-five and sous chef at French Laundry, which was itself one of the best restaurants anywhere. "I thought I knew food and cooking," he recalls, but the dishes that emerged from the elBulli food "lab" left him "disoriented, surprised, and amazed. Completely blown away." He continues,

> Trout roe arrived, encased in a thin, perfect tempura butter. I shot [my companion] a skeptical glance and he immediately returned it. You simply don't deep-fry roe. You can't. It isn't possible.
>
> We popped the gumball-sized bite into our mouths. There was no obvious binder holding the eggs together, and they were still cold and uncooked! How did they hold the eggs together and then dip them into a batter without dispersing them into hundreds of pieces? And how are they uncooked? Whoa.

> A small bowl arrived. "Ah, polenta with olive oil," I thought. "This isn't so out there. This I can understand." But as soon as the spoon entered my mouth an explosion of yellow corn flavor burst, and then all the texture associated with polenta vanished. I laid my spoon down and stared at it with mock calm. I was astonished.
>
> What the hell was going on back there? This is the stuff of magic.[4]

After three days in Spain, Achatz was overcome and inspired. "Everything was new and strange to me: the way the team was organized, the techniques being used, the sights, even the smells. Here was a new cuisine where nothing was routine."[5] He returned from Spain, and as he described it, "the urge to create outside of The French Laundry became irresistible."[6] After a stop as head chef at Trio outside Chicago, he went on to open Alinea.

Are you wondering what high-concept and inedible sounding food has to do with free trade? Everything.

Trade is about the exchange of goods, and that includes ideas. In an increasingly connected world, trade policy affects not only the price and availability of oil from Canada or manufactured goods from China, but new kinds of food and new ways of cooking food. Drive down the street in almost any U.S. city today and you'll see restaurant signs offering international cuisines from Chinese to Mexican to Ethiopian. Even "traditional American" fare is constantly enriched by new ideas from around the world.

The blockbuster film *Gravity* was conceived and directed by a man—Alfonso Cuaron—who grew up in Mexico. Leo Tolstoy's *War and Peace*, one of the greatest novels ever written, comes from Russia. My favorite author of fiction, Somerset Maugham, was from

England. Life is infinitely enriched by openness to ideas and culture from all over the globe. American students in eighteenth-century Paris learned medical techniques that were advanced well beyond what they could have learned at home. The abolitionist politician Charles Sumner studied alongside black students at the Sorbonne and recorded in his journal in 1838 that "the distance between free blacks and whites among us is derived from education, and does not exist in the nature of things."[7]

Arthur Laffer likes to explain free trade by asking whether Americans would refuse a cure for cancer because it was not produced at the Mayo Clinic in Minnesota. Would the United States be weakened if a pill that cures heart disease were discovered in Prague?

Microsoft is based in Redmond, Washington, but are the citizens of New York, Los Angeles, or Morgantown, West Virginia, worse off for "importing" Windows? What about the residents of Paris, Madrid, and Tokyo? Just as the exploits of Michael Jordan and LeBron James have created basketball fans around the world, free trade lets the Jordans and Jameses of software, food, and clothing compete to meet the needs of the citizens of the world by maximizing their comparative advantage.

Think about that for a moment. In daily life, people comparison shop locally for restaurants, computers, and clothes. Borders open to foreign goods allow us to comparison shop all over the world. Even better, everyone gets a raise with each paycheck. Thanks to global competition, no business can ever become too bold about raising its prices. With the businesses of the world competing for your trade, the purchasing power of your paycheck grows.

But isn't the price of free trade lost jobs? Once again, the economic evolution of the world has been about unrelenting job destruction—and that's a good thing. People no longer have to work from dawn to dusk to grow enough food to survive. With free trade, innovators can eliminate backbreaking work. They can make our clothes, computers, and phones with televisions on them so we don't have to.

If free trade really caused hard times and unemployment, then New York and Hong Kong would stand as devastated monuments to its horrors. The wealth of these cities, which import almost everything, is a sign that trade enriches people.

Remember that no act of saving ever detracts from demand. What is saved is either lent out or invested in businesses focused on creating the next gadget, restaurant, and healthcare cure. Open trade increases people's purchasing power, allowing them to save more. Saving is the only path to individual wealth, and entrepreneurs cannot be entrepreneurs without access to savings.

Free trade also brings peace. The *New York Times* columnist Thomas Friedman has famously noted that no country with a McDonald's in it ever invaded another country with a McDonald's in it. When trade is free, producers around the globe have a rooting interest in the success of the countries to which they export. They'll prefer trading with them to fighting with them.

War closes markets, destroys wealth, and brings tragedy to families. When people are unable to expand their sales to foreign countries, the horrors of war, at least in the near term, are less repellent, since war with a closed country does not cost anyone customers. Trade brings people together as they exchange products, ideas, and cures for lethal diseases.

Most of all, trade is about liberty. People go to work to produce what they need to trade for unmet personal wants. When governments impede trade, they make that work less worthwhile and deny people the freedom to seek the best product and best price irrespective of national origin. Free trade is about our right to exchange with anyone without answering to politicians. If that doesn't deserve our support, what does?

PART IV

Money

CHAPTER NINETEEN

A Floating Foot, Minute, and Second Would Give You Ugly Houses, Burnt Wings, and Slow NFL Draft Picks

A currency, to be perfect, should be absolutely invariable in value.
—David Ricardo, *Proposals for an Economical and Secure Currency*

As their name suggests, Buffalo wings were invented in Buffalo, New York. Late one night in 1964, Teressa Bellissimo, the owner of the Anchor Bar, deep-fried and basted with hot sauce the part of the chicken that cooks had usually tossed. Fifty years later, Americans consume an estimated 1.25 billion wings on Super Bowl Sunday. Progress in a market economy is defined by the leap and the information gained (bad news can be as valuable as good) from the risk taken. Bellissimo made a major leap in 1964, and her discovery of what to do with chicken wings changed how Americans (and foreigners) eat.

Wings have become so popular that there is a National Buffalo Wing Festival in—you guessed it—Buffalo, New York, each Labor Day weekend. Matthew Reynolds and Ric Kealoha won the 2013 competition, a victory immortalized in the Hulu documentary *The Great Chicken Wing Hunt*. The *Wall Street Journal* described the preparation of their "medium-hot, crisp and tender wings." Included in the blue-cheese dressing were two tablespoons of finely chopped onion, a quarter-cup of parsley, and one cup of mayonnaise. The Reynolds-Kealoha Buffalo sauce was made with one teaspoon of celery salt and one tablespoon of honey mustard, and the wings were fried in thirty-two ounces of vegetable oil. The sauce was cooked for three to four minutes over medium heat, sautéed for five minutes, left to simmer for fifteen minutes, then another fifteen minutes with the honey mustard. The wings were fried for eight to ten minutes in vegetable oil heated to 375 degrees.

The result of this cookery is surely tasty but hardly high cuisine.[1] Still, the successful preparation of something as simple as wings requires precise measurements. Imagine what would have happened if Reynolds' and Kealoha's tablespoons and measuring cups constantly changed size or if the duration of a "minute" was elastic. Thanks to the standardization of the tablespoon, cup, ounce, and minute, we can reliably cook chicken wings and all the other things that make life worth living.

On a far more serious level of culinary art, Grant Achatz's cooking lab would be reduced to chaos without unchanging units of measure. There would be no Alinea, and Achatz would be back in St. Clair "flipping eggs." Without standard measures, one of the world's greatest chefs would be like a Lamborghini without wheels.

The construction of a house or office building is possible because a foot is standard. Without exact measurements, there would be plenty of oddly shaped houses, doors wouldn't fit in their door frames, and the leaning tower of Pisa wouldn't be unusual.

In the NFL, scouts and coaches spend months each year preparing for the draft, stopwatches in hand, timing prospective players in the forty-yard dash. Here the difference between 4.43 seconds and 4.73 seconds is substantial. Millions of dollars in salaries are at stake, along with the coaches' careers.

They say football is a game of inches, and those inches are won and lost by the speed, strength, and jumping ability of players scouted and drafted. In the NFL, a third of a second in the forty-yard dash determines whether a defensive end reaches a quarterback or a left tackle blocks an onrushing linebacker. A vertical inch determines whether a cornerback tips away a spiraling pass. The Seattle Seahawks made it to Super Bowl XLVIII thanks to cornerback Richard Sherman's speed, but also because of his ability to leap high enough to tip Colin Kaepernick's pass to Malcolm Smith as time was running down.

But if the second, pound, and inch weren't fixed units of measure, NFL teams would frequently find themselves working with imperfect information about players and, as a result, on the losing side of matchups. As it is, the draft is an inexact science—in 1998, many scouts rated the number-two pick, Ryan Leaf, a better quarterback than number-one Peyton Manning. But if no one really knew how fast or big the players were, draft day would simply be a crap shoot.

If units of measure were variable, surely restaurants, football teams, and construction companies would adjust, but the cost would be immense. They could hire mathematicians to calculate the constant changes in the length of a minute, second, and foot in hopes of mitigating the uncertainty. But the absurdity of that scenario is obvious. A standardized minute, pound, and foot are essential to much that we do. Their invariability permits a great deal of productivity and innovation. George Gilder would refer to them as "low entropy" inputs that allow a lot of "high entropy" leaps to new economic information.

All this speculation about a world without fixed units of measure would be pointless if it weren't for what President Richard Nixon did on August 15, 1971. On that infamous date, he foisted on the economy a dollar without a fixed value. Since then, the greenback has floated up and down every second of the day. The foolishness of this policy is hard to minimize.

In *The Wealth of Nations*—the masterpiece that laid the groundwork for the rise of modern capitalism—Adam Smith observed that the "sole use of money is to circulate consumable goods."[2] That was a throwaway line, for no serious thinker had ever considered money as anything but a measure. Money came into existence because men needed a way to measure the value both of their production and of the consumable goods they sought in exchange for the fruits of their labor. Smith was stating the obvious.

Smith would laugh at all the commentary in the media today about the need for a "strong dollar" or a "weaker dollar to boost exports" or the importance of convincing the Chinese to "boost" the value of the yuan. To Smith, that would be the equivalent of saying "increase the length of a meter" or "shorten the minute" or, because Kim Jong-Un is bothered by his diminutive five-foot-six-inch stature, there is a need to "devalue the foot" so the North Korean dictator can stand ten feet tall. Just as the foot is never long or short, money should be neither strong nor weak. The foot is a standardized tool to measure actual things, and money should have the same constancy.

The vintner makes wine, and the baker bakes bread, and while the vintner might want bread, the baker might not want wine in exchange. This asymmetry in trade gives money its purpose. If the baker were a teetotaler, he could still trade with the vintner, who would offer money for the bread. Money is an acceptable medium of exchange. The baker can take the money he receives from the vintner to the butcher in order to buy meat. Trade is the exchange of products for products. But money permits different people with different wants to trade easily with one another.

I work as an editor and as a writer, and while the McDonald's on Wisconsin Avenue in Washington, D.C., does not want my writing and editing, *Forbes* and RealClearMarkets do. They pay me in dollars for my work as a writer and editor, and as those dollars are an accepted medium of exchange, I am able to exchange my work as a writer and editor for all the Quarter Pounders and fries that I can afford.

Money is not wealth. It is a *measure* of wealth. The salaries that my employers pay me in dollars are their measure of my worth to them. My work is my demand for money, but as the chapters on trade made clear, people produce in order to consume. The supply of work enables the consumption of the work product of others. So while my work is my demand for money, what it really represents is my demand for all the things I do not have.

My ability to specialize in the kind of work I'm good at—one of the benefits of free trade—makes me more productive, so my employers' measurement of the worth of my work is higher. I would struggle if I had to work in the high-tech business. I would end up as a gofer for the geniuses at Dell or Apple and would languish at the low end of the pay scale. But thanks to open markets, I get to focus on writing and editing, for which my employers pay me a good salary, and with those dollars I am able to buy my computers and phones from Dell and Apple.

If I had to add a shower to my apartment, I'd be in trouble. Thanks to money, I can trade my writing and editing skills for the shower that I want; even if my contractor has no interest in my work at *Forbes* and RealClearMarkets. Now, let's say a contractor tells me the new shower will cost ten thousand dollars, and because of a busy schedule, he can't complete the job for six months. Let's then say that I agree to those terms, but to make sure he finishes the job, I offer five thousand dollars up front and five thousand upon completion of the work. This deal would make sense except for one problem.

Until 1971, the dollar's value was defined by gold. Specifically, a dollar was worth one thirty-fifth of an ounce of gold. To be sure, there were variations in the gold standard during the U.S. dollar's first two centuries. But the United States stuck to the gold standard because the only good money is money that is a constant measure of value, just as a foot and minute are constant measures of length and time. The obvious question, then, is why gold?

That question is easy to answer. Gold has had the most stable value of any commodity in history. It was not an accident that a world in need of "money" for the purpose of exchange settled upon gold. Other commodities, including seashells and cigarettes, have been tried, but since perfect money is that which is invariable in value, the sovereigns of the world have always gravitated to gold.

John Stuart Mill stated in his *Principles of Political Economy*, "As it is much easier to compare different lengths by expressing them in a common language of feet and inches, so is it much easier to compare values by means of a common language of pounds, shillings, and pence."[3] But if the baker is going to have enough faith in that "language" to rely on it in exchanging his bread, it must be stable. Gold provided money with credibility precisely because it was, and is, so stable. Gold, said Mill, is "among the least influenced by any of the causes which produce fluctuations of value."[4] More recently, the economist and investor Nathan Lewis wrote in his masterly book *Gold: The Monetary Polaris*:

> A gold standard system has a specific purpose: to achieve, as closely as possible in an imperfect world, the Classical ideal of a currency that is stable in value, neutral, free of government manipulation, precise in its definition, and which can serve as a universal standard of value, in much the manner in which kilograms or meters serve as standards of weights and measures.[5]

Lewis, like Mill, acknowledges that gold is not perfectly invariable in value in the way that a foot is always a foot. But after many centuries of effort to find the most stable definer of money, he says, "nobody has found a better way" to provide money with a stable value than gold.[6]

In recent years, gold has been especially volatile. But its gyrating and mostly rising price is measured in dollars that are themselves *without definition*. A rise in gold signals a decline in the value of the dollar, and a decline in gold signals a rising dollar. Until 1971, the supply of dollars was managed by pegging the price of an ounce of gold at thirty-five dollars. There were some wiggles in that price, particularly during the Johnson and Nixon administrations, but generally the dollar's value was maintained at one thirty-fifth of an ounce of gold. A market commodity known for its stability, as opposed to government bureaucrats, managed the supply of dollars.

Let's go back to my agreement with the contractor, who will get the other five thousand dollars when he finishes installing my shower in six months. I am hardly driving a hard bargain, but since the dollar is no longer defined by gold, it is possible that six months from now the dollar will be worth less, maybe a lot less. If so, the weaker dollar will turn our voluntary and mutually enhancing exchange into a good deal for me but a bad one for him.

On the other hand, what happens if the dollar rises in value during those six months? It has happened before. When the 1980s began a dollar bought as little as 1/875 of an ounce of gold.[7] By 1982, a much stronger dollar bought one three hundredth of an ounce. If there's a big jump in the dollar's value over the six months that the contractor is adding the shower, then I'll be paying more than I had intended. Now you can see why gold has been used to define money for so many centuries and for much of American history. Allowing money to fluctuate undermines what makes it useful in the first place.

This is not to say that people stopped producing and consuming once the dollar was set afloat back in 1971. But this monetary mistake has prevented a great deal of economic progress. When the dollar—and by extension all other currencies—lost its gold-based stability, it was as if someone broke into Alinea's kitchen just before the dinner rush, removed the temperature dials from the ovens, smashed every timer, and left with every measuring cup and measuring spoon. Suddenly contracts written in dollars, pounds, and yen were left with wildly fluctuating values. Wages once carefully measured in those currencies became less certain, as did investments and returns on investment. Money, which had been a "low-entropy" measure of value, lost its purpose. They do not call the 1970s the "malaise decade" for nothing. The global economy had to st cooking without a thermometer, timer, and teaspoons. Clever minds have come up with ways to mitigate the problems of the *floating* dollar, but the economic costs have nevertheless been enormous.

Wall Street, in lower Manhattan, where investment banks were once concentrated, is a symbol for the financial business that now takes place all over the country. In many ways, Wall Street is a positive symbol because its firms provide important services. But Wall Street changed substantially after 1971, and the change wasn't for the better. When the U.S. dollar was pegged to gold, most of the world's currencies were pegged to the dollar, so they too were on the gold standard. When President Nixon severed the dollar from gold, currencies around the world began to fluctuate. If one day a "minute" was fifty-one seconds, thirty seconds the next, and forty-five seconds the following day, there would be chaos in Grant Achatz's cooking lab, where precise timing is essential. That's what happened in the world economy when the value of money began changing every day.

Nobody stopped producing or trading. Human needs and desires and the urge to produce and consume are too powerful. Instead, Wall Street came up with a way to work around the new elasticity of its standards of measure: currency trading.

As the *Wall Street Journal*'s Craig Karmin noted in his 200 book, *Biography of the Dollar*, "the currency market is the bigg t market in the world, with a daily trading volume of $3.2 trilli "[8] More importantly, it is "also one of the newest."[9] He ex ns, "Throughout the nineteenth and first half of the twentieth ury, the world's major currencies were tied to a gold standard, r than trading directly against one another in an open market."[10] 197 there "was no need for a foreign exchange market beca rencies were pegged to a dollar rate and could only be changed n unusual circumstances."[11]

Toyota wants to sell cars in the United States, but since it sells those cars for constantly fluctuating dollars, it must hedge against changes in the greenback's value. Apple, Dell, and Microsoft sell their products globally for yen, pounds, and Australian dollars, and as all three are also floating currencies, they must protect their earnings in those currencies against a decline in their value. People are still trading products for products, and currency remains the facilitator of the exchange, but the foreign exchange market has exploded with activity meant to subdue the chaos bred by currency's constant fluctuation.

When I worked in Goldman Sachs's Private Client Services division, a client of mine, along with his partners, sold a business to a Japanese buyer in 2001. The payment was in yen and was spread over five years. If the transaction had taken place in 1970, when the yen was pegged to the dollar at 360 to one, my client would have done nothing further. But since the value of the yen was fluctuating, my client and his partners needed to protect themselves from such fluctuations over the five years of the sale. We were able to hedge the five-year yen payout against any declines, but the transaction took weeks to complete. The loss of productivity for all involved was stounding, and it should have been completely unnecessary.

Economic growth is about matching human capital with invest-nt. Fluctuating money has led a great deal of human capital to m ate to Wall Street in order to trade the chaos. The work done to mi te the economic uncertainty caused by floating exchange rates is n sary: global trade and investment would not occur nearly as freq y without it. But floating money has redirected many of our nancial minds to jobs that, while highly paid, amount to facilitator work. It's a tragic waste. The "seen" is bright and hard-working traders making good money at banks, investment banks, and hedge funds. The "unseen" is what these people could have accomplished if their talents hadn't been diverted to compensating for the instability of our currency. How many advances in medicine or technology did we forego because of the useless necessity of currency trading?

* * *

The most important commodity in the world is probably oil. It's at the root of much of the world's turmoil, and people all over the world watch breathlessly as its rising or falling price changes the geopolitical balance of power. And the instability of the all-important price of a barrel of oil is almost entirely a result of the floating dollar. Remember: despite what you read in the paper, there have never been "oil shocks." Since 1971, an ounce of gold has fairly consistently bought about fifteen barrels of oil. Gold is the constant. A rise in its price does not signal greater scarcity but a falling dollar. When gold falls, it signals a rising dollar. When the dollar weakens and gold rises, the price of oil goes up.

As Steve Forbes has observed, "When the dollar was fixed to gold between the mid-1940s and 1971, the price of oil barely fluctuated."[12] Which is exactly what you'd expect. With a stable dollar, oil was stable and cheap. Just as there was no need for a currency trading market before 1971, there was little need to hedge against volatility in commodities that were priced in dollars.

When the dollar started floating, commodity trading took off alongside currency trading. Leo Melamed, the former chairman of the Chicago Mercantile Exchange, wrote in 2007 that the breakdown of the postwar Bretton Woods gold standard "provided the rationale for the launch of financial futures by the Chicago Mercantile Exchange."[13] Much as floating money lured many bright minds into the currency trading market, it lured others into the commodity pits, and the economy lost even more talent to a business whose only purpose was to tame the chaos stirred up by a floating dollar.

While oil, soybean, wheat, and meat prices were fairly flat under a gold-defined dollar, commodities went on a wild ride once the dollar lost its anchor. It is popular today to demonize hedge funds and other products of financial wizardry, but a drifting dollar made the complicated evolution of finance inevitable. To offer one example, airlines need certainty about fuel prices. A floating dollar has taken jet fuel on a turbulent path, and airlines have had to divert precious resources from serving customers to working with traders in order to stay on the right side of the fuel market.

Historians of the U.S. automobile industry will trace its long-term decline to the early 1970s. American carmakers were best at producing big, air-conditioned, gas-guzzling cars. That was their comparative advantage. When the dollar lost its link to gold in '71 and went into a free-fall, oil prices soared. Suddenly the big cars that GM, Ford, and Chrysler were adept at manufacturing were not so attractive to buyers. For a sense of how the price of a gallon of gas has changed, watch *The Last Picture Show*, set in the 1950s. Be sure to notice the posted price for gasoline. There are many authors of the American auto industry's struggles, but a large if usually ignored factor is hiding in plain sight. The industry's sickest periods were in the 1970s and the 2000s, when the dollar weakened and oil spiked.

Some argue, against all the evidence, that a weak dollar has helped U.S. carmakers export their products. But as Douglas Irwin of Dartmouth College has pointed out, American car producers have to import much of what they need to build those cars:

> ...30 percent of the car's value is due to assembly in Korea, 17.5 percent due to components from Japan, 7.5 percent due to design from Germany, 4 percent due to parts from Taiwan and Singapore, 2.5 percent due to advertising and marketing services from Britain, and 1.5 percent due to data processing in Ireland. In the end, 37 percent of the production value of this American car comes from the United States.[14]

A cheaper dollar means more expensive imports. Remember, no consumer good is made by one person or one company. Everything we enjoy is the result of cooperation among myriad individuals around the world. If the dollar is weakened, moreover, American workers—including auto workers—will demand more pay. Finally, all American companies are in the business of earning dollars. How then is a weaker dollar good for them, and how do they attract investment if investors know those dollars will be devalued?

It's the American consumer who suffers most of all from a floating dollar. Businesses can at least work with traders to mitigate the damage of corrupted money, but not the average consumer. A dollar that bought 1/250 of an ounce of gold in 2001 now buys less than 1/1200, but with most Americans lacking the means or sophistication to protect themselves from a falling dollar, they have had to endure nosebleed gasoline prices, not to mention rising grocery bills. And that's only part of a tragic story.

Inflation is nothing more than a falling dollar, and gold is the most reliably objective measure of its health. In the next chapter we'll see how the meanings of inflation and deflation have become so perverted as to obscure the monetary errors of these last thirteen years. Then we'll look at the devastating and widespread economic consequences of a falling dollar. The floating currency is one of the most damning indictments of the economics profession and the political class that ought to have protected the dollar.

CHAPTER TWENTY

Do Not Be Fooled by Rising and Falling Computer, Flat Screen, and VHS Prices: They Are Not an Inflation or Deflation Signal

Let it therefore be remembered (and occasions will often rise of calling it to mind) that a general rise or a general fall of values is a contradiction; and that a general rise or a general fall of prices is merely tantamount to an alteration in the value of money....
—**John Stuart Mill**, *Principles of Political Economy*

Bret Swanson is a futurist based in Indianapolis, and a longtime collaborator with George Gilder. Swanson founded a research firm several years ago called Entropy Economics. "Entropy," says Gilder, is "the process by which the entrepreneur translates the idea in his imagination into a practical form."[1] That is, entrepreneurs perpetually pursue the creation of high-entropy concepts that will transform our lives—cancer cures, computer tablets, or transportation innovations.

Entrepreneurs seek to improve our lives and usually hope to grow wealthy in the process. Translating their ideas into marketable form, however, requires an economic environment or background that is low-entropy—that is, steady, open, and predictable. That low-entropy setting is really what this book is about. Human beings have unlimited desires, and satisfying those desires is easier when politicians remove the barriers to production. In modern times, government has become a high-entropy barrier to production. I am trying to make the case for reversing our course on taxes, regulation, trade, and money. In all four areas, we need maximum freedom from government meddling to achieve maximum growth.

I have shown (1) that taxes are a penalty placed on work and investment in new companies. Moreover, government spending itself is a tax. It is the extraction of resources from the private sector that robs entrepreneurs of capital, and the average worker of wages. (2) Regulation can't succeed because the less talented and informed are trying to anticipate what even the sharpest minds in a given field have a difficult time predicting. (3) Trade is the reason people go to work every day, to get what they do not possess. Taxes on imports are taxes on the purpose of work, and they impede the productive specialization that free trade fosters. Finally, (4) money allows producers to measure the value of what they are exchanging and investing in (more on investment in the next chapter). When it is unstable as a measure, the economy loses the honest price signals that organize economic activity.

Gilder and Swanson seek to make taxes, regulation, trade, and money low-entropy inputs to commerce, as unintrusive and as unnoticeable as possible. So do I. If government intervention in the economy were substantially limited, entrepreneurs could productively pursue the high-entropy concepts that will raise living standards. Some of the government's worst economic mischief is the result of monetary policy based on a fundamental misunderstanding of inflation and deflation.

At a conference organized in 2009 by Applied Finance Group, with which I am professionally affiliated through their mutual fund arm, Toreador Research & Trading, Swanson displayed a 1989 ad for the Tandy 5000 desktop, the "most powerful computer ever!" Monitor and mouse were not included in the $8,499 price. This once great computer, of course, would not come close to passing muster now. Today's most basic Dell desktop is infinitely faster, offers far more features, including the monitor and mouse, and is just $449.99. In the year 2000, a fifty-inch flat-screen high-definition television cost twenty thousand dollars.[2] Today a fifty-inch flat-screen high-definition television sells at BestBuy.com for $549.99.[3]

Stories like this abound in market economies. The original hand-held cellular phone, the Motorola DynaTAC 8000X, which we recalled in chapter seven, was rolled out in 1983 at a price of $3,995.[4] As amusing as it is to look back on those technological relics of the '80s, we know that it won't be long before we're scoffing at the iPhone 6, which will seem primitive and expensive.

In the 1970s, a Sony Betamax was a luxury item that cost over a thousand dollars. The VHS video format ultimately proved more appealing to consumers than the Betamax. Yet today's consumers would surely laugh at popping a videocassette into a bulky VCR in order to watch a film. Now there are DVD players and streaming video. Sony's HDMI DVD player is listed at less than fifty dollars at Walmart.com, and that includes the cost of delivery.

These stories are a reminder that today's luxuries of the rich are a preview of what everyone will enjoy eventually, and sooner rather than later if government is a low-entropy input in the economy. They also show that the rich—who provide the capital for the entrepreneurial ideas of others—are consumer "guinea pigs." Acquiring the latest innovations at high prices, they act as "venture capitalist" buyers, creating the incentives for entrepreneurs to figure out how to sell expensive goods at low prices. But what do all these stories about relentlessly falling prices say about inflation and deflation? *Very little.*

What these stories *do* tell us is that falling prices, far from being deflationary, reveal new wants. As Mill wrote, "life is highly favorable to the growth of new wants, and opens a possibility of their gratification."[5] Flat-screen televisions available for a few hundred dollars indicate that consumers are now searching for the next big thing. Ultra-high-definition televisions have now reached the market, retailing at around twenty-five thousand dollars, but it's a fair bet that within a few years that price will be dramatically lower.

Falling prices by themselves are not deflationary, because no act of saving ever subtracts from demand. Plummeting television prices merely free up money for new, previously unattainable wants, sending those prices up. And if the money saved on televisions isn't spent on other consumer goods, it will be available, through savings, to someone else—either a consumer with short-term demands or the entrepreneur who has figured out a way to make ultra-high-definition televisions that can be sold for five hundred dollars.

News about the Federal Reserve today often concerns central bankers who fear deflation. Their constant focus on consumption makes Fed officials worry that falling prices will cause consumers to delay their purchases, driving prices down further and weakening the economy. But this is a mirage. To save *is not* to not consume, as the Fed believes. Saving simply shifts consumptive ability to others. As we saw in chapter six, banks "borrow" money from savers in the form of a deposit, or liability, and they immediately turn that liability, in the form of a loan to someone else, into an asset.

Falling prices are normal in a market economy, and they do not deter consumption. The first Apple iPhone retailed at around five hundred dollars, but consumers can now buy a much more advanced model from their wireless service providers at a fraction of that cost. Consumers are well aware that prices have a tendency to fall, particularly in the highly competitive world of technology. Yet despite the history of falling prices, consumers lined up to buy the first Apple iPhone, as they lined up, more recently, to buy the iPhone 6.

The price of admission to the first Super Bowl, played in 1967, was twelve dollars.[6] In 2014 the face value of a Super Bowl ticket was one thousand dollars, but the average price actually paid was $3,552.[7] Is this what economists mean by inflation? Many economists probably *do* think it is inflation, but it is not.

If the demand for certain goods, like Super Bowl tickets, becomes so strong that the price rises substantially, consumers have less money to demand other goods, driving the prices of those goods down. Prices are constantly adjusting to a multitude of factors, such as consumer preferences and enhanced productivity. Rising and falling prices, therefore, tell you many things about the market, but they don't tell you much about inflation or deflation, which is a change in the value of money.

If oranges are discovered greatly to reduce the possibility of heart failure, then demand for oranges will skyrocket. But if people are paying more for oranges, then they'll have less money to spend on other goods, the prices of which will decline. There is no inflation here, just a change in what consumers desire. You can buy a VHS recorder for next to nothing nowadays because no one wants it, but no one would call that deflation. Furthermore, markets always adjust to changing demand. If soaring demand for hotel rooms in Las Vegas drives prices up, the market is signaling entrepreneurs to build more hotels in Vegas. Prices, regardless of their direction, are a poor measure of inflation or deflation.

What about globalization, or the arrival of the less developed world into the global capitalist system? The most dramatic manifestation of globalization has been China's turn away from dogmatic collectivism and its embrace of a market economy. Shouldn't the entrance into the world market of hundreds of millions of Chinese consumers, hungry after decades of deprivation for the goods we enjoy in the West, drive up prices? Ben Bernanke, the recently departed chairman of the Federal Reserve, seems to think so.

In a speech before the Stanford Institute for Economic Policy Research in March 2007, Bernanke opined that "there seems to be little basis for concluding that globalization overall has significantly reduced inflation."[8] His point was that all those new workers would increase demand for goods and services and consequently drive up prices.

What Bernanke missed is that all demand is a function of supply. A visitor to China beholds the beautiful sight of formerly poor people enjoying an increasingly middle-class, and even upper middle-class, way of life, with all the consumption that comes with it. But Chinese demand for goods and services is a result of Chinese workers themselves supplying commensurate goods and services to the world economy. The increased supply and the increased demand balance each other, neutralizing the pressure on prices from these entrants to the labor force.

Quite comically, some economists argue that the Chinese *don't consume enough*,[9] showing how fraudulent the economics profession has become. It cannot be emphasized enough that savings provides capital for entrepreneurs and that the act of saving shifts consumptive ability from one person to another. It is the purest form of wealth redistribution, a fact almost totally lost on economists.

There are others who argue that China's embrace of capitalism will cause deflation. Bernanke's predecessor as Fed chairman, Alan Greenspan, asserted as much in his 2007 book, *The Age of Turbulence*, writing that "the rising rate of worker migration to the export-oriented coastal provinces imparted an ever-increasing wage (and price) disinflation to the developed economies."[10] No doubt the Chinese are producing all sorts of goods for us to enjoy, but they are not doing so in order to remain poor. The Chinese, like anyone else, are producing in order to consume. Their production brings with it commensurate demands, whether through their own consumption, or through their shifting of consumption to others through savings.

Every day that the Chinese go to work, Americans get a raise. But as I have emphasized, falling prices of certain goods (including those made in China) are not deflation. Instead, falling prices give rise to new demands that previously did not exist. The prices of consumer goods are a poor measurement of inflation pressures.

It is widely believed in the economics profession that economic growth is the source of inflation. This theory is easily disprovable, but it is very popular, particularly at the Fed, so let's examine it further.

The theory that inflation is the result of total demand's outstripping total supply is expressed in the Phillips curve. In a speech given in 2008, former Fed vice chairman Donald Kohn said, "A model in the Phillips curve tradition remains at the core of how most academic researchers and policymakers—including this one—think about fluctuations in inflation." Kohn added, "Bringing overall inflation immediately back to the low rate consistent with price stability could be associated with a much higher rate of unemployment for a short time."[11] Get it? The Fed thinks that when unemployment falls too low, its job is to engineer an economic slowdown to keep inflation in check.

Kohn is correct that he is hardly alone in believing that growth is the cause of inflation, and that's a serious indictment of both the Fed and the economics profession. In *The Age of Turbulence* Greenspan repeatedly states that a growing economy and falling unemployment are the source of inflation. "[G]ood growth, high optimism, and full employment," he observes, are "all reasons to be leery of inflation."[12]

Bernanke is singing in the same choir as Kohn and Greenspan. In a 2003 speech made while he was vice chairman at the Fed, Bernanke spoke about the possibility of future inflation, warning that "the effective slack in the economy may be less than we now think, and inflationary pressures may emerge more quickly than we currently expect." In a *Wall Street Journal* column published in July 2005, a few months before his nomination as Fed chief, Bernanke asserted that we had the "highest level of employment that can be sustained without creating inflationary pressure."[13] But is any of this true?

The best place to start is employment. Bernanke, Greenspan, and Kohn are all on record as believing that if unemployment gets too low, inflationary pressure will result. At first glance, this makes sense. If there is a labor shortage, employers presumably have to offer higher wages to current and prospective workers, and higher labor costs will push up the price of goods.

But these assumptions do not hold up under further inspection. First, the number of prospective workers is not static. If rising demand for workers sends wages up, workers on the sidelines will be more willing to offer their services. Recently, for example, rising wages in oil-patch states such as Texas and North Dakota[14] have drawn able-bodied workers from other states.[15]

The Fox Business News host Lou Dobbs has made a second career out of criticizing American companies that have moved jobs overseas. In chapter sixteen I made the case that "outsourcing" or "offshoring" results in better and higher paid work in the United States, but leaving that argument aside, as long as U.S. companies continue to find an abundant supply of labor around the world, a tight labor market at home won't put pressure on American wages. Simply put, when policymakers suggest that falling unemployment in the United States is inflationary, they ignore American companies' access to a worldwide labor force.

Markets, moreover, innovate their way around labor shortages. Most Americans no longer encounter another human being when they buy movie and airplane tickets or when they make bank deposits or withdrawals. More and more big-box retailers and grocery stores offer self-service checkout lines requiring no cashiers. In addition to these adaptations, the American labor force increases through immigration.

After Bernanke became chairman of the Fed in 2006, a stream of press releases from the Federal Open Market Committee offered variations of the following statement: "While the Fed expects inflation to moderate, a high level of resource utilization has the potential to sustain those [inflationary] pressures." The Fed's thinking here is that if the economy really starts growing, excessive demand might exhaust producers' manufacturing capacity, causing prices to rise.

This concern might seem reasonable at first, since supply and demand certainly affect pricing. But capacity, like the labor force, is not static. Looming capacity shortages are a signal for producers to increase the very capacity that the Fed assumes is fixed. Manufacturers, moreover, constantly enhance their production techniques to get more out of their existing assets. Compare a Ford factory from the early twentieth century with one today. Production becomes more efficient.

Finally, American companies have access to world capacity to make the finished products that their customers want. When the Fed worries that domestic capacity is a source of inflationary pressure, it assumes that American manufacturing capacity is limited to the fifty states. It is not.

The assertion that economic growth, which allows people to work and prosper, is the cause of inflation is based on the assumption that the U.S. economy, or any country's economy, is an island. But the world economy is so interconnected that wage and capacity pressures do not drive prices up. Even if they did, rising prices in one area simply reduce demand in other areas. After that, economic growth is about production. The idea that productive economic activity could be inflationary defies the basic economic law that all demand originates from supply.

What about the Consumer Price Index, the most familiar "measure" of inflation, calculated by the U.S. Bureau of Labor Statistics? The CPI measures changes in the price level of a market basket of consumer goods and services purchased by households. Of course, that description shows why it fails as a useful measure of inflation. If people are paying more for Super Bowl tickets, then they have less money to purchase clothes or cigarettes. And if improved productivity makes flat-screen televisions cheaper, there is more money to purchase Nike sneakers and the next new thing from Apple.

If the CPI is heavy on technology products like computers and cellphones, the index will be lower than it would be if it were weighted toward gasoline and ground beef. Even more distorting is the so-called "Core CPI," which leaves out food and energy. Those commodities, priced in dollars and therefore priced minute by minute in commodity markets, are the most sensitive to changes in the value of the dollar. Yet they are left out of the inflation calculation.[16] A CPI heavily weighted toward gasoline and food alone would tell an inflation tale over the last dozen or so years that computers and phones would not.

Worse, producers can raise prices without actually raising prices. In 2009, Skippy peanut butter jars were indented, reducing the contents by 9 percent, but the price of each jar remained the same. Steve Forbes, who makes a daily visit to Starbucks to buy their pastries, observed back in 2009 that while Starbucks had held the line on pastry prices, the size of the pastries had shrunk.[17]

And then consider the Tandy 5000 computer, priced at $8,499 in 1989, and today's vastly more powerful Dell desktop that retails for under five hundred dollars. Since there is no reasonable way to compare the two computers, the idea of using consumer prices to chart inflation becomes rather difficult. Likewise, the gadgetry in a 2015 BMW 535i will be substantially advanced beyond that in a 2012 model, let alone a 2009. Using a basket of goods to gauge pricing pressures raises far more questions than it answers.

After that, the CPI is whatever federal bureaucrats want it to be. The *Wall Street Journal* reported in 2011, "Food accounts for 47% of the basket of products that make up India's consumer-price index and 34% of China's."[18] Rest assured that if the U.S. CPI were that heavily weighted toward food and gasoline ("the things we all buy," as is often said), CPI inflation in the United States would be very high at the moment.

Prices of goods and labor move up and down all the time for all manner of reasons. Trying to "divine" inflation or deflation from the price of computers and televisions, from levels of unemployment, from globalization, or from baskets of goods selected by the federal government is a fool's errand. Worse, it can be dangerous. It is widely known that the Fed, ever focused on consumption, wants CPI inflation of 2 percent per year. Really? So the Fed wants prices to double in thirty-six years? People should ignore it.

Inflation is a decline in the value of the dollar—nothing more and nothing less. The best measure of the dollar's value is the price of gold simply because it is priced in dollars and is the commodity least influenced by supply and demand. Gold is the constant, and that is why market actors happened on it as the best way to stabilize the value of money.

In July 2001, a dollar bought roughly 1/266 of an ounce of gold.[19] In the fall of 2014, a dollar bought roughly 1/1200 of an ounce of gold. The dollar has been substantially devalued these last thirteen years, meaning we've had serious inflation. In the next chapter we'll see why that's a problem.

CHAPTER TWENTY-ONE

True Inflation Is Currency Devaluation, and It Is a Cruel Blast to the Past

As for future stuff, it cannot be produced without investments in financial assets. The shift into tangibles thus prefigured a decline in production.
—Brian Domitrovic, *Econoclasts: The Rebels Who Sparked the Supply-Side Revolution and Restored American Prosperity*

If you wish to destroy a nation you must first corrupt its currency.
—Adam Fergusson, *When Money Dies*

The networks that televise the Super Bowl can command enormous rates for ads during the telecast. In 2001, the cost to air a thirty-second commercial was $2.1 million. By 2014, the rate had ballooned to *four million dollars*.[1] The number speaks not just to the rising popularity of the NFL's signature event, but also to the health of the various networks that bought the rights to the game over the years.

Still, by now you may have developed a bit of healthy skepticism about the price of anything in dollars. If I cut the length of the foot in half in order to be twelve feet tall, I'll still be six feet tall. That's how you should think of the dollar. While the dollar for most of American history had a fixed value in terms of gold, over the last four decades it has floated freely. Do those Super Bowl ad rates mean much?

At the end of January 2001, a dollar bought 1/264 of an ounce of gold. By Super Bowl Sunday in 2014, that same dollar was a shadow of its former self, buying only 1/1250 of an ounce.[2] Most economists and pundits will tell you that there has been no inflation since 2000, and according to a Consumer Price Index that excludes the commodities most likely to signal monetary error, they may be right.

But the economic consequences of the dollar's substantial decline over the last thirteen years demand attention, especially in light of America's monetary experience since 1971. Devaluation of money *is* inflation, and the floating dollar's forty-three year story is worth a brief review.

Watching ESPN one night, I was struck by a comment from Hall of Fame quarterback Steve Young. He said that he and the late Bill Walsh had come to the conclusion that a careful study of the quarterbacks' footwork in a game film will invariably reveal who won and who lost. A keen and seasoned football eye would need to see only the quarterbacks' movements from the ankles down—to the exclusion of everything else—to know the outcome of the game.

Likewise, if you were forced to live in a cave with no access to the outside world but were provided with just one economic indicator to follow the economy's health, you'd want that indicator to be the dollar's value in gold. As the 1980s Bundesbank president Otmar Emminger once asserted, "the dollar is the most important price in the world economy."[3] Yes, it is, and the most telling indicator of the dollar's price is its price in gold. Supplied with this knowledge, a cave-dweller would have a pretty good sense of the United States' economic health and that of the rest of the world.

When President Nixon made the fateful decision to sever the dollar's link to gold in 1971, he wanted a weaker dollar. Presidents always get the dollar they desire. Unlinked to gold, the dollar began to fall as gold rose.

The financial writer John Brooks noted presciently in the *New York Times* that "the president and his advisers, in making their draconian move, did not understand what they were doing."[4] Agreed. It quickly became apparent that Nixon and his advisors had unleashed economic chaos. The prices of commodities that had historically been flat and nominally cheap (a barrel of oil at $2.30) eventually soared. There were no "oil shocks" in the early 1970s, but there were dollar shocks. From 1972 to 1973 alone, the price of a barrel of oil rose over 300 percent, meat prices were rising at an annual rate of 75 percent, and the price of a bushel of wheat rose over 240 percent.[5]

The Fed funds rate rose over 450 basis points from 1971 to 1973, but the housing market was undeterred. It is economically revealing that housing emerged as the top asset class during Nixon's second term. Investors are always seeking the best return. When they put capital to work, they are buying future dollar income streams. But with the dollar in free fall, stock and bond income streams representing future wealth creation are not as attractive as they have been. So investors ask themselves a very blunt question: Why commit capital to future wealth creation if the returns will come in severely devalued dollars? In these circumstances, investment flows into the hard assets that are least vulnerable to devaluation—land, art, rare stamps, anything tangible. This is wealth that *already exists*. The migration of investments into existing wealth as a protection against dollar devaluation is a strong signal that production of wealth *which does not yet exist* will not be funded. Devaluation provokes a blast to the past, a boon for assets that the economy has already created.

The housing boom under Nixon was a troubling economic signal. The Austrian School economist Ludwig von Mises referred to the "flight to the real," which occurs in periods of devaluation. Nixon's monetary blunder made stock and bond markets unappealing, and housing and other hard assets were the beneficiaries. A house is tangible. You can live in it. In short, it is safe.

The problem with everyone's pouring into housing is that it is consumption, like Vince Young's three-hundred-thousand-dollar party. The purchase of a house will not make you more productive, it will not open up foreign markets, and it will not lead to cures for cancer. Investments in houses, land, art, and other tangibles is the equivalent of the prevent defense in football—a conservative strategy meant to avoid calamity. The problem is that economies need risk takers—entrepreneurs willing to try something new paired with intrepid investors willing to back new ideas that might deliver big returns (or not).

With the dollar in decline, investors went into prevent mode to protect their wealth from devaluation. Without aggressive investment in imaginative new ideas, Nixon's economy sputtered badly, leaving him vulnerable to his political foes when Watergate erupted.

The dollar's fall continued into Jimmy Carter's presidency. Despite a sharp drop in the value of the dollar against gold and the Japanese yen throughout the 1970s, Carter's Treasury secretary Michael Blumenthal intimated in a speech in June 1977 that the dollar was overvalued against the yen.[6] This was a fairly explicit signal that President Carter wanted a weaker greenback, and the markets complied. Although gold was trading at roughly $140 an ounce[7] when Carter entered office, it was at roughly $220 an ounce by 1979,[8] and it hit $875 an ounce by January 1980.[9]

Unsurprisingly, "oil shocks" again accompanied the dollar's fall. The price of a barrel of oil jumped 43 percent from 1975 to 1979. Yet those "shocks" were by no means global. Some countries chose not to mimic America's currency devaluation. Over the same four years, a barrel rose only 1 percent in Deutschemarks and 7 percent in Japanese yen. In Swiss francs the cost of a barrel actually fell.[10]

In a decade marked by a declining dollar, stock market indices like the S&P 500 nearly flattened. Entrepreneurial enterprise dried up. There were three hundred high-tech start-ups in 1968, but none in 1976.[11] Initial public offerings, which represent companies of the future, averaged twenty-eight per year from 1974 through 1978; by comparison, there were 953 in 1986 alone.[12] High capital gains taxes were a big part of the problem, but dollar devaluation is very much a tax on investment. Remember that investors are buying future dollar income streams when they commit money to the stock market.

The investors who went into prevent mode did well enough. David Frum describes the 1970s this way: "If you had the nerve to borrow a lot of soggy cash, and then use it to buy hard assets—land, grain, metals, art, silver candlesticks, a book of Austro-Hungarian postage stamps—you could make a killing in the 1970s." Frum further notes that when *Forbes* magazine "published its first list of the 400 richest Americans in 1982, 153 of them owed their fortunes to real estate or oil. (On the 1998 list, by contrast, only fifty-seven fortunes derived from real estate or oil.)"[13]

In his classic *Wealth and Poverty*, first published in 1981, George Gilder summed up the decade that had just ended: While "24 million investors in the stock markets were being buffeted by inflation and taxes, 46 million homeowners were leveraging their houses with mortgages, deducting the interest payments on their taxes, and earning higher real returns on their down payment equity than speculators in gold or foreign currencies." Gilder also cited a 1978 *Fortune* magazine study that found that half the new multi-millionaires were in real estate.[14] Oil was a good investment too. The Rolls-Royce dealership in oil-rich Midland, Texas, emerged as one of the brand's most profitable dealerships in the world.[15]

You might think that the average American doesn't follow the dollar, let alone the dollar's price in terms of gold, and you'd be right. But the average American *does* follow the market's price signals. During stock market booms there is plenty of conversation about stocks among regular people, but in the soggy-dollar '70s the talk was about money made on housing and in the oil-patch. Americans reoriented their investments into the areas least vulnerable to devaluation. Oil, housing, and hard assets soared, while the stock market, which represents the funding of future wealth creation, flattened.

In the 1970s the American economy mimicked Michael Jordan's move from basketball, where he was the best, to baseball, where he was not very good. The rush into housing was about getting by, not pursuing stunning advances in the human condition. The flood of investment into the American oil patch was the equivalent of LeBron James's suspending his basketball career to play tight end. Rather than being content to import oil that others produced at a low profit margin and devoting our own energy and resources to high-margin technology businesses, we let oil signals, which were distorted by a falling dollar, lure us into low-margin work and investments.

The American fascination with housing consumption caused a capital shortage for businesses. A flat stock market and a malaise-ridden decade told the tale of the falling dollar's damage. Fortunately, relief arrived in the person of Ronald Reagan.

For our purposes, the most important thing about Reagan's 1980 campaign was his declaration, "No nation in history has ever survived fiat money, money that did not have precious metal backing."[16] As we learned with Nixon and Carter, presidents always get the dollar they want. The dollar fell to an all-time low in January 1980, when gold hit $875 an ounce, but the decline reversed itself. As Reagan's victories in the Republican primaries started to accumulate, the price of gold fell as the dollar strengthened. Markets always price in the future, and the expectation of a new president who was explicit in his belief that unlinking the dollar from gold had been a mistake sent the dollar into a rally.

Under President Reagan, economic policy improved a great deal. Deregulation—already begun under President Carter—continued, the top marginal income tax rate was reduced from 70 percent to 28 percent, and the value of the dollar, reflected in the plummeting price of oil (ten dollars a barrel by 1986), was rising.[17] While Reagan often erred when it came to free trade, getting three out of four of the basics of economic growth correct is not bad.

Early in his presidency, the economy fell into a major recession. But recessions are cleansing and necessary. Though undoubtedly painful in the short term, recessions indicate that an economy is on the mend. A recession is an economy's cleansing itself of all the bad businesses, bad investments, and labor misallocations that brought on the trouble. That is why when government stays out of the way, recessions turn into impressive rebounds. The recession of the early '80s was the equivalent of Michael Jordan's ending his baseball flirtation and returning to championship form in basketball.

A stronger dollar made housing and energy less attractive to investors and revived their hope in future dollar income streams, so they returned to the stock market. With the president no longer talking down the dollar as Nixon and Carter had done (Gerald Ford's presidency was too short to take into account for our purposes here), investors were finally comfortable about scrapping the prevent defense in favor of imaginative investing in future production and wealth creation. The IPO market that had lain dormant in the '70s quickly took off. While Reagan did not restore the dollar to its proper role as a stable measure of value defined in gold, a rising greenback throughout much of his presidency was a boon to the economy. In the booming 1980s, the S&P 500 soared 222 percent as the price of gold declined 52 percent.[18] The decade-long dollar nightmare was over, and high-profit-margin companies like Microsoft and Cisco were again the beneficiaries of Americans' investment.

George H. W. Bush's presidential election was, in many ways, the electorate's way of giving Reagan a third term. But where things get most interesting from an economic and monetary perspective is the presidency of Bill Clinton. In 1999, near the end of Clinton's second term, the liberal historian Richard Reeves acknowledged, "Reagan, in fact, is still running the country. President Clinton is governing in his shadow, trying, not without some real success, to create a liberal garden under the conservative oak."[19]

Clinton did raise income tax rates in 1993, but in taking the top marginal rate from 31 percent to 39.6 percent he was conceding that the days of 70 percent marginal rates were over. And Clinton actually cut the capital gains tax—the price of investment in new companies—from 28 percent to 20 percent in 1997.[20] On trade policy, Clinton worked with Republicans to ratify the North American Free Trade Agreement, which liberalized trade between the United States, Canada, and Mexico.[21]

Clinton was at his best on dollar policy. In Robert Rubin, who joined the cabinet in 1995, Clinton had a secretary of the Treasury who truly believed that a strong dollar was in America's best interest. Rubin backed this belief with action, or better yet, *inaction*. As the economists Ronald I. McKinnon and Kenichi Ohno wrote approvingly in 1997, not once after Rubin's arrival "did a responsible official in the American government complain that the dollar was too high."[22] Presidents always get the dollar they want, and as the Clinton administration was fairly explicit about its desire for a strong dollar, the greenback and the economy took off.

Even conservatives applauded Clinton's dollar policy. Inflation—by definition a devaluation of the dollar—is a cruel blow to investments that have already been made. The free-market economist Lawrence Kudlow happily acknowledged in 1996 that Clinton got it right with the dollar:

> The single most significant, inter-galactic, extra-celestial, interplanetary, and spiritual force behind the global stock market rally is the decline of inflation to rates not seen in over thirty years. While many industrial nations, including the U.S., have imposed anti-growth and anti-saving tax increases in recent years, fiscal drag has been offset by a steady decline of inflation. Inflation is a tax on money, wealth creation, income, and work effort. Inflation is a devastating tax on savings. But low inflation is a tax-cut. By enhancing the value of financial assets, price stability rewards patient savers and investors. It is a stimulant to capital formation, new business start-ups and growth. Growth does not cause inflation, low inflation causes growth.[23]

In those eight sentences, Kudlow explained the Clinton boom. The importance of the administration's support of the dollar from the mid-1990s on cannot be minimized. Many conservatives still suggest that Bill Clinton was simply lucky to be president during the rise of the internet. This is faulty thinking.

The internet boom was inseparable from Clinton's dollar policies. Investors become defensive when money is falling in value, and they seek safety. But if they know their investments will not suffer erosion by devaluation, they become willing to take risks. The strong Clinton dollar was the low-entropy background for the high-entropy innovation that was occurring in Silicon Valley.

The dollar is the most important price in the world, and often its value drives the direction of global currencies. With the dollar strong, other currencies followed on the way to a global boom. I must repeat that money is nothing more than a unit of measure. In a perfect world, money is neither weak nor strong but only stable. So while the United States did not return to an invariable dollar during the Reagan-Bush-Clinton era, Nathan Lewis has observed that from 1982 to 2000, "the dollar's value was crudely stable vs. gold around $350/oz."[24]

From that stability came an economic boom. During the 1980s and '90s, the tax penalty imposed on work fell, the tax of government spending was lighter, regulation was less intrusive, freedom to trade was expanded, and the dollar was strong and stable. These are the *basic necessities for economic growth*. The stock market rally that began in the '80s continued into the '90s, and the S&P 500 rose 314 percent in the latter decade.[25]

So what happened? How did such a wildly prosperous economy sink into slower growth, flat stock markets, and financial crisis in the 2000s? Why has the richest nation on the planet seemingly lost its economic confidence?

Just as Steve Young and Bill Walsh would look at the quarterbacks' footwork, we can look at the dollar. Presidents get the dollar they want, and with the election of George W. Bush in 2000, weak-dollar policies came into favor to the misfortune of the United States and the world. Treasury secretaries are mouthpieces for the dollar, and that is why they are coached so heavily about what they utter. What they say can move the dollar. Bush's first Treasury secretary, Paul O'Neill, announced that a strong dollar was not a priority. His successor, John Snow, continued this lurch toward cheap money, asking at a G-8 meeting in 2007, "What's wrong with a weak dollar?"[26]

The Bush administration imposed tariffs on foreign steel, softwood lumber, and shrimp. Carter (and, it must be said, Reagan) had perennially complained about the weak Japanese yen, and George W. Bush followed suit by complaining about a weak Chinese yuan. This was an explicit signal that the administration wanted a weak dollar, and markets predictably complied. No investor is going to fight a president who has control over Federal Reserve appointments. And whatever your opinion about the wars in Afghanistan and Iraq, war and good money are not always correlated.

And so the dollar began to decline. It bought 1/266 of an ounce of gold when Bush was inaugurated in 2001, and by July 2008 it bought 1/940 of an ounce.[27] The price of oil during this period predictably soared, eventually reaching an all-time high of $145 per barrel. It had been as low as ten dollars a barrel in 1998 and twenty-five dollars a barrel in 2001. These were not "oil shocks," but dollar shocks. In dollar terms, the price of a barrel rose 459 percent. Measured in other currencies, oil was still spiking, though not as much. In Swiss francs, a barrel had risen 216 percent, and it was up 198 percent in euros.[28]

Commodities are priced every second of the day in markets around the world. They are priced in dollars, and with the dollar's fall against gold, it was not just oil that was spiking. Odd headlines—"States battle rise in copper thefts"[29] and "Copper: Hot loot for some thieves"[30]—pointed to the problem. When the copper in a penny became more valuable than the penny itself, one congressman floated a bill to overturn a U.S. Treasury ban on melting pennies.[31] It was the slow-growth 1970s all over again. The wealth of yesterday became more attractive than the wealth of tomorrow, which is funded in the stock market.

Stocks did move up in the early years of the Bush administration, but the gains were not what investors had grown accustomed to in the 1980s and '90s. Google's IPO was the only notable one. As *Bloomberg* reported in May 2008, "Take away ExxonMobil Corp, Chevron Corp. and ConocoPhillips and profits at U.S. companies are the worst in at least a decade."[32]

Around this time, oil-patch states such as Texas and North Dakota were the recipients of an influx of people chasing an oil boom that was driven by a weak dollar. Harvard graduates were earning less money out of college than graduates of the South Dakota School of Mines & Technology.[33] It's true that brilliant engineering advances like fracking and horizontal drilling opened up vast reserves of previously unattainable oil and natural gas. But oil is plentiful at the market price around the world. In rushing headlong back into energy's relatively low profit margins, Americans were repeating the 1970s, when lower-margin economic activity gained at the expense of work that was far more profitable. A Michael Jordan basketball economy had once again become a Michael Jordan baseball economy.

And just as they did in the '70s, Americans started speculating in housing. It offered better returns than the stock market, and you can live in a house. The rush into housing was as bad an economic signal in the 2000s as it had been in the 1970s. As Adam Smith wrote in *The Wealth of Nations*,

> Though a house, therefore, may yield a revenue to its proprietor, and thereby serve in the function of a capital to him, it cannot yield any to the public, nor serve in the function of a capital to it, and the revenue of the whole of the people can never be in the smallest degree increased by it.[34]

Housing is about consumption of wealth, but investment in wealth that does not yet exist is what makes the economy grow.

What caused the flood of investment into housing? The answer popular on the Left is that banking deregulation drove it. The favorite answer on the Right seems to be that Alan Greenspan's decision to cut the Fed funds rate to 1 percent in 2003 made money easy and fed the boom. Others point to Fannie Mae, Freddie Mac, and the income tax deduction for mortgage interest payments. Let's look at each of these arguments.

The deregulation explanation simply doesn't hold water. John Allison points out, "Financial services is a very highly regulated industry, probably the most regulated industry in the world."[35] Banking came under even more regulation in the 2000s, including Sarbanes-Oxley and the Patriot Act.

Some on the left blame the near-total repeal of the Depression-era Glass-Steagall regulations, which separated securities services from commercial banking. This explanation is no more accurate than the argument about deregulation. Hybrid banks and investment banks were the healthiest financial institutions in 2008. They were the ones asked to acquire a failed Bear Stearns (J. P. Morgan), the failed Merrill Lynch (Bank of America), and the failed Wachovia (Wells Fargo). But the most important problem with this explanation is painfully obvious: banks ran into trouble not because of their exposure to investment banking services or because of underwriting or because of dealing in securities (which banks are still prohibited from doing).[36] They imploded because of mortgage lending and exposure to mortgages, and the partial repeal of Glass-Steagall *had nothing to do with that*. As Gregory Zuckerman has pointed out, federal regulators *encouraged* the mortgage madness.[37] Regulators are always the last to see problems. If they weren't, they wouldn't be regulators but billionaire speculators shorting the shares of errant banks.

The argument that a low Fed funds rate caused the rush into housing fails because it presumes that artificially low interest rates represent "easy money." That's like saying that if the government decreed that Ferraris would cost only ten thousand dollars then everyone could go out and buy a Ferrari. There wouldn't be any Ferraris to buy because the Ferrari company couldn't afford to make them if it had to sell them at that price. Likewise, low interest rates drove a lot of savers out of the market.

Furthermore, as we saw when we looked at regulation, John Paulson ultimately made billions betting against the housing house of cards. The employee who initially brought the lucrative trade idea to him, Paolo Pellegrini, had carefully studied interest rates and home prices. In tracking interest rates over the decades, he "concluded that they had little impact on house prices."[38]

Housing soared in the 1970s when interest rates were sky-high. Looking back on the housing boom of that earlier decade, George Gilder writes:

> What happened was that citizens speculated on their homes.... Not only did their houses tend to rise in value about 20 percent faster than the price index, but with their small equity exposure they could gain higher percentage returns than all but the most phenomenally lucky shareholders.[39]

What about Fannie Mae and Freddie Mac and the mortgage interest deduction? All three should have been abolished a long time ago. The last thing government should ever do is subsidize consumption of any market good, particularly one that makes people less mobile. Alexis de Tocqueville observed in the nineteenth century that Americans are "restless amid abundance."[40] Government subsidies of housing consumption give people an incentive to remain stationary, whereas, historically, they have moved all over the country in search of the best job opportunities. Stationary citizens are easy to tax (this may explain why government is so eager to subsidize housing), and they can't pursue jobs elsewhere when the opportunity beckons.

More to the point, the view that Fannie, Freddie, and the mortgage interest deduction caused the housing boom ignores its *global* nature. Housing soared in Great Britain without a Fannie Mae or Freddie Mac and despite the abolition of the British mortgage interest deduction in the 1980s.[41] In Canada, it is difficult to attain a home mortgage, yet housing boomed there as well. Blaming the low Fed funds rate is unsatisfactory because interest rates were higher around the world.

So what caused the migration of investment into housing? If you paid careful attention to my discussion of the 1970s, you already know. The rest of the world mimicked our weak dollar policies, and when money is devalued, housing is always one of the safer places to go. History is simply littered with instances of investors seeking shelter in housing amid periods of monetary devaluation. Housing is the classic inflation hedge. In *When Money Dies*, a tragic account of the collapse of the mark in post–World War I Germany, Adam Fergusson writes, "Anyone who was alive to the realities of inflation could safeguard himself against losses in paper currency by buying assets which would maintain their value: houses, real estate, manufactured goods, raw materials and so forth."[42]

Looking at the British pound's decline in the 1970s, David Smith writes in *The Rise and Fall of Monetarism* that the sector "which investors chose above all others was property development."[43] And a Bank of England quarterly bulletin observed, "There was [in the 1970s] no other general area of economic activity which seemed to offer as good a prospective rate of return to an entrepreneur as property development."[44]

In his classic history of the Federal Reserve, *Secrets of the Temple*, William Greider asserts that the economy of the Carter years "particularly benefited the broad middle class of families that owned their own homes."[45] Housing is a relatively safe investment, one that holds its value better than stocks do when money is in decline.

A global housing boom occurred during the Bush years because the dollar was in free fall. That fall, moreover, caused a run on paper currencies all around the world. Housing, oil, and real estate drove the 1970s economy when the dollar sank, and a return to 1970s-style dollar policy during George W. Bush's presidency generated a similar result.

Remember, when the dollar is weak, there is a tendency to migrate toward the tangible, to wealth that already exists. Investors go to their prevent defense. When money is stable or strong, investors do not worry as much about their investments' being eroded by inflation, so they are intrepid.

The truth about the 2000s is that if we defined inflation the way it has always been defined—a decline in the value of money—there would be a broad acknowledgement that we had suffered a serious bout of inflation, a bout from which we are still suffering. Inflation, far from being the result of strong economic growth, is the ultimate growth retardant. Inflation, as Brian Domitrovic said, is the process whereby investment goes into tangibles such as housing instead of into the stocks and bonds that will lead to new wealth creation. The economic weakness of so much of the 2000s is all the evidence of inflation we need. Like a quarterback's footwork, the dollar price of gold tells the tale.

The next question is why the moderation of the housing rush in 2008 caused a financial crisis. The answer is *it didn't*, as we'll see in the next chapter.

CHAPTER TWENTY-TWO

If They Tell You They Predicted the "Financial Crisis," They're Lying

A man must learn from his mistakes ... from MAKING THEM, not from being saved from them.
—**Shelby Foote**, letter to Walker Percy, 1952

Experience ... was merely the name men gave to their mistakes.
—**Oscar Wilde**

"Your No. 1 client is the government," John J. Mack, Morgan Stanley's chairman and chief executive from 2005 to 2009, told current CEO James Gorman in a recent phone call. Mr. Gorman, who was visiting Washington that day, agreed.
—***Wall Street Journal***, September 10, 2013

In a December 2012 television interview with Ben Affleck, who had just turned forty, Barbara Walters asked the talented actor-screenwriter-director, "If you could give advice to your twenty-five-year-old self, what would you say?" Perhaps she expected him to rue the myriad errors that had reduced him to a Bentley-driving, J-Lo-dating, bad-script-chasing joke after he won a best screenplay Oscar for *Good Will Hunting*. As Ross Douthat summed up those years, "Affleck spent the next decade embodying Hollywood as we wish it weren't. He starred in bad action movies, mediocre dramas, lousy comedies, and bloated *Titanic* wannabes. He made not one but two bad movies with Michael Bay...."[1] And that's going easy on Affleck. The attachment of the painfully overexposed Affleck's name to any project in the early 2000s was a box-office death sentence, and most people think his career bottomed out with 2003's universally panned *Gigli*. Then he made *Argo*, which won the Academy Award for best picture soon after his interview with Walters.

Affleck didn't answer as you might have expected—that he'd tell his younger self to avoid the bad scripts and embarrassing tabloid covers. Instead, he said that his mistakes had made him, that he wouldn't change much of anything, and that failure is ultimately the best teacher. Affleck's answer was entirely correct.

Affleck's story of redemption speaks to the value of letting failure run its course. Indeed, what a shame if Affleck's falls had been cushioned, if he'd been bailed out, because bail-outs perpetuate the very actions that lead to failure in the first place. It's reasonable to suppose that Affleck's decline as an actor spurred his desire to reinvent himself as a director, that the painful attention of his tabloid joke phase helped restore his focus as he sought to prove his countless critics wrong. Failure is merely a harsh word for the experiences that animate the constant drive for self-improvement.

Ben Affleck's story brings us back to the end of the last chapter. Housing was all the rage by the mid-2000s, signaling that the economy was in trouble. The manic flow of investments into housing was related to the eventual "financial crisis," but indirectly. There would have been no rush to housing if the dollar been strong and stable. With a healthy dollar, stocks and bonds, which fund future wealth creation, would have won out over consumption, as they did in the

1980s and '90s. The over-consumption of housing was bad for the economy, so a correction of that over-consumption, which was a barrier to growth, would not have been a "crisis."

It's unfortunate that six years after the "financial crisis," we're still pairing the words "financial" and "crisis." Despite what the mainstream media tell you, the crisis was decidedly not financial, nor was it caused by a crackup in the housing market, nor was it caused by the failure of Lehman Brothers.

Recall the economic impact of the bankruptcy of Blockbuster Video in 2010—there wasn't much to report. Any sensible observer recognizes that the bankruptcy of the video rental behemoth was an example of a healthy capitalist system's working as it should, replacing one form of commerce with a better one. The same is true of the more spectacular bankruptcy of Enron, which was financially connected to firms all around the world. Its collapse barely disturbed the markets or the global economy.

It's true that Blockbuster was irrelevant by the time it went bankrupt, while banks such as Lehman, Citi, and Bear Stearns were relatively large. Yet the size of those banks made their decline even *healthier* for the economy than the end of Blockbuster. Successful economies are about the efficient allocation of capital, and a large business that is destroying capital hurts an economy more than a small one. Historically, if failure was unthinkable, then we would have bailed out buggy manufacturers at the expense of the nascent car makers Ford and GM. Commodore and Kaypro, two long-dead computer makers, would have been saved at the expense of Apple and Dell. And Ben Affleck would have received a government subsidy to write, direct, and act in—God forbid—*Gigli II*.

Bear, Lehman, and Citi did not collapse because they were effectively using the capital entrusted to them. They imploded because the markets had decided they were *not* using it well. So how could the failure of one, or even all three, have caused what is now known as a financial crisis? A former senior Fed official told me *off the record* in 2013 that Citi has been bailed out five times in the last twenty-two years. Can anyone explain why bailing out this most errant of banks is economically beneficial or how it has deterred a "financial" crisis?

As a matter of logic, Citi's fall could only *help* the economy by eliminating a massive waster of capital. The surest way to foster a financial crisis is to perpetuate the failed practices of Citi, not to mention Lehman and Bear, by propping them up with taxpayer funds. As will become apparent, that is exactly what happened.

Many financial institutions were exposed to the housing market, and it is still said that a moderation of home prices in 2007 led to an economy-crushing crisis in 2008. Really? That view assumes that massive lending for the consumption of a good that does not make people more efficient, does not lead to cancer cures or software discoveries, and does not open up foreign markets for trade is somehow a source of economic dynamism. In truth, the rush of capital from 2001 until 2007 into housing instead of productive entrepreneurial ventures was a *recipe for recession*.

The multitude of pundits who say the "crisis" was born of a housing correction are turning basic economics on its head. Even the most ardent defenders of bank bailouts acknowledge that mortgage lending had grown out of control by 2007. How could a correction of this imbalance have caused a crisis, or even an economic slowdown? Let's return to reality: the 2007 housing moderation signaled an economy fixing itself. This included bankrupting the financial institutions whose errors had made all the housing consumption possible.

An economy robbed of failure is also robbed of success, because failure provides knowledge about how to succeed. Failure is the healthy process whereby a poorly run entity is deprived of the ability to do more economic harm. In sporting terms, it means that Mike Shula is relieved of his Alabama Crimson Tide coaching duties so that Nick Saban can take over.

The implosion of Bear Stearns in 2008 was beneficial because it was the kind of development that is necessary for economic growth. The firm was not going to disappear. If it had been allowed to go under, the management of its assets would have ended up in the hands of people more skilled. Sadly, the Bush Treasury and the Bernanke Fed blinked. Laboring under the delusion that Bear's failure would precipitate a financial meltdown, the government brokered an economy-weakening deal in which J. P. Morgan acquired Bear in return for the Fed's exposing itself to Bear's undesirable balance sheet. At that point, a frequently inept federal government turned a healthy corporate implosion into a crisis.

If Bear had folded, better managers would have acquired its assets at a very cheap cost, enhancing their odds of success. Failure contains the seeds of success because quality assets that have been poorly managed are purchased cheaply. USC football's revival under Pete Carroll initially cost the university little since Carroll, having been fired by the Jets and the Patriots, was a "damaged" asset. In fact, his reputation was in free-fall. Getting him on the cheap enabled USC to reap huge dividends when the football team's return to glory opened the wallets of the university's alumni.

The failure of Bear Stearns would have signaled to Lehman, Citi, and everyone else that bailouts were not an option. A struggling bank would need to find a buyer soon to avoid Bear's fate. Investment banks have been failing *regularly* for as long as they have existed, so the resolution of these institutions' difficulties would have been an orderly process.

Instead, the bailout of Bear, and especially the bailout of Bear's counterparties, signaled to the market that the feds were ready and willing to "save" ailing financial institutions. Thus informed, the management of Lehman Brothers made no provisions for bankruptcy. Lehman, you must remember, was in trouble because it had deployed the funds entrusted to it in a faulty way. Its implosion in a normal—yes, *capitalist*—world would have been cause for cheer. But since capitalism's abundant powers of self-healing were being overridden by slow-growth government intervention, its collapse created crisis conditions.

When their assumption that the government would prevent the failure of an institution like Lehman was upended by the firm's bankruptcy, investors panicked, and the market became turbulent. None of this had anything to do with capitalism. It had everything to do with blinding the markets by intervention. It was as if the New York Jets prepared all week to play the New England Patriots without Tom Brady and Rob Gronkowski, only for the two to show up at game time ready to play. Or imagine being told to study for a history exam on the Revolutionary War but finding only questions about the Civil War on the exam. Panic erupted because of a lack of preparation. The element of surprise—the result of the wrongheaded bailout of Bear—turned Lehman's decline into a crisis.

Once the blaze was ignited, the Securities and Exchange Commission fanned it into a forest fire by banning the short-selling of nine hundred different financial shares. Think about that for a moment. The entrance of short sellers into the market signals the arrival of massive buying power. When short sellers "short" a stock, they borrow the shares from an owner and then sell them on the assumption that they can buy them cheaply down the line and return the borrowed shares to the owner. For short sellers to profit, they must eventually re-enter the market to *buy* the shares they borrowed. But rather than allow the buyers whose shorts would eventually put a floor under a falling market, the SEC banned them when they were needed most.

To put this in perspective, ask yourself what was the biggest economic story of the thirty years prior to 2008? The overwhelming victory of free markets over central planning. Doubters need only Google the image of South Korea and North Korea at night. But in 2008, a Bush administration that talked a big game about capitalism and markets ran from both as fast as it could—allegedly to save capitalism and free markets. Do you recall Ronald Reagan's famous quip that the scariest words in the English language are "We're from the federal government and we're here to help"?

Bailouts are never free. Even if they were, they would still be disastrous. The bailouts of financial institutions in 2008 clearly signaled that government intervention in the economy was coming back—*with a vengeance*. Thus John Mack's admonition to his successor as head of Morgan Stanley, "Your no. 1 client is the government." When a business accepts a government bailout, it is no longer in the business of profit. Instead, it is serving political masters who do not care about profits and who view businesses as social concepts whose wealth is subject to redistribution.

Given the stupendous failures of central planning in the twentieth century, is it any wonder that the markets cracked up in 2008? They had tried to eliminate poorly run financial institutions and had signaled thereby that further lending for housing consumption would cease. Markets were working well to end the crisis of financial institutions' chasing bad housing investments, but rather than allow markets to work, the Bush administration renounced them.

"Your No. 1 client is the government" was not a response to a "financial" crisis in 2008 but to the major problems ahead. When poorly run institutions were not allowed to fail as the consumption of housing decreased, the markets correctly convulsed as they priced in the perpetuation of faulty banking practices, Fed encouragement of more housing consumption, and the rise of the federal government as the top client of U.S. finance.

The crisis was only "financial" insofar as the bailouts weakened banks and other financial institutions that would have gained strength through failure. Silicon Valley is not the richest place in the United States because businesses there always succeed. It thrives because there has been constant failure for the last fifty years. The failures authored great success in Silicon Valley because laggards were not allowed to consume precious capital for too long.

The bailouts weakened the financial institutions that animate our economy by robbing their managers of the knowledge gained from mistakes. A great deal of talent has migrated out of the banks and into hedge funds, which are unregulated and were not bailed out in 2008. New York City is still the center of global finance, and its enormous wealth is there for all to see. But the "unseen" is how much wealthier New York would be and how much more innovative finance would be if the taxpayers weren't always there to save financial institutions from their mistakes.

Perhaps you are skeptical about my assurances that the markets would have righted themselves in the absence of government intervention. You may recall Ben Bernanke's dire warning to Congress as it considered the bailouts: "I spent my career as an academic studying great depressions. I can tell you from history that if we don't act in a big way, you can expect another great depression, and this time it is going to be far, far worse."[2] That line sent a chill down a lot of spines in 2008.

But consider what Howard E. Kershner wrote about the horrid outlook for Germany after World War II:

> After the war the Russian Communists dismantled many industrial plants in Germany and hauled away a great deal of the movable wealth not only from East Germany, but in a lesser degree from West Germany as well. This unfortunate country had been more nearly destroyed than any other in Europe. She had suffered the loss of many millions of her strongest young men and had seen a great part of her homes, factories and business buildings destroyed. City after city had reduced to a mere skeleton and people were living in caves, cellars, quonset huts and three or four families crowded into a dwelling intended for one.[3]

Japan faced similar challenges in the aftermath of the same war. Human capital is the single most important ingredient for economic growth—nothing else comes close—and Japan had lost at least a generation of its best and brightest human capital. Atomic bombs had reduced two of its major cities to rubble. Yet within a few years of the war's end, Japan was booming again. And "in a few short years," wrote Kershner, "Germany became the most prosperous country in Europe, if not in the world."[4] Whatever economic displacement the United States might have faced at the end of 2008 was nothing compared with the total economic devastation that Germany and Japan faced at the end of 1945, yet those two countries returned to prosperity fairly quickly. Not only that, the banks that Bernanke deemed essential to America's economic health accounted for only 20 percent of financial lending in 2008.[5] Indeed, most lending occurs outside of the banking system, from company to company, and from company to customer.

Bernanke's assessment of the urgency of saving those errant banks was wildly exaggerated. The actions taken by Bernanke, President Bush, Treasury Secretary Paulson, and Congress did not just weaken a banking system they were trying to save. They created a crisis in the process that was not at all financial and had everything to do with government error.

Likewise, anyone who says he predicted the "financial crisis" deserves to be met with skepticism. In fact, no one did any such thing. As early as mid-2006, and many times after that, I wrote about the rush into housing in various cities, deploring it as a negative economic signal. In a column published on June 12, 2006, I noted that the housing boom of the Bush era made the economic climate of his presidency similar to that of Jimmy Carter's.[6] And in October 2007 I wrote:

> Lastly, it should be remembered that housing's greatest decade as an asset class occurred during the inflationary, malaise-ridden 1970s. With the dollar in free fall, housing served as a classic hedge for unsophisticated investors eager to shield their wealth amidst the dollar's fall. That real estate became the asset of choice of the new millennium wasn't so much a signal of a flush economy, but more realistically was the result of renewed dollar weakness that once again made Americans very risk averse.[7]

Did I foresee a "financial crisis"? Not by a long shot. All I predicted was basic economics.

The hedge fund manager John Paulson raised a $147 million fund to buy insurance on mortgages and mortgage securities that he felt would eventually go bust. Paulson wound up making billions off his trades, but did he predict the financial crisis? No. Mortgages, home construction, and housing purchases represent consumption. Paulson simply predicted an economically healthy market correction. Mass consumption of housing usually signals a capital deficit for businesses eager to attain financing to fuel their growth. Paulson's riches, therefore, were not the *cause* of a crisis but provided a valuable signal to the markets that further consumption of housing and investment in mortgage-backed securities was a bad idea.

What about those people who kept saying that housing was headed for a collapse in the years leading up 2007 and 2008? Did they predict a crisis? No, they did not. For a falling market for consumption goods to cause that kind of crisis, we'd need to rewrite basic economics.

To paraphrase Joseph Schumpeter, there are no entrepreneurs without capital, so any correction of manic consumption could hardly have created a crisis. And contrary to most of the media narrative to this day, by 2007 and 2008, housing prices had not corrected all that much. As Michael Lewis noted in *The Big Short*, for the mortgage skeptics eventually to profit, "[h]ome prices didn't even need to fall. They merely needed to stop rising at the unprecedented rates they had the previous few years for vast numbers of Americans to default on their home loans."[8]

If a correction in the mortgage and housing markets didn't cause a financial crisis, what did? First, I want to repeat that there was nothing "financial" about the crisis. To have predicted the "financial" crisis, you would have had to predict the failure of Bear Stearns or some other financial institution. Having done so, you would have had to foresee a bailout of Bear or a similar institution. After that, you would have had to predict that, the markets having priced in bailouts for everyone, a panic would ensue when an even larger financial institution (Lehman Brothers, as it turned out) was allowed to collapse. Lehman caused the markets to convulse only insofar as the markets were surprised that it was allowed to go bankrupt. Investors panic when they can't tell what's going on. Lehman was a crisis only for investors lacking a clear understanding of the hapless Bush administration's policies regarding the failure of financial institutions.

Next, you would have had to sense months ahead of time that the Bush administration would not only blink on bailouts that were wholly unnecessary, but that it would make matters worse by banning short sellers too. And then having predicted a series of anticapitalist errors, you would have had to understand the unhappy consequences for the global economy of this misbegotten intervention and that calls for massive re-regulation of the economy would quickly rise to the top of governmental priority lists, scaring markets even further. Finally, you would have to have known that those same governments would do everything possible to blunt the market corrections that would have quickly revived the global economy. *No one* predicted the various government mistakes in response to the markets' attempts to correct themselves, so no one can be said to have predicted the "financial crisis."

Nouriel Roubini is famous for supposedly having foreseen the carnage. He did not predict the mistaken government intervention that convulsed the markets, but he was correct in drawing a connection between housing health and the eventual "crisis." The problem with Roubini is that he turned Adam Smith and John Stuart Mill upside down. According to Roubini, an eventual housing moderation or collapse would on its own have been the undoing of the financial system and the economy.

No, it would not have been. The economy's problem in the early 2000s was the capital deficit that was starving productive new ventures as the housing market, goosed by Bush's devalued dollar, boomed. The problem was global because the devaluation of the U.S. dollar is often a worldwide event.

Roubini predicted a crash of the housing market. But if he had truly understood the situation, he would have seen how the economy would benefit from such a correction, provided that the businesses and financial institutions most exposed to that sector were allowed to fail. Instead, Roubini called for a stimulus package triple the size of the one President Obama and Congress foisted on the economy. He also said that U.S. banks should be nationalized.[9] Roubini's reputation as a prophet of doom was made by the government intrusion that he advocated. And if we had followed his advice in the wake of the crisis, it would have been worse.

Perhaps someone somewhere predicted the government errors that turned a healthy correction into a horror show, but I have never seen any evidence of it. Count on it—if someone self-assuredly contends that he predicted the carnage of the "financial crisis," *he's lying*.

Capitalism cannot cause a financial crisis because capitalism is about markets constantly correcting errors. It is government intervention that can and often does cause crises, 2008 being a notable example. Writing about countries in dire straits, John Stuart Mill observed with warranted optimism,

> The possibility of a rapid repair of their disasters, mainly depends on whether the country has been depopulated. If its effective population have not been extirpated at the time, and are not starved afterwards; then, with the same skill and knowledge which they had before, with their land and its permanent improvements undestroyed, and the more durable buildings probably unimpaired, or only partially injured, they have nearly all the requisites for their former amount of production.[10]

Capitalist societies can rebound from anything. In particular, they can bounce back from bank failures that do not exterminate human capital or destroy their infrastructure. An interfering government is the only barrier to any society's revival, and that is why the global economy cratered amid all the government intervention in 2008. As Mill put it,

> The only insecurity which is altogether paralyzing to the active energies of producers, is that arising from the government, or from persons invested with its authority. Against all other depredators there is a hope of defending one's self.[11]

Government is the only impediment to astonishing prosperity in the United States and everywhere else. Without government's tax, regulatory, trade, and monetary barriers to man's natural desire to produce, the only limit we face is the limit of our imagination. Indeed, government *is* the crisis when it comes to slow growth. Any guarantee of future prosperity requires taming not commerce but government.

CHAPTER TWENTY-THREE

Conclusion: "Do-Nothing" Politicians Deserve a Special Place in Heaven

I'm telling you that the cure is the disease. The main source of illness in this world is the doctor's own illness: his compulsion to try to cure and his fraudulent belief that he can. It ain't easy to do nothing, now that society is telling everyone that the body is fundamentally flawed and about to self-destruct.
—The Fat Man, *House of God*

If you see ten troubles coming down the road, you can be sure that nine will run into the ditch before they reach you.
—Calvin Coolidge

From 1920 to 1921, the U.S. economy endured a recession far more brutal than the one that set in from 1929 to 1930.[1] There is a reason that history books do not spend much time on the 1920–1921 recession, however—it was very short.

It was so brief because the federal government got out of the way. Good doctors often allow the body to heal itself, and smart politicians allowed the economy to do the same. Today's conventional wisdom is that governments must spend with abandon during times of economic hardship, but in 1920–1921 federal spending was slashed. While the government had consumed $6.4 billion of precious capital in 1920, by 1923 the government's burden on the economy had been reduced to just under $3.3 billion.[2] This was textbook growth economics. Governments have no resources, so during times of weakness, it is essential for them to reduce what they consume to free up always limited capital for the private sector.

Today's conventional wisdom also says to devalue the currency during trying economic times, but "the gold standard was unshaken" in the early 1920s, notes Benjamin Anderson in his essential book, *Economics and the Public Welfare.*[3] Since investors are buying future dollar income streams when they commit capital, devaluing money during downturns runs off investors when you need them most.

Recessions are the cure for what's wrong with an economy. They cleanse it of the bad businesses, bad investments, and labor mismatches that got it in trouble in the first place. When the 1920–1921 recession hit, a wise political class sat back and did nothing other than lower taxes slightly and slash spending. Unemployment dropped from 11.2 percent in 1921 to 1.7 percent by 1923, and the Roaring '20s took off.

In 1929 and 1930, the U.S. economy dipped again. Eager to shield Americans from the near-term pain of recession, Presidents Herbert Hoover and Franklin D. Roosevelt decided to intervene. Their interventions gave us the sixteen-year debacle known as the Great Depression. That disaster was not a creature of capitalism but the result of running away from it. Indeed, Hoover and Roosevelt violated the principles of growth in all four areas of economic policy—taxes, trade, regulation, and money.

First, they told entrepreneurs and investors—the people most essential for an economic recovery—that there was no point in taking risks because the government would confiscate most of the rewards. Hoover raised the top income tax rate from 25 percent to 62 percent, and then Roosevelt took it all the way up to 83 percent.[4]

Perhaps the most disastrous component of Roosevelt's Depression-extending program was the Undistributed Profits Tax of 1936, which imposed a tax of up to 74 percent on earnings that businesses saved, whether for plant expansion, research on new products, or a rainy day.[5] You'll recall that Henry Ford, who incorporated the Ford Motor Company in 1903, perfected his manufacturing process through the constant reinvestment of profits. If the Undistributed Profits Tax had been in place then, the profits that he plowed back into his revolutionary enterprise would have been confiscated. There might have been no mass-produced Model T and a very different American auto industry.

Hoover and Roosevelt also increased government spending, which is a tax like any other. Rather than leaving credit and capital in the private sector, where they could fund real growth, government devoured them itself. Federal spending doubled on Hoover's watch, and Roosevelt took it from there, saddling the economy with a seven-billion-dollar budget deficit in 1934.

Second, they imposed job-killing regulations. Hoover called on businesses not to reduce wages despite market signals telling them to do just that. If Walmart is struggling to sell televisions, it needs to reduce its prices to attract buyers. But Hoover kept the price of labor at an artificially high rate, so businesses were unable to add workers.

Roosevelt in turn passed the Fair Labor Standards Act, which introduced a minimum wage, maximum work week, and guaranteed overtime, imposing a cost of labor that should be set by markets and pricing workers out of the labor force altogether. Private employment was hurt even more by Roosevelt's various make-work programs, in which the federal government paid artificially high wages for work that often had no discernible economic value. Every dollar the government pays an individual is an extra dollar businesses must pay to lure him into private-sector work. With government forcing wages above what the market would bear, unemployment was abnormally high throughout the 1930s.

Third, Hoover signed the Smoot-Hawley Tariff, raising taxes on imports and provoking other countries to raise taxes on U.S. exports. "I almost went down on my knees to beg Herbert Hoover to veto the asinine Smoot-Hawley tariff," recalled Thomas W. Lamont, the head of J. P. Morgan. Graeme Howard, the European head of General Motors, sent a telegram to Washington warning that Smoot-Hawley would lead to the "MOST SEVERE DEPRESSION EVER EXPERIENCED."[6] The tariff shrank the foreign markets of the best U.S. companies while subsidizing America's weakest producers. While free trade allows people to exploit their comparative advantage, taxes on trade encourage the opposite.

Fourth, Roosevelt set about devaluing the dollar. It bought one-twentieth of an ounce of gold when he reached the White House, but he soon devalued it to one-thirty-fifth of an ounce. Investors, who seek future dollar income streams when they commit their capital to businesses, were promised that the reward for their job-creating investments would be devalued dollars.

It is instructive to compare the economic policies of the Depression era with those of today. The parallels are striking. The doldrums in which our economy has been stuck since the panic of 2008 are the result of government intervention, not capitalism itself. Presidents George W. Bush and Barack Obama have replayed the Hoover-Roosevelt follies.

On September 25, 2008, Bush told the nation:

> I'm a strong believer in free enterprise, so my natural instinct is to oppose government intervention. I believe companies that make bad decisions should be allowed to go out of business. Under normal circumstances, I would have followed this course. But these are not normal circumstances. The market is not functioning properly. There has been a widespread loss of confidence, and major sectors of America's financial system are at risk of shutting down.[7]

There is something odd here. Markets are not a living, breathing organism any more than an economy is. Markets are simply people with differing views on the price of just about everything. For that reason, markets cannot be said to function properly or improperly; they just *function*. Markets are a constantly changing source of information.

In 2008, the individuals who constitute the markets concluded that consumption of housing was overdone. The market result was failure of financial institutions too exposed to the housing market, along with defaults by individual consumers who had bought more house than they could afford. The market was correcting investments that were bad for the economy and were themselves the results of government error. The markets that Bush claimed were "not functioning properly" were in fact correcting Bush's mistakes.

President Bush, Fed Chairman Bernanke, Treasury Secretary Paulson, and Congress led the charge of government intervention, blocking the natural way in which markets correct for errors. In doing so, they created a crisis.

Before plunging into his destructive program of intervention, Bush would have been smart to consult the thinking of the early-twentieth-century social critic Albert Jay Nock, who cautioned,

"Any contravention of natural law, any tampering with the natural order of things, must have its consequences, and the only recourse for escaping them is such as entails worse consequences."[8] The short-term consequence of Bush's tampering with the markets' natural order was a financial crisis that was by definition a creation of the political class. The long-term consequence was an anemic recovery.

Learning nothing from Bush's errors, Barack Obama promptly revealed that his own misunderstanding of how economies grow rivaled that of Bush. In his first State of the Union address he said:

> I can assure you that the cost of inaction will be far greater, for it could result in an economy that sputters along not for months or years, but perhaps a decade. That would be worse for our deficit, worse for business, worse for you, and worse for the next generation. And I refuse to let that happen.[9]

Full of the hubris all too common in politicians, Obama continued the intervention in an economy which should have been allowed to correct itself. Although Obama signed an extension of the 2003 Bush tax cuts in 2010, he initially passed a suffocating $787 billion federal spending bill, an economic chokehold on a nation that was trying to recover from its errors. And at the end of 2012, Obama finally got his tax hikes, increasing the penalties on work and investment.

Obama introduced a regulatory reign of terror in the energy, finance, and healthcare industries. His preposterously named Affordable Care Act, requiring businesses with fifty employees or more to offer expensive health insurance plans that have nothing to do with insurance, is dying of its myriad contradictions, but it has substantially raised the cost of hiring workers.

The Bush and Obama administrations both made our trading partner China an enemy even though the growth of its economy has done wonders for every American. Each day the Chinese get up to go to work, Americans get a raise. Nevertheless, the Obama administration levied a tariff on Chinese tires, while the Bush administration imposed tariffs on steel, softwood lumber, and shrimp from any country. The only winners were businesses with close Washington ties. The losers were the American people, who saw their paychecks diminished by government edict.

And then there is the dollar. It bought 1/266 of an ounce of gold when Bush entered office. By the time he departed, the greenback had shrunk to 1/880 of an ounce. Under Obama, the dollar's slide continued to an all-time low of 1/1900 of an ounce. The message to investors: Intrepid capital commitments intended to create the wealth of the future will endure erosion by dollar devaluation.

The economy has been weak for much of the last thirteen years, and the weakness is reflected in stock indices that basically sit where they did in 2000, when the dollar was much stronger. The sources of the weakness are obvious for all to see: taxes on work and investment are up, the tax that is government spending has reached new records, regulation has run wild, trade has been choked, and the dollar has been in free-fall.

All of which brings us to Ben Bernanke, the mercifully departed former Fed chairman who drove the short rate for credit to zero, the last thing a central banker should have done. Interest rates are a price like any other, and in free markets, interest rates are simply the way that markets match the needs of savers and borrowers. But just as apartments in Manhattan would be scarce if Mayor Bill de Blasio capped rents at one hundred dollars per month, credit is scarce for all but the biggest governments and businesses because

Bernanke told savers that they would get nothing in return for their savings.

Bernanke's policy of buying up Treasuries and mortgage bonds—"quantitative easing"—simply propped up government consumption and delayed a necessary housing correction. Wouldn't life be simple if the Fed's purchases of Treasuries and mortgages could hatch the Googles and Apples of the future? Back in the real world, the way to foster the companies of the future is to get the four basics right, with the Fed doing as little as possible.

But Bernanke's gravest economic sin was thinking that meddling with the economy could dull the pain of recession or avoid another one. He ignored the necessity of recessions for economic recovery. By blocking the natural direction of the economy, Bernanke prevented a powerful rebound. Those who should know better have called Bernanke the leading scholar of the Great Depression, yet his every action at the Fed revealed an economist who learned all the wrong lessons from that disaster.

Writing in the midst of the Great Depression, Nock observed, "The present paralysis of production, for example, is due solely to State intervention, and uncertainty concerning further intervention."[10] That diagnosis is as accurate for the U.S. economy since 2008 as it was for the economy of the 1930s, and that's why we can be optimistic about our economic future.

Americans have not run out of ideas, work ethic, or entrepreneurial spirit. Our problem is the government, which continues to violate the four basic economic truths that I have discussed in this book. The reasons for the economy's struggles are obvious, and that is why people should be giddy about the future.

It seems that once a generation Americans become careless in their voting. In the 1930s, we violated the basics of growth, only to rediscover them with the free trade and sound money that prevailed after World War II. In the 1970s the economy suffered from tax and monetary blunders. But the economic agonies of the Nixon, Ford, and Carter presidencies awakened the electorate, who turned to Ronald Reagan and eventually extended his economic policies with Bill Clinton.

Two decades of prosperity made Americans complacent. The result was Presidents Bush and Obama and their economic wreckage. Fortunately, Americans have woken up again. They are increasingly skeptical of government, and there is a good chance that such unhappiness will influence the outcome of the 2016 presidential election.

Until then, there is reason for hope. In February 2014, Facebook purchased a fifty-five-employee company called WhatsApp for nineteen billion dollars. However that acquisition works out, it is a reminder of Americans' growing ability to create wealth in an interconnected global economy. The future wealth creation to which the WhatsApp purchase points will make today's market look puny. And WhatsApp is a sign that Americans have not forgotten how to innovate.

The economy is set to grow in the years ahead because President Obama's presidency ended for all practical purposes in 2012. Crippled by the spreading failure of Obamacare, he has lost the power to do more harm. He will leave office with the economy growing precisely because he will have passed no further substantial legislation before his departure.

Obama's presidency, and Bush's before it, has done wonders for the freedom movement. Americans are far more skeptical about government in 2014 than they were in 2000. This should lead to the election of a much less interventionist president in 2016, and boom times thereafter. What we don't know is whether Americans will again forget why economies grow once this next economic boom takes place.

In the hope that Americans won't forget, I have tried to make the basic ingredients for economic growth understandable. Our economy is ailing today because the state has grown too large and intrusive. But economics is easy, and its lessons are all around us. Once we citizens force the political class to get the basics right, everyone will soon see that *economic growth* is easy too.

ACKNOWLEDGMENTS

A short book could be written naming all the people who helped me over the years and whose encouragement, support, and sharing of knowledge led to this. It would be more than presumptuous to say that I stand on the shoulders of giants, but it would be true to say many giants have made what I do possible. In advance, all errors within *Popular Economics* are surely mine. So here goes.

Thank you to Alan Reynolds, a senior fellow at the Cato Institute, not just for reading my first attempt at a public op-ed in 2003 but also for introducing me to *National Review*'s Kathryn Jean Lopez. Your introduction got me started, after which *National*

Review's Chris McEvoy and *TechCentralStation*'s Nick Schulz generously gave me my first chances to write for an audience beyond a small circle of friends.

Thank you to the *Wall Street Journal*'s editorial page for sparking my interest in economic policy back in the late 1980s. Thomas Sowell's brilliant 1989 collection of op-eds, *Compassion Versus Guilt*, was the first book I ever purchased on economics, and his essay within *Compassion*, "India Versus Hong Kong," remains the standard when it comes to clear explanations about the wonders of economic freedom.

Big thanks to CNBC's Larry Kudlow, whom I first started watching back in the late 1980s on the *McLaughlin Group* and who gave me my first shot at television. Larry taught me the four basics of economic growth, which he had learned from the great Arthur Laffer. Art, if it's possible, I've actually learned more from you about monetary policy than tax policy. Thank you for all your encouragement all these years.

Art wrote *The Financial Analyst's Guide to Monetary Policy* decades ago with Chuck Kadlec and Victor Canto, and this essential book is rarely far from me. It was from Chuck, who taught me so much about everything economic, that I learned the essential truth, "Bull markets don't die of old age; they succumb to policy failure." Chuck, we all miss you and hope you hurry back.

George Gilder, widely known and revered for his brilliance, was the writer most often quoted by Ronald Reagan. I too have quoted George Gilder more than anyone else, but that doesn't begin to describe his influence on this book. George's essential insight that economic growth is a function of information, and more specifically, the "leap," is at the heart of *Popular Economics*. I also owe a substantial debt to George's frequent collaborator, Bret Swanson. Bret, without your thinking the chapters on inflation wouldn't be what they hopefully are.

It is no exaggeration to say that Nathan Lewis knows more about money and correct monetary policy than any person alive. His books and op-eds on monetary policy have had an enormous influence on me, and without him, the chapters on money would be far less informative. Professor Richard Salsman of Duke University—one of the few who can talk money on Nathan's level—years ago introduced me to the clear monetary thinking of the brilliant and generous Judy Shelton. Marc Miles likewise requires mention for having exposed the folly of the quantity theory of money in his essential book, *Beyond Monetarism*.

John Allison turned BB&T into a global banking behemoth before taking over as president of the Cato Institute. Allison's book, *The Financial Crisis and the Free Market Cure*, was very useful as I set out to write my chapters on regulation. Thank you to Allison for reminding readers not just why regulations are a problem, but of greater importance, why they quite simply cannot work.

David Malpass of Encima Global, who seems to have been teaching everyone about the economics of growth for years and years, has always been patient in teaching me. Amity Shlaes, an early contributor to RealClearMarkets, was always encouraging when very few were. Her wonderful book *The Forgotten Man* informs many parts of mine. The Heritage Foundation's Steve Moore has brought the notion of tax simplification to life for many. His help and influence are apparent in my chapters on taxes.

RealClearPolitics founders John McIntyre and Tom Bevan require prominent mention. They took a Gilderian "leap" into the internet back in the early 2000s when many short-term thinkers had left it for dead. Their entrepreneurialism made RealClearMarkets possible, and better yet, they made it possible for me and many others to have a voice in what some like to call the "new media." Thank you to David DesRosiers for the introduction.

Then there are the great thinkers who left us too soon. Simply put, I wouldn't have much to say without the amazing insights of Warren Brookes and Jude Wanniski, whose fingerprints are all over this book. And while I was never lucky enough actually to meet Robert Bartley, he was kind enough to correspond with me by email on occasion. His masterwork, *The Seven Fat Years*, is one of the best books on economics ever written, and *Popular Economics* is indebted to his insight and style.

There are also the giants of centuries past—Adam Smith, John Stuart Mill, Frédéric Bastiat, and Jean-Baptiste Say—who laid the foundations for the clear economic thinking that has rendered the free parts of the world wildly prosperous.

Steven Hayward is perhaps best known for his brilliant two-volume classic, *The Age of Reagan*. Though known as a work of history, it's arguably even better for its economics. Without Hayward's books, *Popular Economics* would be considerably blander.

The president of H. C. Wainwright Economics, David Ranson, hired me away from Wall Street back in 2002. David can articulate economic policy as few can, and for years I have benefitted from his insight through reports and monthly HCWE conference calls. Rafe Resendes of Applied Finance Group invited me to speak at an AFG conference in 2007, when no one was asking me to give speeches. Rafe, thank you and the whole AFG/Toreador Research & Trading team for believing in me when few did.

Thanks to Harry Binswanger for his forceful writing style that is uncompromising in its proper elevation of the productive, and to Jerry Bowyer for patiently reminding me that the most important form of protest is survival. Thanks to Richard Miniter's prolific writing for the inspiration it provided and to Diana Furchtgott-Roth for telling me how to get the book started.

I've been sharing ideas on economic policy with Chuck Smithers, Cedric Muhammad, Steve Shipman, Reuven Brenner, Louis Woodhill and Paul Hoffmeister more than with anyone else these last ten years, and their thinking informs the chapters on money and taxes. Louis and Paul, I can't wait for your books on monetary policy, and, Reuven, your many books were instrumental to me as I wrote mine. Your frequent discussion of the "vital few" constantly informs how I think and write.

John Batchelor, Ralph Bristol, Bill Cunningham, and Crane Durham have been hosting me on their radio shows for years. Thanks to all of you for finding me, and thank you for your many excellent questions that were hopefully answered in this book.

Russell Redenbaugh could and should write his own book, but until then, I'm grateful for his energetic promotion of economic thinking from the Classical school. If that thinking were implemented now, we would quickly enjoy a major economic rebound. Russell and his partner at Kairos Capital Advisors, James Juliano, not only believe in Classical thinking, but they've taken the extra—and courageous—step of very successfully applying it to the allocation of capital.

I know Russell thanks to Rich Karlgaard at *Forbes*. Rich has taught me so much for so long about economic policy, but more than that, he's been a great friend who welcomed me into the commentariat back when few would give me the time of day. So did his fellow publisher at *Forbes*, Tim Ferguson. Tim has always been willing to meet with me during my frequent visits to New York, and he introduced me to David Asman at Fox News. Big thanks to David, someone fortunate enough in his great career to have worked for both

Robert Bartley and Warren Brookes, as well as to the whole *Forbes on Fox* team: Elizabeth MacDonald, John Huber, Tia Tiryaki, Allegra Zagami, Sabrina Schaeffer, Mike Ozanian, Bruce Japsen, Carrie Sheffield, and my favorite lefty in the world, Rick Ungar. Rick, I'll make a libertarian of you yet! And to the late producer of *Forbes on Fox*, Annie Goodman, you left us way too soon. Thank you for giving me a chance.

Jeff Beckel and Greg Parr, friends since college, patiently unearthed the facts and statistics I desperately needed when I started writing op-eds. Thanks, Jeff and Greg, for giving my rants empirical backing. Big thanks as well to the rest of my college-era crew, which includes John Cragar, Chase Belew, Jim Doran, Mike Ferry, Robert Elms, Mark Griffin, Guy Heartfield, Steve Leininger ("if it's in the newspaper, it's priced") and Nico Vilgiate. You've all suffered my stridency for decades.

Cari Erickson, Neal and Susan Erickson, and Scott and Staci Richardson have been amazing friends and a constant source of encouragement from up in Minneapolis, and in Cari's case, all over the world. To say that you've all been intensely generous to me is the definition of understatement. And to Ian and Siobhan Gilday in London, thank you for relaying to me so much financial knowledge over the years, and for giving me a place to stay during frequent visits. Millie Gilday, thank you for always agreeing with me!

On all too many nights, Patrick Simpson-Nairn and his wife, Stephanie, have had to listen to me talk monetary policy in the Hamptons and many other exciting locales. Patrick's knowledge of Nike was valuable as I wrote *Popular Economics*. Thank you, and Peter Shea too, for not reaching for the hemlock during all those policy conversations.

Patrick Chauvin and Myles King have had to endure the same in Washington, D.C., and at the Greenbrier. Thank you for being such generous hosts to Kendall and me. Patrick's expertise in the field of housing has informed my own views. Myles, we all can't wait to visit the King's Road! Major thanks to Todd Dorfman and Anneli Werner not just for all the encouragement, but for all the advice on marketing and style; advice that led to the crucial creation of my website.

Lesley Albanese deserves special mention for being such a great work colleague, an even better friend, and for having convinced Ed Crane, the beloved founder of the Cato Institute, to hire me in 2003. To say that Ed has made this book possible gives this champion of liberty way too little credit. Ed, I internalized far more of what you explained to me about policy over the years than you'll ever imagine, and I'd like to think the chapters on government spending and the nature of taxation have your common sense all over them.

But perhaps the biggest gift Ed has given to me is allowing me get to know the many great supporters of Cato, whose knowledge substantially improved *Popular Economics*. The list is long, but it includes Rob Arnott, Cliff Asness, Scott and Vanessa Barbee, John Brynjolfsson, John Dalsheim, William Dunn, Jeff and Jill Erber, Jim Fitzgerald, Roger and Elizabeth Hagans, Nathan and Anita Hanks, Ken and Eileen Leech, Scott Grannis, Dick Kessler, Dean Zarras, Daniel Shuchman, Herb Stiles, David and Laura Thayer, Joel Trammell, Ruth Westphal, Jay and Sally Lapeyre, and Peter Goettler.

In particular, long-time Cato-ites Bob and Ruth Reingold have been amazingly kind to me, and their grandson Louis and granddaughter Juliette taught me how to ski Aspen's double-blacks. Louis also patiently taught me the realities of the business world during freezing lift rides. Bob, your explanation of the prosperity that results from assets' being allowed to reach their proper market level *no matter the level* informs much of what I wrote about a 2008 crisis that had nothing to do with finance. Thank you also for introducing me to Parkinson's Law, but more than anything, thank you for teaching me about life.

Richard and Sue Ann Masson have been incredibly kind and generous to Kendall and me for years. Richard, it was an email exchange about Jude Wanniski back in 2005 that seemingly got me in the door for our first meeting. You were lucky enough to have known him, and I hope my book lives up to all that he taught us.

Hall and Letty McAdams, it's no stretch to say that you watched me grow up. Without a hint of hyperbole, my life would be very different, and much poorer, without a certain visit to Little Rock in 2003. The two of you extolled my virtues to Kendall back when she was more than a bit skeptical, and then just about everything I presume to know about banking I owe to many late-night conversations that included too few cigarettes and way too many drinks. I hope the book will reveal that amid all the revelry, I took good notes.

Cato's Tim Reuter was instrumental in making *Popular Economics* happen. He was an essential sounding board, occasional researcher, and a nice editor too. Tim, I can't wait to read your many books. Tom Spence of Regnery took my rough draft and made it eminently more readable. Thanks to Tom, even those who disagree with me might think I'm smart.

My wife, Kendall, naturally rates numerous mentions, including for bringing me into her wonderful family. Her parents, Scott and Susan Brodarick, have been generous and encouraging in-laws. I'm so lucky to have them, as well as my new brother-in-law, Taylor, and his lovely, soon-to-be wife, Beth. Taylor will forget more than I'll ever know in one sitting of Trivial Pursuit.

And then there's my own family. A day doesn't go by when I don't remind myself of how lucky I was to be raised by my parents, Peter and Nancy. Their goodness and generosity to me had and has no limits, and their encouragement of my decision to pursue a different career in writing meant everything. I can't believe my good fortune to have them as my parents, and if that weren't enough, I've also got a wonderful sister in Kim. She forgets this, but it was Kim who taught me the politics of housing when we were in grade school, and as I hope the chapters on housing will reveal, her wise words stuck with me. Thank you, Kim, for always being so supportive of me despite my frequently obnoxious ways. Steve Streich, thanks for being the brother I never had. I think you'll mostly agree with what I have to say.

An extra-special mention is reserved for Steve Forbes. Certain people elevate us in life, and outside of my family no person has had a bigger impact on me. Steve could so easily have been aloof toward me given my worship of him, but instead he welcomed me into Forbes, and most of all, for years he's been unwavering in his encouragement of my writing. Kendall constantly reminds me to try to be like Steve, because Steve is not just an amazing thinker whose thoughts have so thoroughly informed this book, but because he's easily the kindest and most gracious person either one of us has ever met. I'll never be able to pay him back for all the great things he's done for me, but it won't be for lack of trying. And then to his daughter Catherine, thank you for doing all that you do to constantly elevate the Forbes brand. Kendall and I are so lucky to be able to call you a great friend.

Last, but surely not least, thank you to my wife, Kendall. Without you I'm surely nothing. You're easily the best thing that's ever happened to me, and I can say with certainty that without you there is no book. I surely took a step up in April of 2014, and I'll spend the rest of my days trying to vindicate your decision to marry me.

NOTES

Introduction

1. Bret Swanson, “Tyler Cowen’s Techno Slump,” *Forbes*, January 27, 2011.

Chapter One: Taxes Are Nothing More Than a Price Placed on Work

1. Keith Richards, *Life* (New York: Little, Brown and Company, 2010), 289.
2. Ibid.
3. Ibid., 102.
4. Ibid., 103.
5. Richard Verrier, “Making film deals with tax credits,” *Los Angeles Times*, December 26, 2013.
6. Ibid.
7. Rob Lowe, *Stories I Only Tell My Friends* (New York: Henry Holt, 2011), 131.
8. Verrier, “Making film deals with tax credits.”

9. Ibid.
10. Andy Kessler, "The Transportation Trustbuster," *Wall Street Journal*, January 25, 2013.
11. Alexis Tsotsis, "Uber Gets $32M From Menlo Ventures, Jeff Bezos, And Goldman Sachs," *Tech Crunch*, December 7, 2011, http://techcrunch.com/2011/12/07/uber-announces-32-million-in-funding/.
12. Source: *Forbes 400*, http://www.forbes.com/profile/jeff-bezos/.
13. Robert Bartley, *The Seven Fat Years* (New York: The Free Press, 1992), 142.
14. Enrico Moretti, *The New Geography of Jobs* (New York: Houghton Mifflin Harcourt, 2012), 60.

Chapter Two: When We Tax Corporations, We Rob Them of Their Future

1. Mary Bellis, "The Duryea Brothers—Automobile History," About.com Inventors, http://inventors.about.com/od/dstartinventors/a/DuryeaBrothers.htm.
2. Mark Spitznagel, *The Dao of Capital* (Hoboken, NJ: Wiley, 2013), 178.
3. Ibid., 180.
4. Tim Reuter and Brian Tan, "The Fall and Rise of Detroit? Cartels, Cronies, and Uber Cars," *Forbes,* June 5, 2013.
5. Spitznagel, 182.
6. Ibid., 181.
7. "Corporate Tax By Country," *Global Finance*, http://www.gfmag.com/component/content/article/119-economic-data/12526-corporate-tax-by-country.html#axzz2qsTDvRLv.
8. Spitznagel, 185.
9. Ibid., 185–86.
10. William Friedkin, *The Friedkin Connection* (New York: HarperCollins, 2013), 149.
11. Ibid., 151
12. George Gilder, *Wealth and Poverty* (Washington, DC: Regnery Publishing, 2012), 354.
13. Merrill Matthews, "About Those Tax Breaks for Big Oil...," *Wall Street Journal*, April 2, 2013.
14. The Tax Foundation, State Corporate Tax Rates from 2000–2013.
15. Matthews, "About Those Tax Breaks for Big Oil..."
16. Ludwig von Mises, *Human Action* (Atlanta, GA: Foundation for Economic Education, 1998), 649.

Chapter Three: Government Spending Did Not Create the Internet, and Has Never Created a Job

1. Allan Sloan, "A plea to learn about Bezos's personal politics," *Washington Post*, August 15, 2013.
2. Kara Swisher, "New Yorker: Bezos' Initial Google Investment Was $250K in 1998 Because 'I Just Fell in Love With Larry and Sergey,'" October 5, 2009, *All Things D*,

http://allthingsd.com/20091005/new-yorker-bezos-initial-google-investment-was-250000-in-1998-because-i-just-fell-in-love-with-larry-and-sergey/.

3. Ibid.
4. Julianne Pepitone and Stacy Cawley, "Facebook's first big investor, Peter Thiel, cashes out," CNNMoney, August 20, 2012, http://money.cnn.com/2012/08/20/technology/facebook-peter-thiel/.
5. Dawn Kawamoto, Ben Heskett, and Mike Ricciuti, "Microsoft to invest $150 million in Apple," CNET, August 6, 1997, http://news.cnet.com/2100-1001-202143.html.
6. http://www.waymarking.com/gallery/image.aspx?f=1&guid=25aaa5cd-3321-4841-8f38-8d20b12eb62f&gid=3.
7. C. J. Maloney, *Back to the Land* (Hoboken, NJ: John Wiley & Sons, 2011), 2.
8. Ibid., 181.
9. Dennis Cauchon, "Federal pay ahead of private industry," *USA Today*, March 8, 2010.
10. Tim Harford, "Adapt: Why Success Always Starts with Failure" (New York: Picador, 2012), 10.
11. Robert L. Bartley, *The Seven Fat Years* (New York: The Free Press, 1992), 142.
12. Joe Stephens and Carol D. Leonnig, "Solyndra tried to influence Energy Department, e-mails show," *Washington Post*, November 16, 2011.

Chapter Four: It's the Spending, Stupid: Budget Deficits Really Don't Matter

1. John Balassi and Josie Cox, "Apple wows market with record $17 billion bond deal," *Reuters*, April 30, 2013, http://www.reuters.com/article/2013/04/30/us-apple-debt-idUSBRE93T10B20130430.
2. John Letzing "Google makes its first debt offering," MarketWatch, May 16, 2011, http://www.marketwatch.com/story/google-makes-its-first-debt-offering-2011-05-16.
3. List of National Debt by Country, http://www.economicshelp.org/blog/774/economics/list-of-national-debt-by-country/.
4. Niall Ferguson, "The Shutdown Is a Sideshow. Debt Is the Threat," *Wall Street Journal*, October 4, 2013.
5. Mark Steyn, *After America* (Washington, DC: Regnery Publishing, 2012), 6.
6. Rich Cohen, "The Girls of Winter," *Vanity Fair*, February 2014.
7. J. Rentilly, "This Is Spinal Tap," *American Way*, March 1, 2014.
8. Erin Egan, "HOF Inductee Russell Maryland Has Plenty of Love for the U," *USA Today*, July 20, 2012.

Chapter Five: Capital Gains Are the Elusive Jackpot That Drive Innovation

1. *Forbes*.
2. Brent Shrotenboer, "The NFL's super plan to get even bigger," *USA Today*, January 31, 2014.

3. Jim Dent, *King of the Cowboys* (Avon, MA: Adams Publishing, 1995), 94.
4. Ibid., 94–95.
5. Ibid., 97.
6. Ibid., 104.
7. Ibid., 98.
8. Ibid., 110.
9. Ibid., 109.
10. Keith Richards, *Life* (Boston: Little, Brown and Company, 2010), 289.
11. Robert L. Bartley, *The Seven Fat Years* (New York: Free Press, 1992), 143.
12. Dent, 98.
13. Jackie MacMullan, "Robert Kraft steady at the helm," ESPNBoston.com, January 15, 2014, http://espn.go.com/boston/nfl/story/_/id/10295274/robert-kraft-navigated-new-england-patriots-20-years-highs-lows.
14. *Forbes*, http://www.forbes.com/nfl-valuations/.
15. MacMullan, "Robert Kraft steady at the helm."

Chapter Six: The Best Way to Spread the Wealth Around Is to Abolish the Estate Tax

1. Robert Barnes, "Obama Talks to Joe the Plumber—And About Him," *Washington Post*, October 22, 2008.
2. Michael Freeman, *ESPN: The Uncensored History* (Lanham, MD: Taylor Trade Publishing, 2000), 5.
3. Ibid., 5.
4. Ibid., 57.
5. Ibid., 7.
6. Ibid., 59.
7. Ibid., 62.
8. Famous Entrepreneurs, "J. Paul Getty," http://www.famous-entrepreneurs.com/j-paul-getty.
9. Freeman, 49.
10. "How Steinbrenner Saved His Heirs a $600 Million Tax Bill," *Wall Street Journal*, July 13, 2010.
11. Howard E. Kershner, *Dividing the Wealth: Are You Getting Your Share?* (Greenwich, CT: Devin-Adair, 1971), 31.
12. Warren T. Brookes, *The Economy in Mind* (New York: Universe Books, 1982), 69.

Chapter Seven: Wealth Inequality Is Beautiful

1. Al Neuharth, "Why Larry King still is 'The King' on air," *USA Today*, April 19, 2007
2. Ibid.
3. Elisabeth Dunn, "From the dole to Hollywood," *Daily Telegraph*, June 30, 2007.

4. Dominick Dunne, *The Way We Lived Then* (New York: Crown, 1999), 200, 201, 208.
5. Bernie Brillstein, Where Did I Go Right? (Beverly Hills, CA: Phoenix Books, 2008).
6. David Whitford, "Fire In His Belly," CNNMoney, May 12, 1997.
7. Reuven Brenner, *History: The Human Gamble*, (Chicago: University of Chicago Press, 1983), 4.
8. Steven F. Hayward, *The Age of Reagan—Part I* (New York: Prima Publishing, 2001), 7.
9. Ibid.
10. Steven F. Hayward, *The Age of Reagan—Part II*, (New York: Crown Forum, 2009), 31.
11. Bret Swanson, "How much would an iPhone have cost in 1991?", TechPolicyDaily.com, February 3, 2014, http://www.techpolicydaily.com/communications/much-iphone-cost-1991/.
12. Thomas Sowell, "The Inequality Bogeyman," *National Review Online*, January 28, 2014, http://www.nationalreview.com/article/369586/inequality-bogeyman-thomas-sowell.
13. Richard Salsman, "Why Do Takers Like Obama And Gingrich Attack Makers Like Romney?," Forbes.com, December 15, 2011, http://www.forbes.com/sites/richardsalsman/2011/12/15/why-do-takers-obama-and-gingrich-attack-creators-like-romney/.
14. Jason Kelly, *The New Tycoons* (Hoboken, NJ: Bloomberg Press, 2012).
15. Alan Reynolds, "The Truth about the 1 Percent," *National Review Online*, November 11, 2013, http://www.nationalreview.com/article/363701/truth-about-1-percent-alan-reynolds.
16. espn.com.
17. Ibid.
18. Lawrence Dorr, *Die Once Live Twice* (Napa, CA: Silverado Books, 2011), 46.

Chapter Eight: Savers Are an Economy's Most Valuable Benefactors

1. David Crook, "Dorothy Stratten Memorial Bankrupts Bogdanovich," *Los Angeles Times–Washington Post News Service*, December 26, 1985.
2. Peter Bogdanovich, "Living Under a Paper Moon," *Wall Street Journal*, January 9, 2014.
3. Crook, "Dorothy Stratten Memorial Bankrupts Bogdanovich."
4. Zach Kruse, "Analyzing How Vince Young Went From Rookie of the Year to Roster Scrub," *Los Angeles Times*, August 28, 2012.
5. Rob Demovsky, "Vince Young released by Packers," ESPN.com, September 1, 2013, http://espn.go.com/nfl/story/_/id/9618913/vince-young-released-green-bay-packers.
6. Ruth Manuel-Logan, "Vince Young Blows Through $26 Million," NewsOne, January 23, 2014, http://newsone.com/2847223/vince-young-bankrupt.
7. Rana Foroohar, "Janet Yellen: The 16 Trillion Dollar Woman," *Time Magazine*, January 20, 2014.

8. Eric Morath, "Wages Lurk as 2014 Growth Spoiler," *Wall Street Journal*, February 1–2, 2014.
9. John Stuart Mill, *Principles of Political Economy* (Amherst, NY: Prometheus Books, 2004), 387.
10. Tim Harford, *Adapt: Why Success Always Starts With Failure* (New York: Farrar, Straus and Giroux, 2011), 10.
11. Adam Smith, *The Wealth of Nations* (New York: Modern Library), 374.
12. Foroohar, "Janet Yellen: The 16 Trillion Dollar Woman."
13. Howard E. Kershner, *Dividing the Wealth: Are You Getting Your Share?* (Old Greenwich, CT: Devin-Adair Company, 1971), 32.

Chapter Nine: Job Creation Requires Perpetual Job Destruction

1. Sally Denton and Roger Morris, *The Money and the Power* (New York: Alfred A. Knopf, 2000), 145.
2. Denton and Morris, *The Money and the Power*, 8.
3. Ibid., 364.
4. John D. Gartner, *The Hypomanic Edge* (New York: Simon & Schuster, 2005).
5. Enrico Moretti, *The New Geography of Jobs* (Boston: Houghton Mifflin Harcourt Publishing, 2012), 23.
6. Alana Semuels, "Detroit's abandoned buildings draw tourists instead of developers," *Los Angeles Times*, December 25, 2013.
7. Walter Isaacson, *Steve Jobs* (New York: Simon & Schuster, 2011), 339.
8. Ibid., 325.
9. Ibid., 339.
10. Ibid., 339.
11. Ibid., 502.
12. Annie Lowrey, "Readers Without Borders," *Slate*, July 20, 2011, http://www.slate.com/articles/business/moneybox/2011/07/readers_without_borders.html.
13. Kyle Smith, "Jesse Jackson Jr. Vs. Apple's iPad," Forbes.com, April 20, 2011, http://www.forbes.com/sites/kylesmith/2011/04/20/jesse-jackson-jr-vs-apples-ipad/.
14. Moretti, *The New Geography of Jobs*, 49.
15. Ibid., 76.
16. Ibid., 61.
17. Ibid., 61.
18. Henry Hazlitt, *Economics In One Lesson* (New York: Three Rivers Press, 1979), 73.
19. Mike Florio, "Carter brings Buddy Ryan and his wife into Hall of Fame with him," NBCSports.com, August 3, 2013, http://m.nbcsports.com/content/carter-brings-buddy-ryan-and-his-wife-hall-fame-him.

20. Brian McCardle, "Cris Carter thanks Buddy Ryan and his wife, brings them into Hall of Fame with him," Philly.com, August 4, 2013, http://www.philly.com/philly/blogs/pattisonave/Cris-Carter-brings-Buddy-Ryan-and-his-wife-into-NFL-Hall-of-Fame-with-him.html.
21. Mark Maske, "Redskins release Chris Cooley," *Washington Post*, August 28, 2012.
22. Benjamin M. Anderson, *Economics and the Public Welfare* (Indianapolis: Liberty Press, 1979), 171.

Chapter Ten: Conclusion: Bulldoze the U.S. Tax Code

1. Post Staff Report, "Schumer takes aim at Facebook co-founder Eduardo Saverin as he proposes law to tax expats," *New York Post*, May 17, 2012.
2. Mark Leibovich, *This Town* (New York: Blue Rider Press, 2013), 171.

Chapter Eleven: Appalachian State Almost Never Beats Michigan, and Government Regulation Almost Never Works

1. Pat Forde, "Appalachian State earns role as conquering hero," ESPN.com, September 1, 2007, http://sports.espn.go.com/espn/columns/story?id=3001214.
2. Ibid.
3. Tommy Bowman, "Eight former Appalachian State players will begin the season on NFL rosters," *Winston-Salem Journal*, September 4, 2013, http://www.journalnow.com/sports/asu/app_trail/eight-former-appalachian-state-players-will-begin-the-season-on/article_b84a2e72-1599-11e3-bf0f-001a4bcf6878.html.
4. Forde, "Appalachian State earns role as conquering hero."
5. John Allison, *The Financial Crisis and the Free Market Cure* (New York: McGraw-Hill, 2013), 5.
6. Gregory Zuckerman, *The Greatest Trade Ever* (New York: Broadway Books, 2009), 45.
7. Ibid., 45.
8. Ibid., 233.
9. Allison, *The Financial Crisis and the Free Market Cure*, 31.
10. Peter J. Wallison, *Bad History, Worse Policy* (Washington, DC: AEI Press, 2013), 422.
11. Michael Lewis, *The Big Short* (London: Allen Lane, 2010), 106.
12. Zuckerman, *The Greatest Trade Ever*, 153.
13. Ibid., 153.
14. Lewis, *The Big Short*, 156.
15. Robert L. Bartley, *The Seven Fat Years* (New York: The Free Press, 1992), 265.
16. Thomas Adam, ed., *Germany and the Americas: Culture, Politics, and History* (Santa Barbara, CA: ABC CLIO, 2005), 250.

17. Michael E. Ross, "It Seemed Like a Good Idea at the Time," *U.S. News and World Report*, April 22, 2005.
18. Ibid.
19. Tony and Michelle Hamer, "The Edsel: A Legacy of Failure," www.About.com, Classic Cars, http://classiccars.about.com/od/classiccarsaz/a/Edsel.htm.
20. Warren T. Brookes, *The Economy In Mind* (New York: Universe Books, 1982), 153.
21. Ibid., 152.
22. T. A. Heppenheimer, *Turbulent Skies* (Hoboken, NJ: Wiley, 1995), 8.
23. Brookes, *The Economy In Mind*, 172.
24. James Ostrowski, "If Washington Hears About This…," *Wall Street Journal*, date unknown.
25. Brookes, *The Economy In Mind*, 172.
26. Clyde Wayne Crews Jr., "The 10,000 Commandments" (Washington, DC: Competitive Enterprise Institute, 2014).
27. Allison, *The Financial Crisis and the Free Market Cure*, 170–71.

Chapter Twelve: Antitrust Laws: The Neutering of the Near-Term Excellent

1. Wheeler Winston Dixon, *Death of the Moguls: The End of Classical Hollywood*, (New Brunswick, NJ: Rutgers University Press), 147.
2. David Leonhardt, "Why 'Avatar' Is Not the Top Grossing Film," *New York Times*, March 1, 2010.
3. Robert Evans, *The Kid Stays In the Picture* (New York: Hyperion, 1994), 216.
4. Ibid., 218
5. Ibid., 216.
6. Marc Gunther and Bill Carter, *Monday Night Mayhem* (Sag Harbor, NY: Beech Tree Books, 1988), 29.
7. Ibid., 179
8. Ibid., 227.
9. Ibid., 274.
10. Steven F. Hayward, *The Age of Reagan, Part II* (New York: Crown Forum, 2009), 343.
11. Brett Martin, *Difficult Men*, (New York: The Penguin Press, 2013), 65.
12. Ibid., 239.
13. David Snow, "Facebook and the Era of Access," PrivCap.com, May 18, 2012.
14. ProFootballReference.com: http://www.pro-football-reference.com/years/1983/draft.htm.
15. Nicholas Dawidoff, *Collision Low Crossers* (New York: Little, Brown and Company, 2013), 97.

16. Rick Newman, "15 Companies That Might Not Survive 2009," *U.S. News & World Report*, February 6, 2009; Stephanie Clifford, "Other Retailers Find Ex-Blockbuster Stores Just Right," *New York Times*, April 8, 2011.
17. Adam Thierer, "Do Regulators Read the Papers? The Blockbuster Antitrust Fiasco Revealed," The Technology Liberation Front, April 18, 2005, http://techliberation.com/2005/04/18/do-regulators-read-the-papers-the-blockbuster-antitrust-fiasco-revisited/.
18. Mike Spector & Peter Lattman, "Hollywood Video Closes Its Doors," *Wall Street Journal*, May 3, 2010.
19. Todd Leopold, "Your late fees are waived: Blockbuster closes," CNN, November 6, 2013, http://www.cnn.com/2013/11/06/tech/gaming-gadgets/blockbuster-video-stores-impact/.
20. Ibid.
21. Charisse Jones, "American gets $425 million for slots at DCA, LaGuardia," USA Today, March 10, 2014.
22. Tim Arango, "How the AOL–Time Warner Merger Went So Wrong," *New York Times*, January 10, 2010.
23. Adam Thierer, "A Brief History of Media Merger Hysteria: From AOL/Time Warner to Comcast/NBC," The Technology Liberation Front, December 2, 2009.
24. Tim Arango, "How the AOL-Time Warner Merger Went So Wrong," *New York Times*, January 10, 2010.
25. Adam Thierer, "A Brief History of Media Merger Hysteria: From AOL/Time Warner to Comcast/NBC," The Technology Liberation Front, December 2, 2009, http://techliberation.com/2009/12/02/a-brief-history-of-media-merger-hysteria-from-aol-time-warner-to-comcast-nbc/.
26. Tim Arango "How the AOL-Time Warner Merger Went So Wrong," *New York Times*, January 10, 2010.
27. Jeff Erber, "Ignore the Pundits, Comcast/Time Warner Merger Is a Good Thing," RealClearMarkets, February 19, 2014, http://www.realclearmarkets.com/articles/2014/02/19/ignore_the_pundits_time_warnercomcast_merger_is_a_good_thing_100910.html.
28. Henry Hazlitt, *Economics In One Lesson* (New York: Three Rivers Press, 1946), 105.
29. Dominick T. Armentano, *Antitrust: The Case for Repeal*, (Auburn, AL: Mises Institute, 1999), 40–41.
30. Ibid., 41.
31. John Tamny, "The Fatal Conceit of Anti-Trust Laws," *National Review Online*, March 13, 2006, http://www.nationalreview.com/articles/217033/fatal-conceit-anti-trust-laws/john-tamny.

32. Tim Harford, *Adapt: Why Success Always Starts With Failure* (New York: Farrar, Straus and Giroux, 2011), 8.

Chapter Thirteen: Conclusion: Don't Dismiss College Dropouts Delivering Alternative Weeklies

1. Andrew Ross Sorkin, "Prophecies Made In Davos Don't Always Come True," *New York Times*, January 21, 2013.
2. Rick Jervis, "How SXSW put itself on the map," *USA Today*, March 7–9, 2014.
3. Mike Moraitis, "Kurt Warner's Grocery-Store Checker to NFL MVP Story a Tale of Perseverance," *Bleacher Report*, May 21, 2012, http://bleacherreport.com/articles/1190204-kurt-warners-grocery-store-checker-to-nfl-mvp-story-a-tale-of-perseverance.
4. Parmy Olson, "Exclusive: The Rags-To-Riches Tale Of How Jan Koum Built WhatsApp Into Facebook's New $19 Billion Baby," Forbes.com, February 19, 2014, http://www.forbes.com/sites/parmyolson/2014/02/19/exclusive-inside-story-how-jan-koum-built-whatsapp-into-facebooks-new-19-billion-baby/.
5. L. Gordon Crovitz, "A WhatsApp Message for the Feds," *Wall Street Journal*, February 24, 2014.

Chapter Fourteen: "Trade Deficits" Are Our Rewards for Going to Work Each Day

1. Geoffrey Bocca, *The Moscow Scene* (New York: Stein and Day, 1976), 36.
2. Ibid., 37.
3. Ibid., 39.
4. Hedrick Smith, *The Russians* (New York: Ballantine, 1976), 83.
5. Ibid., 250–51.
6. Ibid., 696.
7. Ibid., 622.
8. Mary Anastasia O'Grady, "Costa Rica's Tough Unions Make It a Cafta Holdout," *Wall Street Journal*, July 15, 2005.
9. Ibid.
10. Donald Boudreaux, *Globalization* (Santa Barbara, CA: Greenwood Press, 2008), 15.
11. Ken Auletta, *The Streets Were Paved with Gold* (New York: Random House, 1975), xii.
12. Robert L. Bartley, *The Seven Fat Years* (New York: Free Press, 1992), 54.

Chapter Fifteen: Comparative Advantage: Could LeBron James Play in the NFL?

1. Bill Barnwell, "Could LeBron James Really Play in the NFL?," Grantland.com, August 5, 2013, http://grantland.com/features/bill-barnwell-examines-lebron-james-possibility-success-nfl/.
2. John Clayton, "Two positions in transition," ESPN.com, June 20, 2013, http://espn.go.com/nfl/story/_/id/9407254/nfl-fullback-tight-end-positions-transition?src=mobile.

3. NBA Player Salaries, 2014–2015, National Basketball Association, ESPN, http://espn.go.com/nba/salaries.
4. Spotrac, http://www.spotrac.com/rankings/nfl/tight-end/.
5. Badenhausen.
6. Monte Burke, "Average Player Salaries in the Four Major American Sports Leagues," Forbes.com, December 7, 2012, http://www.forbes.com/sites/monteburke/2012/12/07/average-player-salaries-in-the-four-major-american-sports-leagues/.
7. Ryan Rosenblatt, "Tony Gonzalez Contract: Tight-end's 2-year deal worth $14 million, according to report." SB Nation, March 15, 2013, http://www.sbnation.com/nfl/2013/3/15/4108754/tony-gonzalez-contract-atlanta-falcons.
8. "Michael Jordan: The Stats," InfoPlease, http://www.infoplease.com/ipsa/A0779388.html.
9. Walter Isaacson, *Steve Jobs* (New York: Simon & Schuster, 2011), 62.
10. Ibid., 85.
11. Ibid., 102–3.
12. Ibid., 397.

Chapter Sixteen: "Outsourcing" Is Great for Workers, and as Old as the Pencil

1. Johan Norberg, "The Noble Feat of Nike," YaleGlobal Online, June 13, 2003, http://yaleglobal.yale.edu/content/noble-feat-nike.
2. Ibid.
3. Enrico Moretti, *The New Geography of Jobs* (Boston, MA: Houghton Mifflin Harcourt, 2012), 10.
4. Robyn Meredith, *The Elephant and the Dragon* (New York: Norton, 2007), 59.
5. Moretti, *The New Geography of Jobs*, 11.
6. Ibid., 60.
7. Ibid., 122.
8. Ibid., 85.

Chapter Seventeen: "Energy Independence" Would Be Economically Crippling; "Global Warming" Is a Crippling Theory

1. Daniel Estrin, "Could Israel be another Middle East oil giant?" *BBC News*, September 30, 2011, http://www.bbc.com/news/magazine-15037533.
2. Warren T. Brookes, *The Economy In Mind* (New York: Universe Books, 1982), 97.
3. John Tamny, "Is There An Oil Story Behind the Iranian Elections?" RealClearPolitics, June 17, 2009, http://www.realclearpolitics.com/articles/2009/06/17/is_there_an_oil_story_behind_the_iranian_elections_97040.html.
4. Benjamin M. Anderson, *Economics and the Public Welfare* (Indianapolis: Liberty Press, 1949), 37.

5. Thomas K. McCraw, *Prophet of Innovation* (Cambridge, MA: Belknap Harvard, 2007), 329.
6. Jerry Taylor and Peter Van Doren, "Oil Weapon Myth," *Cato Institute*, December 5, 2001, http://www.cato.org/publications/commentary/oil-weapon-myth.
7. Robert L. Bartley, *The Seven Fat Years* (New York: Free Press, 1992), 32.
8. Mark Perry, "Exxon Paid Almost $1M Per Hour in Income Taxes and Its Effective Tax Rate Was 42.3%," Carpe Diem Blog, April 28, 2011, http://mjperry.blogspot.com/2011/04/exxonmobil-paid-almost-1m-per-hr-in.html.
9. Dan Senor and Saul Singer, *Start-Up Nation*, (New York: Twelve, 2009), 11.
10. John Tamny, "Oil, the Dollar and Comparative Advantage," *Investor's Business Daily*, July 16, 2008, http://news.investors.com/071608-487382-oil-the-dollar-and-comparative-advantage.htm?p=2.
11. Perry.
12. Ibid.
13. Merrill Matthews, "About Those Tax Breaks for Big Oil ...," *Wall Street Journal*, April 2, 2013, http://online.wsj.com/news/articles/SB10001424127887324789504578380684292877300.
14. Peter Maass, *Crude World: The Violent Twilight of Oil* (New York: Vintage Books, 2010), 134.

Chapter Eighteen: Conclusion: Free Trade Is the Path to Knowledge, Liberty, World Peace, and Big Raises

1. Grant Achatz and Nick Kokonas, *Life, On the Line* (New York: Gotham Books, 2011), 287.
2. Ibid., 257.
3. Ibid., 23.
4. Ibid., 102.
5. Ibid., 103.
6. Ibid., 103.
7. Tim Reuter, "How American Expatriates In Paris Built The United States", Forbes.com, January 24, 2014, http://www.forbes.com/sites/timreuter/2014/01/24/how-american-expatriates-in-paris-built-the-united-states/.

Chapter Nineteen: A Floating Foot, Minute, and Second Would Give You Ugly Houses, Burnt Wings, and Slow NFL Draft Picks

1. Joshua David Stein, "Where the Best Wings Roam," *Wall Street Journal*, February 1–2, 2014.
2. Adam Smith, *The Wealth of Nations* (New York: Modern Library, 2013), 370.

3. John Stuart Mill, *Principles of Political Economy* (Amherst, NY: Prometheus Books, 2004), 457.
4. Ibid., 459.
5. Nathan Lewis, *Gold: The Monetary Polaris* (New Berlin, NY: Canyon Maple Publishing, 2013), 5.
6. Ibid., 5.
7. Robert L. Bartley, *The Seven Fat Years* (New York: Free Press, 1992), 108.
8. Craig Karmin, *Biography of the Dollar* (New York: Crown Business, 2008), 19.
9. Ibid., 39.
10. Ibid., 39–40.
11. Ibid., 40.
12. Steve Forbes, "Powerful Antiterror Weapon," *Forbes*, October 6, 2006, http://www.forbes.com/global/2006/1016/015.html.
13. John Tamny, "Futures Shock," *TCS Daily*, May 11, 2007, http://www.ideasinactiontv.com/tcs_daily/2007/05/futures-shock-1.html.
14. Douglas Irwin, *Free Trade Under Fire* (Princeton, NJ: Princeton University Press, 2002), 18.

Chapter Twenty: Do Not Be Fooled by Rising and Falling Computer, Flat Screen, and VHS Prices: They Are Not an Inflation or Deflation Signal

1. George Gilder, *Knowledge and Power* (Washington, DC: Regnery Publishing, 2013), 23.
2. Damon Darlin, "Falling Costs of Big-Screen TV's to Keep Falling," *New York Times*, August 20, 2005, http://www.nytimes.com/2005/08/20/technology/20tvprices.html?pagewanted=print&_r=0.
3. BestBuy.com. http://www.bestbuy.com/site/50-class-49-1-2-diag-led-1080p-120hz-hdtv/8976104.p;jsessionid=8E4458DE9969C1CA49AF6869DA963B5B.bbolsp-app01-132?id=1218960138258&skuId=8976104&st=flat%20screen%20tv&cp=1&lp=11.
4. Steven F. Hayward, *The Age of Reagan: Part II* (New York: Crown Forum, 2009), 31.
5. John Stuart Mill, *Principles of Political Economy* (Amherst, NY: Prometheus Books), 40.
6. Stephen Smith, "Super Bowl ticket prices: A historical look," CBS NEWS.com, February 3, 2012, http://www.cbsnews.com/news/super-bowl-ticket-prices-a-historical-look/.
7. Chris Isidore, "Super Bowl ticket prices heat up," CNNMoney.com, February 2, 2014, http://money.cnn.com/2014/01/31/news/economy/super-bowl-tickets/.
8. John Tamny, "Globalization and Inflation," *The American Spectator*, March 6, 2007, http://spectator.org/articles/45710/globalization-and-inflation.
9. Rachel Ziemba, "The G-20's Crowded Agenda," *RGE Monitor*, September 23, 2009, http://www.economonitor.com/analysts/2009/09/23/rge-monitor-the-g20s-crowded-agenda/.

10. Alan Greenspan, *The Age of Turbulence* (New York: Penguin Press, 2007), 384.
11. John Tamny, "The Phillips Curve Is Dead, Except at the Fed," RealClearMarkets, September 16, 2008, http://www.realclearmarkets.com/articles/2008/09/phillips_curve_is_dead_except.html.
12. Greenspan, *The Age of Turbulence*, 103.
13. Tamny, "The Phillips Curve Is Dead, Except at the Fed."
14. David Muir, James Wang & Maggy Patrick, "Unemployed Flock to North Dakota; What's Their Secret?", ABCNews.com, October 19, 2011, http://abcnews.go.com/US/unemployed-flock-north-dakota-advantage-job-boom/story?id=14772915.
15. A. S., "Texas, Here We Come", *The Economist*, June 16, 2010, http://www.economist.com/blogs/freeexchange/2010/06/migration.
16. Sheyna Steiner, "Is Inflation Higher Than You Think?" Bankrate.com, http://www.bankrate.com/finance/personal-finance/is-inflation-higher-than-you-think-1.aspx.
17. John Tamny, "The True Meaning of Inflation", Forbes.com, January 25, 2010, http://www.forbes.com/2010/01/24/inflation-prices-gold-standard-opinions-columnists-john-tamny.html.
18. John Tamny, "'Low' U.S. Inflation Is a Function of Clever Calculation", *RealClearMarkets*, February 1, 2011, http://www.realclearmarkets.com/articles/2011/02/01/low_us_inflation_a_function_of_clever_calculation_98847.html.
19. Kitco.com. http://www.kitco.com/scripts/hist_charts/monthly_graphs.plx.

Chapter Twenty-One: True Inflation Is Currency Devaluation, and It Is a Cruel Blast to the Past

1. *New York Post*, "Super Bowl Ad Rates: Rates for a 30-second commercial," January 25, 2014.
2. Kitco, http://www.kitco.com/scripts/hist_charts/monthly_graphs.plx.
3. Manuel H. Johnson and Robert Keleher, *Monetary Policy: A Market Price Approach* (Westport, CT: Quorum Books, 1996),
4. Robert L. Bartley, *The Seven Fat Years* (New York: Free Press, 1992), 33.
5. Allen J. Matusow, *Nixon's Economy: Booms, Busts, Dollars, and Votes* (Lawrence, KS: University of Kansas Press, 1998).
6. Ronald I. McKinnon and Kenicho Ohno, *Dollar and Yen: Resolving Economic Conflict Between the U.S. and Japan* (Cambridge, MA: MIT Press, 1997), 15.
7. Kitco.
8. Ibid.
9. Bartley, *The Seven Fat Years*, 108.
10. Warren T. Brookes, *The Economy In Mind* (New York: Universe Books, 1982), 96.
11. Bartley, *The Seven Fat Years*, 67.
12. Ibid., 143.

13. David Frum, *How We Got Here* (New York: Basic Books, 2000),
14. George Gilder, *Wealth and Poverty* (Washington, DC: Regnery Publishing, 2012), 241–42.
15. H. G. Bissinger, *Friday Night Lights* (Cambridge, MA: Da Capo Press, 2000),
16. Bartley, *The Seven Fat Years*, 109.
17. Steve Forbes, "Powerful Antiterror Weapon," *Forbes*, October 6, 2006, http://www.forbes.com/global/2006/1016/015.html.
18. John Tamny, "Gold's Plunge Is Cause for Optimism," *Wall Street Journal*, April 18, 2013, http://online.wsj.com/news/articles/SB10001424127887324485004578427271772508456.
19. Steven F. Hayward, *The Age of Reagan: Part II* (New York: Crown Forum, 2009), 634.
20. Charles Kadlec, "The Dangerous Myth About The Bill Clinton Tax Increase," Forbes.com, July 16, 2012, http://www.forbes.com/sites/charleskadlec/2012/07/16/the-dangerous-myth-about-the-bill-clinton-tax-increase/.
21. Miller Center, "Clinton Signs NAFTA, December 8, 1993," University of Virginia, http://millercenter.org/president/events/12_08.
22. McKinnon and Ohno, *Dollar and Yen: Resolving Economic Conflict Between the U.S. and Japan*, 228.
23. Lawrence A. Kudlow, *American Abundance: The New Economic and Moral Prosperity* (New York: Forbes/American Heritage Custom Publishing, 1997), 42.
24. Nathan Lewis, "The Correlation Between the Gold Standard and Stupendous Growth Is Very Clear," Forbes.com, April 11, 2013, http://www.forbes.com/sites/nathanlewis/2013/04/11/the-correlation-between-the-gold-standard-and-stupendous-growth-is-clear/.
25. Tamny, "Gold's Plunge Is Cause for Optimism."
26. Quin Hillyer, "Catch a Falling Dollar!", *The American Spectator*, November 27, 2007, http://spectator.org/articles/44470/catch-falling-dollar.
27. Source: Kitco.
28. Source: Bloomberg.
29. Kevin Johnson, "States battle rise in copper thefts," *USA Today*, October 30, 2007.
30. Ibid.
31. Ken Dilanian, "Ohio Dem wants to overturn Treasury ban on melting coins," *USA Today*, November 1, 2007.
32. Michael Tsang and Darren Boey, "Oil Producers Mask Decade's Worst S&P 500 Profit Drop," *Bloomberg*, May 19, 2008, http://www.bloomberg.com/apps/news?pid=newsarchive&sid=aB50jeKPl7gE.
33. Joe Richter, "Harvard Losing Out to South Dakota In Graduate Pay: Commodities," *Bloomberg*, September 19, 2012, http://www.bloomberg.com/news/2012-09-17/harvard-losing-out-to-south-dakota-in-graduate-pay-commodities.html.

34. Adam Smith, *The Wealth of Nations* (New York: Modern Library, 1937), 305.
35. John Allison, *The Financial Crisis and the Free Market Cure* (New York: McGraw-Hill, 2013), 5.
36. Peter J. Wallison, *Bad History, Worse Policy* (Washington, DC: AEI Press, 2013), 260.
37. Gregory Zuckerman, *The Greatest Trade Ever* (New York: Broadway Books, 2009), 45.
38. Ibid., 107.
39. Gilder, *Wealth and Poverty*, 241–42.
40. John D. Gartner, *The Hypomanic Edge* (New York: Simon & Schuster, 2005), 12.
41. Nigel Lawson, *The View From No. 11* (New York: Doubleday, 1993).
42. Adam Fergusson, *When Money Dies* (New York: Public Affairs, 1975), 109.
43. David Smith, *The Rise and Fall of Monetarism* (Harmondsworth, Middlesex: Pelican, 1987).
44. Ibid.
45. William Greider, *Secrets of the Temple* (New York: Simon & Schuster, 1989).

Chapter Twenty-two: If They Tell You They Predicted the "Financial Crisis," They're Lying

1. Ross Douthat, "Emotional Rescue," *National Review*, November 12, 2012, https://www.nationalreview.com/nrd/articles/331659/emotional-rescue.
2. Andrew Ross Sorkin, *Too Big To Fail* (New York: Viking, 2009), 443.
3. Howard E. Kershner, *Dividing the Wealth* (Old Greenwich, CT: Devin-Adair Company, 1971), 133.
4. Ibid., 133–34
5. Thomas E. Woods, *Meltdown: A Free Market Look at Why the Stock Market Collapsed, the Economy Tanked, and Government Bailouts Will Make Things Worse* (Washington, DC: Regnery, 2009).
6. John Tamny, "Blame the Media For Bush's Low Economic Ratings?" *National ReviewOnline*, June 12, 2006, http://www.nationalreview.com/articles/217906/blame-media-bushs-low-economic-ratings/john-tamny.
7. John Tamny, "Misplaced Hand Wringing Over Housing," *TCS Daily*, October 30, 2007, http://www.ideasinactiontv.com/tcs_daily/2007/10/misplaced-hand-wringing-over-housing.html.
8. Michael Lewis, *The Big Short* (New York: Allen Lane, 2010), 65.
9. Tunku Varadarajan, "'Nationalize' the Banks," *Wall Street Journal*, February 21, 2009.
10. John Stuart Mill, *Principles of Political Economy* (Amherst, NY: Prometheus Books, 2004), 98.
11. Ibid., 132

Chapter Twenty-Three: Conclusion: "Do-Nothing" Politicians Deserve a Special Place in Heaven

1. John Tamny and Richard Vedder, "The Role of Labor Policy," Council On Foreign Relations, http://www.cfr.org/united-states/role-labor-policy/p18983.
2. Benjamin M. Anderson, *Economics and the Public Welfare* (Indianapolis: Liberty Press, 1949), 92.
3. Ibid., 92.
4. Ibid., 366.
5. Ibid., 372
6. Amity Shlaes, *The Forgotten Man: A New History of the Great Depression* (New York: Harper Perennial, 2008).
7. Transcript, "President George W. Bush's speech to the nation on the economic crisis," http://www.nytimes.com/2008/09/24/business/economy/24text-bush.html?pagewanted=all&_r=0.
8. Albert Jay Nock, *Our Enemy, The State* (Caldwell, ID: The Caxton Printers, 1935), 197.
9. Barack Obama's 2009 State of the Union Speech, http://www.cnn.com/2010/POLITICS/01/27/sotu.transcript/.
10. Nock, *Our Enemy, The State*, 151.

INDEX

G

H